ANTISEMITISM
ITS HISTORY AND CAUSES

BERNARD LAZARE
Translated from the French

Introduction to the Bison Book Edition
by Robert S. Wistrich

University of Nebraska Press
Lincoln and London

University of Nebraska Press

⌐nited States of America

⌐nis book meets the minimum requirements of
⌐nal Standard for Information Sciences—Permanence of
⌐or Printed Library Materials, ANSI Z39.48-1984.

First Bison Book printing: 1995
Most recent printing indicated by the last digit below:
10   9   8   7   6   5   4   3   2   1

Library of Congress Cataloging-in-Publication Data
Lazare, Bernard, 1865–1903.
[Antisémitisme. English]
Antisemitism: its history and causes / translated from the French of
Bernard Lazare.
p.   cm.
Includes bibliographical references and index.
ISBN 0-8032-7954-X (pbk.: acid free)
1. Antisemitism—History.   I. Title.
DS145.L413   1995
305.892′4—dc20
95-5651   CIP

Originally published in 1894 as *L'Antisémitisme, son histoire et ses causes*.
Reprinted from the 1967 edition published by Britons Publishing Co.,
London, the pagination of which has not been changed in this Bison
Book edition.

INTRODUCTION
Robert S. Wistrich

Bernard Lazare (1865–1903) is probably best remembered today for his pioneering role in the Dreyfus affair. The young Jewish anarchist and literary critic carried the torch of the Dreyfusard cause in its earliest and loneliest phase. Born in Nîmes, in Southern France, into an assimilated Jewish family, he had arrived in Paris in 1886, where he became involved in both the Symbolist and anarchist movements.[1] He was a regular contributor to the libertarian press and in early 1894 he organized a militant campaign to free the imprisoned anarchist Jean Grave. A year later, shortly after the arrest and conviction of Captain Alfred Dreyfus—a French Jewish officer charged with selling military secrets to the Germans—he was asked by the accused's brother, Mathieu, to investigate the case. It was a paradoxical choice, for the Dreyfus family belonged to the wealthy bourgeoisie—the social class whose iniquities the young Lazare had regularly castigated in his polemical journalism. But concerned at the growing antisemitic campaign in France, Lazare agreed to take on the task and by the summer of 1895 had already produced a closely reasoned booklet entitled *Une erreur judiciaire: la vérité sur l'affaire Dreyfus*. Its publication was, however, delayed by Mathieu until November 1896 in the hope that a revision of his brother's case could be secured without a public campaign.

When it finally appeared, *Une erreur judiciaire* had only a limited impact. But it was the first documented exposure of the legal irregularities in the case. Lazare was also the first French commentator to insist that Dreyfus was condemned as a Jew, following a long antisemitic campaign of slander.[2] From very early on, Lazare had suspected that the case was not a simple error of justice but the result of an antisemitic machination. He could see no motive for a patriotic bourgeois Jew like Dreyfus, who had freely opted for French nationality (following the annexation of Alsace in 1871) to betray his country. Dreyfus was very wealthy and his choice of a military career suggested that patriotism and honor were his guiding stars. If there was no motive, then it was doubtful there was a crime.[3]

Lazare paid close attention, moreover, to the virulent campaign against Jewish officers in the French army (and the role of Jews in France in general) which had been running for at least two years in Edouard Drumont's antisemitic newspaper, *La Libre Parole*. It was Drumont's paper which had first announced "the arrest of a Jewish officer" and which kept claiming that the affair would be covered up because the officer was a Jew. The French anti-Semites were on the point of inventing the myth of the "Jewish Syndicate," the theory of a well-oiled conspiracy by Jewish financiers to obscure treasonable Jewish actions—and subsequently to rehabilitate Dreyfus.[4]

In the first two months after Dreyfus's arrest in October 1894, before his first trial for treason, an extraordinary campaign of calumny and vilification against the Jews had been unleashed. The resulting atmosphere of fear, hysteria, and intellectual terror reminded Lazare of some ritual murder cases in the past, which he had carefully studied.[5] To his mind, this poisonous atmosphere had not only precluded the possibility of a fair trial for Dreyfus but it underlined the desire of French society to replace "le Judas classique" by a contemporary Jewish traitor.

Lazare's sensitivity to these points and his intense involvement in the affair as the first Jewish Dreyfusard were major signposts in a complicated odyssey of Jewish self-discovery. Until 1892, his own writings on the "Jewish Question" had betrayed a definite strain of Jewish antisemitism. In an article in September 1890 entitled "Juifs et Israélites," he had sharply differentiated between Jews as worshippers of the Golden Calf—mean, narrow-minded, sly, and unscrupulous—and the "Israelites of France."[6] The latter were honest, upright, decent people who had absorbed the blessings of Latin civilization and were indistinguishable from their French compatriots. They had rightly, in his opinion, rejected any fictitious solidarity linking them with Frankfurt Jewish moneychangers, Galician pawnbrokers, or Russian usurers.[7] The narrow sectarianism of the Talmud and the bizarre Judeo-Germanic patois (i.e., Yiddish) were wholly alien to true Israelites. Lazare's article ended with a startling appeal to Drumont and his friends, to be "just, at last," and to confine themselves to being "anti-Jewish" rather than confuse "juifs" with "Israélites." "On that day," he added, "they would be sure to have many Israelites on their side."[8]

A second article, "La solidarité Juive," published a month later, focused its attack on the *Alliance israélite universelle*. This French Jewish philanthropic organization had been violently slandered by French anti-Semites from Gougenot des Mousseaux to Drumont as the center of a secret Jewish conspiracy for world domination. Lazare's objection was, however, directed more against its policy of granting succour and aid to persecuted Jews in Russia and eastern Europe. As a result, the doors of France had been thrown wide open to a flood of coarse, uncultivated, money-grabbing nomads. Lazare deplored the fact that "thanks to these hordes with whom we are confused, it is forgotten that we have lived in France for nearly 2000 years, like the Franks who invaded this country."[9] As an Israelite of France, he asked himself "by virtue of which supposed fraternity shall I concern myself over measures taken by the Tsar against subjects who seem to him to be doing harmful things?"[10] His firm answer was that "we have nothing in common with those who are constantly being thrown in our face, and we should abandon them." He therefore advised his co-religionists to "halt, to dam up if they can, the perpetual immigration of these predatory, vulgar and dirty Tartars who come to feed unduly on a country which is not their own."[11]

Less than a decade later, Lazare himself would denounce this kind of assimilated Jewish complicity in antisemitism (by seeking to displace it onto east European Jews) with the same vehemence that characterized his outbursts of 1890. He would deplore the disintegration of "Jewish solidarity" as one of the undesirable consequences of emancipation and assimilation. Above all, he would become the unofficial spokesman and defender of the Russian, east European, and other persecuted Jews outside France, whose fate had once been so indifferent to him.

The Dreyfus affair and his interpretation of it were the sources of this metamorphosis, for they brought him to a new awareness of his own pariah status as a Jew in French society. As he put it in an open letter in June 1899 to Ludovic Trarieux (protesting the silencing of his own role in the affair and of its Jewish aspects): "I want it to be known that the first who spoke, the first who stood up for a martyred Jew, was a Jew, who knew to what an outcast, disinherited, ill-starred people he belonged, & drew from this consciousness the will to fight for justice & truth."[12] This insistence on his self-consciously Jewish commitment to Dreyfus was not at all to the taste of the Dreyfus family, of most French Jews at the time, or indeed of most non-Jewish Dreyfusards. It partly explains why after Zola's "J'Accuse" of January 1898, Lazare's role was downplayed and relegated to his tireless, propagandist work behind the scenes. It is also part of the reason for the oblivion into which Lazare's missionary Dreyfusardism fell, until about twenty-five years ago.[13] In the battle for Dreyfus and the French Republic, the emphasis on a distinctively Jewish participation was generally seen as an obstacle rather than as an asset.

This background is vital to fully understand the remarkable, wide-ranging study, *L'Antisémitisme, son histoire et ses causes* (1894), which Bernard Lazare published when he was only twenty-nine. The first systematic study of the question until that time, it was written between 1891 and 1893, some sections of the book having previously appeared as review articles. Remarkably documented, full of original insights and surveying over two thousand years of Jew-hatred with passion, economy, and clarity, this work can still be read with profit as a textbook. However, the book also falls into two distinct parts, whose orientation and emphases are very different, reflecting the changing viewpoints and attitudes of the author. The first seven chapters cover the development of anti-Judaism from Greco-Roman Antiquity to the French Revolution. In this historical section, Lazare is by no means free of the "Jewish" antisemitism that characterised his polemics of 1890, despite his claim to be writing an impartial sociological and historical study. The second half of the book (chapters 8 to 15) explores the legal, socioeconomic, nationalist, and racial factors in modern antisemitism. He concluded that its eventual disappearance was inevitable since it was a vestige of the past, "one of the last, though most long lived, manifestations of that old spirit of reaction and narrow conservatism, which is vainly attempting to arrest the onward movement of the Revolution" (see p. 183, this edition).

Lazare's starting point is that antisemitism is a phenomenon of the Dispersion, of Jewish history outside of Palestine, once the Jews had ceased to be a people defending its land, liberty, and independence. Since it existed among peoples of such diverse origin and

character, in different times and places, the one constant factor in
antisemitism must be the Jews themselves. Indeed, the main thesis
of the historical section is that the Jews were themselves, at least
partly, "the cause of their own ills" (8). The "unsocial" character of
the Jew, fixed and unchanged, rooted in his ritual law and in
Tulmudic teaching, had made him an object of hatred in pagan
antiquity. The Torah prevented social intercourse with foreign
peoples, acceptance of their gods or their laws, and encouraged
exclusivity, arrogance, and the desire to dominate other nations.
Above and outside the law of other peoples, enjoying privileges
and exemptions that allowed them to become a "State within a
State," the Jews naturally provoked the envy and hostility of their
neighbors. Moreover, their Law inculcated in them a sense of pride
and superiority, of being the "chosen people of God," the sole ben-
eficiaries of his Covenant (10). The world would not be happy, according to the Judaic conception, until it came under the universal
hegemony of the Law, i.e., that of the Jews. Such beliefs, reinforced
by Ezra and the Scribes, the Pharisees, and the Talmudists, isolated
the Jews from the rest of humanity and encouraged contempt for
non-Jews (11–12). Antisemitism in pagan antiquity could therefore
be seen as a natural reaction against Jewish exclusivity and excessive pride.

Lazare portrays the masses of Jewish traders and hawkers living
in the dirtiest part of ancient Rome as unsociable and exclusive.
The separatist "ghetto Jew" is already there, having voluntarily, as it
were, cut himself off from society, without the application of any
external pressure (24). Similarly, the medieval Jew in Lazare's account often resembles a greedy Shylock driven by the rationalism
of the Talmud to excel in usury as much as by the severity of civil or
ecclesiastical legislation. The Jew exhibits an insatiable love of gold
and through his money-lending skills sometimes becomes "the
master of [his] masters"(63). Moreover, despite persecution and
humiliation, the Jew still retains his sense of superiority and an
indomitable, tenacious patriotism associated with the mystical fatherland of Zion (71). But we are told that the victory of rabbinical
obscurantism had by the fourteenth century rendered the Jews
hostile to any noble, generous, or progressive ideas. Lazare estab-
lishes a dubious symmetry here between orthodox Jews burning
Maimonedes's *Guide for the Perplexed* and Catholics burning the Talmud; between Jews desiring to live apart and being obliged to wear

distinguishing marks that stigmatized them; between Talmudic obscurantism and the onset of systematic persecution, leading to expulsions and massacres. Lazare's loathing for rabbinical "fanaticism" misled him at times into a false equation of the Synagogue and Church, which in terms of power, status, numbers, and practical effects were hardly equally matched.

Lazare's history seems, moreover, to underestimate seriously the unique characteristics and weight of Christian antisemitism, which was qualitatively different from anything that went before.[14] The tension between the Jews and the early Jewish-Christians is described well enough against the background of the Jewish wars against Rome. But the anti-Judaism of the Gospels and of the Church Fathers, though it is briefly evoked, plays a much more secondary role than it would in any present-day history of antisemitism.[15] The pivotal event of the Crusades and the lasting effects of the anti-Jewish massacres that ensued is somewhat glossed over. Nor is the full extent of the dehumanizing stereotypes that emerged in the Middle Ages, the equation of the Jews with the Devil and the impact of legends like the Antichrist, adequately conveyed.

Nevertheless, in chapter 7, which deals with anti-Judaic literature and prejudices, Lazare does come to grips with some of the myths, legends, and fantasies concocted by Christian theologians and writers. This well documented section does demonstrate the systematic denigration of Judaism by the Church, its prejudices, phobias, obsession with conversion of the Jews and perpetual fear of "Judaisers." Lazare, despite his own bias against traditional Judaism, observes with a certain admiration how the rabbis more than held their own with ecclesiastics during the medieval disputations; how Jews (as well as Arabs) in late medieval Spain laid the seeds of Renaissance humanism, scepticism, and critical inquiry; and how the "Jewish spirit" triumphed with the Protestant Reformation. Opposed to Talmudism and Jewish usury stood the great prophetic texts of the Bible which animated the fanatic German Anabaptists and Cromwell's Puritan warriors, as well as the Jewish revolutionaries of modern times.[16]

This theme of "The Revolutionary Spirit of Judaism" (previously published in the *Revue Bleue* in May 1893) is developed in chapter 12 at greater length. Lazare contrasts the rebellious character of the Jew with the resignation of the Christian and the fatalism of the Muslim. The Jew rejects the consolations of the afterlife and future beatitude in favour of Justice here-and-now, in this life and in this world. The coming messianic age is to be an age of justice, equality, and liberty—ideas that the people Israel was the first to enunciate clearly. Similarly, Lazare asserts that the Jews had always been anarchists as heart, because the premise of their religion was that all government was bad, "since it tends to take the place of the government of God"(146). The Jew could not ultimately accept any authority except his God Yahveh, "the only head of the Jewish commonwealth." Hence, paradoxically, prophetic Judaism encouraged a libertarian ethos and helped to make the Jews a ferment of revolution in modern society. Lazare happily lists the Jewish revolutionaries and socialists in the nineteenth century, including Karl Marx, whom he describes as "inspired by that ancient Hebraic materialism," which dreamed of Paradise on earth. Marx's own anti-Jewish diatribes and baptism are ignored in favor of stressing how much his dialectical spirit of revolt, sarcasm, and invective owed to his ancestry (157). Similarly, the radicalism of Heine, Börne, Lassalle, Moses Hess, and others is largely attributed to their Jewish heritage.

Lazare had no doubt that this revolutionary spirit of the Jews had contributed to the transformation of modern societies and to the erosion of the Christian State. Jews had been at the forefront of liberal, socialist, and anti-clerical movements, thereby aiding those who sought to de-Christianize and secularize contemporary society (175). Since the Middle Ages they had forged the intellectual weapons to sap the dogmas of the Church. Similarly, they had allied themselves with those forces seeking to bring down the *ancien régime*. They had been especially prominent as entrepreneurs, industrialists, and financiers in establishing the basis for the industrial revolution and bourgeois hegemony on the Continent. Though they did not establish on their own the triumph of bourgeois capitalism, they did aid its victory. Thus, the Jews stood at two exposed poles of contemporary society, contributing to the centralization of capital and fomenting ardent opposition to it (155). This, too, was a major cause of conservative and clerical antisemitism, though it was exaggerated (as Lazare himself emphasized) to portray the Jews as the sole motor of modern revolutions.

In the second half of his book dealing with modern antisemitism, Lazare's tone had changed considerably, and the somewhat negative image of the "eternal Jew" that prevailed earlier had been considerably modified. Since the French Revolution, Lazare maintains, the Jew has become emancipated and in the West he has morally and intellectually freed himself of his Talmudic baggage. Antisemitism, too, has become less religious and more concerned with emphasizing economic, political, and nationalist factors. Less impulsive, it seeks to buttress itself with rational, "scientific," and doctrinal arguments. Ethnographic and racial theories in the late nineteenth century begin to postulate an unbridgeable chasm between so-called "Aryans" and "Semites." Lazare effectively exposes the absurdity of these theories of a pure race, whether they are put forward by anti-Semites, or sometimes even by Jews.[17] He now emphasizes that the Jewish type is constantly transformed by different milieux and that there is little in common between emancipated French Jews and their Galician or Russian coreligionists (178).

Modern racial antisemitism is based, so he claims, on a myth of common origins and descent, but behind it lies the same root as in anti-Judaism, "the fear of, and the hatred for, the stranger" (176). Hellenistic Alexandria, Cicero's Rome, Near Eastern Antioch, feudal Christian Europe, or contemporary nation-states, the Jew was always perceived as a stranger because he did not assimilate with the surrounding peoples. As long as he did not submerge himself within the nation, so Lazare still believed in 1894, there could be no solution to the "Jewish question." The modern nationalists sensed this and became anti-Semites because they could reproach the Jews with an exclusivism as intransigent as their own (176–78). Their premise—that the Jews could *never* assimilate—was however adamantly rejected by Lazare in 1894. The nationalist anti-Semites, he argued, had fallen into a fundamental contradiction as a result of their reliance on the pseudo-scientific theory of racism. They had returned these groundless doctrines into a self-fulfilling prophecy. "[A]ntisemitism was born in modern societies, because the Jew did not assimilate himself, did not cease to be a people, but when anti-Semitism had ascertained that the Jew was not assimilated, it violently reproached him for it, and at the same whenever possible it took all necessary measures to prevent his assimilation in the future" (138).

Lazare was optimistically convinced, however, that there was no future for this type of racist antisemitism. Based on xenophobic reflexes, it belonged to the past; lost in delusions and vain nostalgia, it was hostile to social change and therefore incapable of adapting to modernity. The world, so Lazare believed, was inexorably moving towards greater internationalism, economic interdependence, and a more civilized, progressive way of thinking. The Jews themselves had adapted, especially in the West where their religion had become a form of "ceremonial deism," ripe for rationalism and free thought. Even though the bulk of the Jewish nation was concentrated in Russia and eastern Europe where Talmudic and ghetto Judaism was well established, even there one could find signs of revolutionary change. Thus, both Judaism and antisemitism were, he believed, ripe for dissolution (179–82).

True, Lazare did not ignore the wide variety of antisemitic doctrines, movements, and platforms in the late nineteenth century. He discusses the left-wing Hegelians, the antisemitism of the anarchists and early socialists, the writings of Treitschke, Dühring, Stoecker, Marr, and von Schoenerer (116–17). He is familiar with Gougenot des Mousseaux, Gobineau, Renan, and of course, Drumont, whom he respects as a propagandist and polemicist but considers inferior as a thinker to the German anti-Semites. He is also well aware that governmental antisemitism in societies like Tsarist Russia and Rumania, where the Jews are far from emancipated, involves draconian legislation, harassment, and persecution of Jews. Yet Bernard Lazare remains remarkably sanguine, despite his own recital, as if determined to impose a happy ending in spite of the logic of his own story. In his view—one shared by most of the socialist movement at the time—antisemitism would fall through its own contradictions. In France, Germany, and Austria, its anticapitalist demagoguery was already preparing the road to a new world of progress and revolution. "This anti-semitic movement, in its origin reactionary, has become transformed and is acting now for the advantage of the revolutionary cause. Antisemitism stirs up the middle class, the small tradesmen, and sometimes the peasant, against the Jewish capitalist, but in doing so it gently leads them toward Socialism, prepares them for anarchy, infuses in them a hatred for all capitalists, and, more than that, for capital in the absatract" (182). Lazare, like so many on the Left, was at the time convinced that antisemitism was not merely doomed in the long run, it was actually serving the cause of social revolution! At the same time, he postulated the end of the Jewish people, which as it became secularized and modernized would dissolve into the host nation (180). Despite the stirring ode to the "revolutionary spirit of Judaism," this too was in the logic of Lazare's assimilationist beliefs in 1894.

The Dreyfus affair would expose many of these assumptions as illusory, and the explosion of French antisemitism in its wake conclusively demonstrated that it had plenty of life still left in it. Already in November 1894, Lazare gave expression to his growing alarm at the *état d'esprit antisémite* in French society, which had created a "new ghetto" of suspicion against the Jews.[18] In a pamphlet of 1895 entitled *Antisémitisme et Revolution,* he observed that the Catholic bourgeoisie was manipulating antisemitism as a way to rid itself of its Jewish capitalist rivals. But all Jews were threatened by this demagoguery, and they could not wait passively to be stripped of their rights until the Revolution intervened to save them.[19] Much more sharply than in his book, Lazare emphasized to Drumont's followers that the Jews of Russia, eastern Europe, and North Africa formed the most miserable proletariat in the world.

By 1896, in his *Contre l'Antisémitisme,* Lazare stressed above all the clerical role in French antisemitism and its remorseless campaign to deprive the Jews of their rights in the hope of returning them to the medieval ghetto.[20] The assault on the Jewish capitalists was a masquerade, for antisemitism condemned no less vehemently the small Jewish tradesman, the Jewish lawyer, doctor, soldier, scientist, journalist, and writer.[21] It was an engine of war for the Catholic Church and other reactionary forces, directed against the French Republic and the revolutionary tradition. The war against the Jews was but a prelude to a more general crusade against Protestants, free-thinkers, anti-clericals, republicans, socialists, and anarchists.[22]

As a result of the Dreyfus affair, Lazare also came to revise fundamentally his perception of assimilation as a solution to the "Jewish question." He became convinced that this "spurious doctrine" was a symptom of the decadence and powerlessness manifested by French Jewry in the face of organized Jew-hatred.[23] Jewish solidarity had been undermined as the Jewish rich showed themselves willing (according to Lazare) to sacrifice their poorer coreligionists to the anti-Semites, as long as their own wealth and status were not affected. Increasingly, Lazare moved towards a social-revolutionary Zionism as the only answer to the problem posed by antisemitism and the demoralization caused by assimilation in the Diaspora.[24] His Zionism, which spoke in the name of libertarian ideals and the worldwide Jewish proletarian nation, was above all a revolt against the spiritual and psychological dependence produced by assimilation.

Within four years of the completion of his book on antisemitism, Lazare had also settled his accounts with the French socialists. He was disillusioned by the failure of the French Left to condemn antisemitism unequivocally and troubled by its belief that class-hatred and Judeophobia might be reconciled.[25] He angrily exposed the socialist tradition of anticapitalist antisemitism running from Fourier, Proudhon, and Toussenel through Bakunin and Marx to Jaurès and other French socialists in his own time who had flirted with Drumont.[26] Lazare demonstrated that the socialist equation of Jews with parasitic middlemen was wholly misleading, that the "social concept of Judaism" was fundamentally anti-capitalist, and that there were millions of working-class Jews. These polemics showed how far he had come from his earlier belief that the social revolution was being promoted by antisemitism or that its eventual triumph would eradicate the disease once and forever.

It was a great irony that most French Jews were hostile to Lazare's history of antisemitism or embarassed by its often harsh criticisms of Jewry. Anti-Semites, on the other hand, frequently praised it and recommended it as the only book on the subject by a Jew that was worth reading. Drumont considered it a highly informative work, "dominated from beginning to end by a fine effort at impartiality" and a determination "not to yield to the impulses of the race". [28] He believed that Lazare was essentially confirming his own theses, only he was doing so in a different way. Drumont and Lazare would later clash vehemently (they even fought a duel) but the leader of French antisemitism always recognized the quality of his opponent.[29]

The founder of the Action Française, Charles Maurras, was another anti-Semite who admired Lazare's work, especially what he called his "World Directory" of the "Jewish Socialist International." Lazare's emphasis on Jewish "revolutionism," along with his earlier depiction of Jewish religious political exclusivism (the "State within a State") was grist to his mill. In 1907 the Action Française brought out a selected edition of what they thought was best in Lazare's book on antisemitism, naturally underlining those harsh judgments on the eternally unsociable Jew—"anarchist, cosmopolitan, a revolutionary agent but conservative towards himself."[30]

The enthusiasm of anti-Semites, then and now, for Lazare's work is understandable, if one-sided and rather selective. It did not extend to his person or to the monument erected in his memory at Nîmes in 1908—"*la statue infâme*," which to the Action Française represented a symbol of anarchy, disorder, and ruin. It was badly mutilated several times by the nationalist hooligans of the movement, the *Camelots du Roi*.[31]

The anti-Semites naturally ignored Lazare's critique of their theses and the fact that he would have undoubtedly changed and rewritten many things had the book been republished. His resolute and uncompromising struggle for Dreyfus and against the French-anti-Semites after 1894 makes that clear enough. His biographer, Nelly Wilson, put it well when she wrote: "Although *Antisemitism, Its History and Causes* was never rewritten in book form, Bernard Lazare's life was a passionate rewriting of it in action, and the first stage came with the Dreyfus Affair."[32]

Lazare's pioneering study of antisemitism must therefore be judged in the context of his time and in the light of his own personal development. It is evident that he subsequently revised many of his positions—towards the Talmud, Jewish capitalism, the feasibility of assimilation as a solution to the "Jewish question" and its desirability. He realized that his assumptions about the imminent demise of religions, including Judaism, were premature. He recognized that he had underestimated the role of the Church in fomenting and propagating antisemitism both in the past and the present. He came to see the anti-Semites as part of a reactionary clerical and nationalist assault on the Republic which would, if it succeeded, have dire consequences for Jews. He disavowed his naive belief that anti-Jewish agitation could serve the interests of the proletarian revolution by accelerating the disintegration of capitalism. Boldly, he fought the antisemitic stereotypes in his own camp— that of the anarchists and socialists—with mixed success.

Abandoning completely his earlier antipathy to east European Jews whom he had once treated with disdain, he became their most intrepid defender in France. He lacerated the indifference and passivity of the French Jewish bourgeoisie who had rejected their brethren in the illusion that they could thereby escape the rigors of antisemitism. His own combative temperament led him inexorably towards Jewish nationalism, interpreted as a libertarian gospel of auto-emancipation.

Formally speaking, Bernard Lazare never disowned his own history of antisemitism, though he knew that life itself had already modified many of the ideas and conclusions expressed in it. Undoubtedly, had he had the time or inclination, he would have substantially revised the book. Nevertheless, it stands in its own right as an extraordinary work of synthesis, rich in documentation, original in conception, and driven throughout by a desire to penetrate one of the most enigmatic and persistent phenomena of human history.

Writing a hundred years ago, Lazare could not, of course, foresee that racist antisemitism would eventually lead in the middle of the twenty century to the most barbaric genocide in the annals of mankind. He was too much of a rationalist to imagine that a highly civilized nation with the most advanced technology at its disposal would plumb the depths of irrationality in seeking to exterminate the Jewish people systematically. Nonetheless, many of his analyses of the religious, social, economic, and political factors in modern antisemitism remain as pertinent today as when they were first formulated. Above all, Bernard Lazare grasped the necessity of vigorously combating antisemitism as a threat to human rights in general and to the dignity of the Jewish people. Through his writing of this history and his crusade for Dreyfus, he acquired a new self-knowledge and the indomitable courage to fight for justice, truth, and national emancipation.

Notes

1. For biographical details, see Nelly Wilson, *Bernard-Lazare: Antisemitism and Jewish Identity in Late Nineteenth-Century France* (Cambridge: Cambridge University Press, 1978) and most recently Jean-Denis Brédin, *Bernard Lazare: De l'Anarchiste au Prophète* (Paris, 1992). For his anarchist views, see the chapter on Lazare in Michael Löwy, *Redemption and Utopia* (Stanford: Stanford University Press, 1992), 178–99.

2. Bernard Lazare, *Une erreur judiciaire: La vérité sur l'Affaire Dreyfus* (Brussels, 1896), 9, where he writes that "it is as a Jew above all that he [Dreyfus] was prosecuted."

3. Wilson, *Bernard-Lazare*, 122. She quotes an interview given by Lazare to a journalist from the *Figaro* where he stated: "j'ai fait mon enquête; je me suis inquiété de la situation de la famille, de sa fortune, de son honorabilité et immédiatement j'ai vu que le mobile du crime manquait. . . . Pas de mobile, pas de crime."

4. From the moment that he entered the fray, Lazare himself became for the anti-Semites a key intermediary in the so-called "Jewish syndicate."

See Nelly Wilson, "Bernard-Lazare et le Syndicat,'" in G. Leroy, ed., *Les Ecrivains et l'Affaire Dreyfus* (Paris, 1983), 27–33.

5. The two cases which were particularly relevant to Lazare were the Damascus blood libel of 1840 (where France assumed an anti-Jewish posture through its consul in Damascus) and the Tiszla–Eszlar case in Hungary in 1882. Lazare was struck by the analogy between these blood libels and the Dreyfus case: the same system of calumny, use of false confessions, and insinuations about past crimes; the same spreading of lies about the accused's private life; the same intoxication of public opinion through antisemitic fabrications and similar methods of physical and moral torture. See Wilson, *Bernard-Lazare,* 302 n.5. See also Albert S. Lindemann, *The Jew Accused: Three Anti-Semitic Affairs. Dreyfus, Beilis, Frank, 1894–1915* (Cambridge: Cambridge University Press, 1991) for the parallel between the Beilis case in Tsarist Russia and the Dreyfus affair.

6. Lazare, "Juifs et Israélites," *Entretiens Politiques et Littéraires* 1 (September 1890): 176–79.

7. Ibid.

8. Ibid., 178–79.

9. Lazare, "La Solidarité Juive," *Entretiens* (October 1890): 231.

10. Ibid., 230.

11. Ibid. See also Robert S. Wistrich, *Revolutionary Jews from Marx to Trotsky* (London: Harrap, 1976), 131–52.

12. Lazare, "Lettre ouverte à M. Trarieux," *L'Aurore,* 7 June 1899.

13. Despite Charles Péguy's wonderful portrait of Bernard Lazare in his memoir *Notre Jeunesse* (Paris, 1910), he fell into relative oblivion for a long time. The first major effort to rehabilitate him came in Hannah Arendt's short study, "The Jew as a Pariah," in *Jewish Social Studies* 6, no. 2 (1944), which presented him as a conscious pariah who prophetically drew the right conclusions from the Dreyfus affair. Michael R. Marrus in his book *The Politics of Assimilation: The French Jewish Community at the Time of the Dreyfus Affair* (Oxford: Clarendon Press, 1971) was the first historian to provide an overall assessment of his role in the *fin-de-siècle* Franco-Jewish context. Like Arendt, Marrus viewed Lazare as the outstanding Jewish protagonist during the affair.

14. Admittedly, Lazare does deal with Christian antisemitism in chapters 3–5 of his work, but it is only in his polemical *Contre l'antisémitisme* (Paris, 1896) and later writings that he attributes to the Church the decisive role in the propagation of antisemitism. He planned a number of works that were in the end never written on ritual murder, the blood-cult in Christianity, and the use of the Judas legend which would have developed this point. It was the Dreyfus affair which heightened his sensitivity to clerical antisemitism. See Wilson, *Bernard-Lazare,* 207–13.

15. See, for example, Gavin Langmuir, *History, Religion, and Anti-Semitism*

(Berkeley: University of California Press, 1990) and Robert S. Wistrich, *Antisemitism: The Longest Hatred* (London: Thames Methuen, 1991).

16. Lazare, "L'esprit révolutionnaire dans le judaïsme," *Revue Bleue* (May 1893), which is the core of the chapter in his *History of Antisemitism,* and also the discussion in Löwy, *Redemption and Utopia,* 188ff.

17. In chapter 10, devoted to the question of race, Lazare insists that there are no races but only nations with their own historic, moral, and intellectual unity. The Jews are not a race or an *ethnos* but a *nation* made up of common sentiments, thoughts, and an ethical code, despite the great variety of Jewish types.

18. Lazare, "Le nouveau ghetto," *La Justice,* 17 November 1894.

19. Lazare, *Antisémitisme et Révolution* (Paris, 1895), 12.

20. Lazare, *Contre l'Antisémitisme* (Paris, 1896), 4–7.

21. Ibid., 6–8.

22. Ibid., 6. After reading *Contre l'Antisémitisme,* the leading French impressionist painter Camille Pissarro (himself an anarchist, a Jew, and a Dreyfusard) wrote to Lazare expressing his agreement and pleasure "de voir un sémite défendre si éloquemment ces idées." Only a scholar and an anarchist, he ventured, could have spoken out with such conviction and authority. "Vous avex été courageux et vous avez fait votre devoir" (Central Zionist Archives, Jerusalem, K 11/77).

23. Lazare, "Le Nationalisme et L'Emancipation Juive," *L'Echo Sioniste,* no. 11 (20 April 1901): 152. For extracts in English from this and other essays by Lazare dealing with Jewish nationalism, see Arthur Hertzberg, ed., *The Zionist Idea: A Historical Analysis and Reader* (Garden City, NY: Doubleday, 1959), 473ff. Hertzberg was perhaps the first historian to see Lazare's importance in the framework of Zionist ideology, even though his involvement in the movement was relatively brief.

24. Wistrich, *Revolutionary Jews from Marx to Trotsky,* 145–47.

25. Lazare, "La conception sociale du Judaïsme et le Peuple Juif," *La Grande Revue* (September 1899), 596. Also in *L'Echo Sioniste,* 5 October 1899, 47–48. An English translation of this and other selected Jewish writings by Lazare appeared in *Job's Dungheap: Essays on Jewish Nationalism and Social Revolution* (New York: Schocken Books, 1948) with a preface by Hannah Arendt.

26. Lazare was responding to an article by the French Socialist leader and Dreyfusard, Jean Jaurès, which appeared in *La Petite République,* 13 December 1898. In reply to Drumont, Jaurès had indicated that a socialism "nuanced with antisemitism" would have raised no objections on the Left. Lazare was shocked that Jaurès should still identify the Jewish "social concept" with capitalist exploitation. See Robert S. Wistrich, "French Socialism and the Dreyfus Affair," *The Wiener Library Bulletin* , n.s., 28, nos. 35–36 (1975), for the background.

27. Lazare, "La conception sociale . . . ." It is particularly noteworthy that in this essay, Lazare completely revised the hostile characterization of the Talmud to be found in his *History of Antisemitism.*

28. Edouard Drumont, *La Libre Parole,* 10 January 1895, 1.

29. Charles Péguy already noted this paradox in 1910. Apart from Péguy's *Les Cahiers de la Quinzaine,* the only newspaper which treated Lazare according to his true dignity, measure, and grandeur was *La Libre Parole* of Edouard Drumont. True, Péguy pointed out, Drumont regarded Lazare as an enemy but he admired his devotion to the cause of Israel and his greatness of character. This contrasted sharply with the shabby treatment he received at the hands of the Dreyfusard politicians and the official French Jewish establishment. See Péguy, *Notre Jeunesse* (Paris, 1969, re-edition) 91.

30. See *Action Française,* t. XIX, 1907, 177. Also Charles Maurras, "Bernard-Lazare," *Action Française,* 15 September 1908, and his *Au Signe de Flore: La fondation de l'Action Française, 1898–1900* (Paris, 1933) 51–52, 87–89.

31. Wilson, *Bernard-Lazare,* 272–74.

32. Ibid., 109.

CONTENTS

PREFACE

PORTIONS of this book, which at various times appeared in the newspapers and periodicals, received the honour of being noticed and discussed. This has induced me to write the few lines that follow.

It has been my intention to write neither an apology nor a diatribe, but an impartial study in history and sociology. I dislike antisemitism; it is a narrow, one-sided view, still I have sought to account for it. It was not born without cause, I have searched for its causes. Whether I have succeeded in discovering them, it is for the reader to decide.

An opinion as general as antisemitism, which has flourished in all countries and in all ages, before and after the Christian era, at Alexandria, Rome, and Antiachia, in Arabia, and in Persia, in mediaeval and in modern Europe, in a word, in all parts of the world wherever there are or have been Jews—such an opinion, it has seemed to me, could not spring from a mere whim or fancy, but must be the effect of deep and serious causes.

It has, therefore, been my aim to draw a full-size picture of antisemitism, of its history and causes, to follow its successive changes and transformations. Such a study might easily fill volumes. I have, therefore, been obliged to limit its scope, confining myself to broad outlines and omitting details. I hope to take up, at no distant day, some of its aspects which could only be hinted at here, and I shall then endeavour to show what has been the intellectual, moral, economic and revolutionary role of the Jew in the world.

BERNARD LAZARE.

Paris, 25 April, 1894.

ONE

GENERAL CAUSES OF ANTISEMITISM

To make the history of antisemitism complete, omitting none of the manifestations of this sentiment and following its divers phases and modifications, it is necessary to go into the history of Israel since its dispersion, or, more properly speaking, since the beginning of its expansion beyond the boundaries of Palestine.

Wherever the Jews settled after ceasing to be a nation ready to defend its liberty and independence, one observes the development of antisemitism, or rather anti-Judaism; for antisemitism is an ill chosen word, which has its *raison d'etre* only in our day, when it is sought to broaden this strife between the Jew and the Christians by supplying it with a philosophy and a metaphysical, rather than a material reason. If this hostility, this repugnance had been shown towards the Jews at one time or in one country only, it would be easy to account for the local causes of this sentiment. But this race has been the object of hatred with all the nations amidst whom it ever settled. Inasmuch as the enemies of the Jews belonged to divers races, as they dwelled far apart from one another, were ruled by different laws and governed by opposite principles; as they had not the same customs and differed in spirit from one another, so that they could not possibly judge alike of any subject, it must needs be that the general causes of antisemitism have always resided in Israel itself, and not in those who antagonized it.

This does not mean that justice was always on the side of Israel's persecutors, or that they did not indulge in all the extremes born of hatred; it is merely asserted that the Jews were themselves, in part, at least, the cause of their own ills.

Considering the unanimity of antisemitic manifestations, it can hardly be admitted, as had too willingly been done, that they were merely due to a religious war, and one must not view the strife against the Jews as a struggle of polytheism against monotheism, or that of the Trinity against Jehovah. The polytheistic, as well as the Christian nations combatted not the doctrine of one sole God, but the Jew.

Which virtues or which vices have earned for the Jew this universal enmity? Why was he ill-treated and hated alike and in turn by the Alexandrians and the Romans, by the Persians and the Arabs, by the Turks and the Christian nations? Because, everywhere up to our own days the Jew was an unsociable being.

Why was he unsociable? Because he was exclusive, and his exclusiveness was both political and religious, or rather he held fast to his political and religious cult, to his law.

All through history we see the conquered peoples submit to the laws of the conqueror, though they may guard their own faith and beliefs. It was easy for them to do so, for with them a line was drawn between their religious teachings which had come from the gods, and their civil laws which emanated from legislation and could be modified according to circumstances, without inviting upon the reformers the theological anathema or execration; what had been done by man could be undone by man. Thus, if the conquered rose up against the conquerors, it was through patriotism alone, and they were actuated by no other motive but the desire to regain their land and their liberty. Aside from these national uprisings, they seldom took exception to being subjected to the general laws; if they protested, it was against particular enactments which placed them into a position of inferiority towards the dominant people; in the history of the Roman conquests we see the conquered bow to Rome when she extended to them the laws which governed the empire.

Not so with the Jewish people. In fact, as was observed by Spinoza,[1] "the laws revealed by God to Moses were nothing but laws for the special government of the Hebrews." Moses,[2] the prophet and legislator, assigned the same authority for his judicial and governmental enactments, as for his religious precepts, *i.e.,* revelation. Not only did Yahweh say to the Jews, "Ye shall believe in the one God and ye shall worship no idols," he also prescribed for them rules of hygiene and morality; not only did he designate the territory where sacrifices were to be offered, he also determined the manner in which that territory was to be governed. Each of the given laws, whether agrarian, civil, prophylactic, theological, or moral, proceeded from the same authority, so that all these codes formed a whole, a rigorous system of which naught could be taken away for fear of sacrilege.

In reality, the Jew lived under the rule of a lord, Yahweh, who could neither be conquered, nor even assailed, and he knew but one thing, the law, *i.e.*, the collection of rules and decrees which it had once pleased Yahweh to give to Moses—a law divine and excellent, made to lead its followers to eternal bliss; a perfect law which the Jewish people alone had received.

With such an idea of his Torah, the Jew could not accept the laws of strange nations; nor could he think of submitting to them; he could not abandon the divine laws, eternal, good and just, to follow human laws, necessarily imperfect and subject to decay. Thus, wherever colonies were founded by the Jews, to whatever land they were deported, they insisted, not only upon permission to follow their religion, but also upon exemption from the customs of the people amidst whom they were to live, and the privileges to govern themselves by their own laws.

At Rome, at Alexandria, at Antioch, in Cyrenaica they were allowed full freedom in the matter. They were not required to appear in court on Saturday;[3] they were even permitted to have their own special tribunals, and were not amenable to the laws of the empire; when the distribution of grains occurred on a Saturday their share was reserved for them until the next day,[4] they could be decurions, being at the same time exempt from all practices contrary to their religion;[5] they enjoyed complete self-government, as in Alexandria; they had their own chiefs, their own senate, their ethnarch, and were not subject to the general municipal authorities.

Everywhere they wanted to remain Jews, and everywhere they were granted the privilege of establishing a State within the State. By virtue of these privileges and exemptions, and immunity from taxes, they would soon rise above the general condition of the citizens of the municipalities where they resided; they had better opportunities for trade and accumulation of wealth, whereby they excited jealousy and hatred.

Thus, Israel's attachment to its law was one of the first causes of its unpopularity, whether because it derived from that law benefits and advantages which were apt to excite envy, or because it prided itself upon the excellence of its Torah and considered itself above and beyond other peoples.

Still had the Israelites adhered to pure Mosaism, they could, doubtless, at some time in their history, have so modified that Mosaism as to retain none but the religious and metaphysical precepts; possibly, if they had no other sacred book but the Bible they might have merged in the nascent church, which enlisted its first followers among the Sadducees, the Essenes, and the Jewish proselytes. One thing prevented that fusion and upheld the existence of the Hebrews among the nations; it was the growth of the Talmud, the authority and rule of the doctors who taught a pretended tradition. The policy of the doctors to which we shall return further made of the Jews sullen beings, unsociable and haughty, of whom Spinoza, who knew them well, could say : "It is not at all surprising that after being scattered for so many years they have preserved their identity without a government of their own, for, by their external rites, contrary to those of other nations, as well as by the sign of circumcision, they have isolated themselves from all other nations, even to the extent of drawing upon themselves the hate of all mankind."[6]

Man's aim on earth, said the doctors, is the knowledge and observance of the law, and one cannot thoroughly observe it without denying allegiance to all but the true law. The Jew who followed these precepts isolated himself from the rest of mankind; he retrenched himself behind the fences which had been erected around the Torah by Ezra and the first scribes,[7] later by the Pharisees and the Talmudists, the successors of Ezra, reformers of primitive Mosaism and enemies or the prophets. He isolated himself, not merely by declining to submit to the customs which bound together the inhabitants of the countries where he settled, but also by shunning all intercourse with the inhabitants themselves. To his unsociability the Jew added exclusiveness.

With the law, yet without Israel to put it into practice, the world could not exist, God would turn it back into nothing; nor will the world know happiness until it be brought under the universal domination of that law, *i.e.,* under the domination of the Jews. Thus the Jewish people is chosen by God as the trustee of His will; it is the only people with whom the Deity has made a covenant; it is the choice of the Lord. At the time when the serpent tempted Eve, says the Talmud, he corrupted her with his venom. Israel, on receiving the revelation from Sinai, delivered itself from the evil; the rest of mankind could not recover. Thus, if they have each its guardian and its protecting constellation, Israel is placed under the very eye of Jehovah; it is the Eternal's favoured son who has the

sole right to his love, to his good will, to his special protection, other
men are placed beneath the Hebrews; it is by mere mercy that they
are entitled to divine munificence, since the souls of the Jews alone
are descended from the first man. The wealth which has come to
the nations, in truth belongs to Israel, and we hear Jesus Himself
reply to the Greek woman : "It is not meet to take the children's
bread and so cast it unto the dogs."[8] This faith in their predestina-
tion, in their election, developed among the Jews an immense pride.
It led them to view the Gentiles with contempt, often with hate,
when patriotic considerations supervened to religious feeling.

When Jewish nationality was in peril, the Pharisees, under John
Hyrcanus, declared impure the soil of strange peoples, as well as all
intercourse among Jews and Greeks. Later, the Shamaites advocated
at a synod complete separation of the Jews from the heathens, and
drafted a set of injunctions, called *The Eighteen Things,* which
ultimately prevailed over the opposition of the Hillelites. As a result
Jewish unsociability begins to engage the attention of the councils
of Antiochus Sidetes; exception is taken to "their persistence in
shutting themselves up amidst their own kind and avoiding all
intercourse with pagans, and to their eagerness to make that intercourse more and more difficult, if not impossible."[9] And the high
priest Menelaus accuses the law before Antiochus Epiphanes, "of
teaching hatred of the human race, of prohibiting to sit down at the
table of strangers and to show good-will towards them."

If these prescriptions had lost their authority when the cause
which had produced and, in a way, justified them, had disappeared,
the evil would not have been great. Yet we see them reappear in
the Talmud and receive a new sanction from the authority of the
doctors. After the controversy between the Sadducees and the
Pharisees had terminated in the victory of the latter, these injunctions became part of the law, they were taught with the law and
helped to develop and exaggerate the exclusiveness of the Jews.

Another fear, that of contamination, separated the Jews from
the world and made their isolation still more rigorous. The Pharisees
held views of extreme rigour on the subject of contamination; with
them the injunctions and prescriptions of the Bible were insufficient
to preserve Man from sin. As the sacrificial vases were contaminated
by the least impure contact, they came to regard themselves contaminated by contact with strangers. Of this fear were born in-
numerable rules affecting everyday life : rules relating to clothing,

dwelling, nourishment, all of which were promulgated with a view to save the Israelites from contamination and sacrilege; all these rules might properly be observed in an independent state or city, but could not possibly be enforced in foreign lands, for their strict observance would require the Jews to flee the society of Gentiles, and thus to live isolated, hostile to their environment.

The Pharisees and the Rabbinites went still farther. Not satisfied with preserving the body, they also sought to save the soul. Experience had shown them that Hellenic and Roman importations imperilled what they deemed their faith. The names of the Hellenistic high priests, Jason, Menelaus, etc., reminded the Rabbinites of the times when the genius of Greece, winning over one portion of Israel, came very near conquering it. They knew that the Sadducean party, friendly to the Greeks, had paved the way for Christianity, as much as the Alexandrians and all those who maintained that "none but the legal provisions, clearly enunciated in the Mosaic law were binding, whereas all other rules growing from local traditions or subsequently issued, could lay no claim to rigorous observance.[10]

It was under Greek influence that the books and oracles originated which prepared the minds for Messiah. The Hellenistic Jews, Philo and Aristobulus, the pseudo-Phocylides and the pseudo-Longinus, authors of the Sibylline oracles and of the pseudo-Orphics, all these successors of the prophets who continued their work, led mankind to Christ. And it may be said that true Mosaism, purified and enlarged by Isaiah, Jeremiah and Ezekiel, broadened and generalized by the Judaeo-Hellenists, would have brought Israel to Christianity, but for Ezraism, Pharisaism and Talmudism, which held the mass of the Jews bound to strict observances and narrow ritual practices.

To guard God's people, to keep it safe from evil influences, the doctors exalted their law above all things. They declared that no study but that of the law alone became an Israelite, and as a whole life-time was hardly sufficient to learn and penetrate all the subtleties and all the casuistry of that law, they prohibited the study of profane sciences and foreign languages. "Those among us who learn several languages are not held in esteem," said Josephus;[11] contempt alone was soon thought insufficient, they were excommunicated. Nor did these expulsions satisfy the Rabbinites. Though deprived of Plato, had not the Jew still the Bible, could he not listen to the voice of the prophets? As the book could not be proscribed, it was belittled and made subordinate to the Talmud; the doctors declared: "The law is water, the Mishna is wine." And the reading of the Bible was considered less beneficial, less conducive to salvation than the reading of the Mishna.

However, the Rabbinites could not kill Jewish curiosity with one blow; it required centuries. It was as late as the fourteenth century, after Ibn Ezra, Rabbi Bechai, Maimonides, Bedares, Joseph Caspi, Levi Ben Gerson, Moses of Narbonne, and many others, were gone, all true sons of Philo and the Alexandrians, who strove to verify Judaism by foreign philosophy; after Asher Ben Yechiel had induced the assembly of the rabbis at Barcelona to excommunicate those who would study profane sciences; after Rabbi Shalem, of Montpellier had complained to the Dominicans of the *Moreh Nebukhim,* and this book, the highest expression of the ideas of Maimonides, had been burned—it was only after all this that the rabbis ultimately triumphed.[12]

Their end was attained. They had cut off Israel from the community of nations; they had made of it a sullen recluse, a rebel against all laws, foreign to all feeling fraternity, closed to all beautiful, noble and generous ideas; they had made of it a small and miserable nation, soured by isolation, brutalized by a narrow education, demoralized and corrupted by an unjustifiable pride.[13]

With this transformation of the Jewish spirit and the victory of sectarian doctors, coincides the beginning of official persecution. Until that epoch there had only been outbursts of local hatred, but no systematic vexations. With the triumph of the Rabbinites, the ghettos come into being. The expulsions and massacres commence. The Jews want to live apart—a line is drawn against them. They detest the spirit of the nations amidst whom they live—the nations chase them. They burn the Moreh—their Talmud is burned and they themselves are burned with it.[14]

It would seem that no further agency was needed to render the separation of the Jews from the rest of mankind complete and to make them an object of horror and reprobation. Still another cause must be added to those just mentioned: the indomitable and tenacious patriotism of Israel.

Certainly, every people was attached to the land of its birth. Conquered, beaten by the conquerors, driven into exile or forced into slavery, they remained true to the sweet memories of their plundered city or the country they had lost. Still none other knew the patriotic enthusiasm of the Jews. The Greek, whose city was destroyed, could elsewhere build anew the hearth upon which his ancestors bestowed their blessings; the Roman who went into exile took along with him his penates; Athens or Rome had nothing of the mystic fatherland like Jerusalem.

Jerusalem was the guardian of the Tabernacle which received the divine word; it was the city of the only Temple, the only place in the world where God could efficiently be worshipped and sacrifices offered to Him. It was only much later, at a very late day, that prayer houses were erected in other towns of Juda, or Greece, or Italy; still in those houses they confined themselves to the reading of the law and theological discussion; the pomp of Jehovah was known nowhere but at Jerusalem, the chosen sanctuary. When a temple was built at Alexandria, it was considered heretical; indeed, the ceremonies which were celebrated there had no sense, for they ought not to be performed anywhere but in a true temple; so St. Chrysostom, after the dispersion of the Jews and the destruction of their city, was justified in saying : "The Jews offer sacrifices in all parts of the earth except there where the sacrifice is permitted and valid, *i.e.,* at Jerusalem."

All Jews of the period of dispersion sent to Jerusalem the didrachm tax for the maintenance of the temple; once in their lives they came to the holy city, as later the Mohammedans came to Mecca; after their death they were carried to Palestine, and numerous craft anchored at the coast, loaded with small coffins which were thence forwarded on camel's back.

It was because in Jerusalem only, in the land given by God to their ancestors, their bodies would be resurrected. There those who had believed in Yahweh, who had observed his law and obeyed his word, would awake at the sound of the last trumpet and appear before their Lord. Nowhere but there could they rise at the appointed hour; every other land but that washed by the yellow Jordan was a vile land, fouled by idolatry, deprived of God.

When the fatherland was dead, when adversity was sweeping Israel all over the world, after the Temple had perished in flames, and when the heathens occupied the holiest ground, mourning over bygone days became everlasting in the soul of the Jew. It was over; they could no longer hope to see on the day of mercy the black buck carry away their sins into the desert, neither could they see the lamb killed for the passover night, or bring their offerings to the altar; and, deprived of Jerusalem during life, they would not be brought there after death.

God ought not to abandon his children, reasoned the pious; and naive legends came to comfort the exiles. Near the tombs of the Jews who die in exile, they said, Jehovah opens long caverns through which the corpses roll as far as Palestine, whereas the pagan who dies there, near the consecrated hills, is removed from the chosen land, for he is unworthy of remaining there where the resurrection will take place.

Still that did not satisfy them. They did not resign themselves to visiting Jerusalem merely as pitiable pilgrims, weeping before the ruined walls, many of them so maddened by grief as to let themselves be trampled upon by horses' hoofs, embracing the ground while moaning; they could not believe that God, that the blessed city had abandoned them; with Judah Levita they exclaimed: "Zion, hast thou forgotten thy unfortunate children who groan in slavery?"

They expected that their Lord would by his mighty right hand raise the fallen walls; they hoped that a prophet, a chosen one, would bring them back to the promised land; and how many times, in the course of ages, have they left their homes, their fortunes— they who are reproached of being too much attached to worldly goods—in order to follow a false Messiah who undertook to lead them and promised them the return so much longed for! Thousands were attracted by Serenus, Moses of Crete, Alroi, and massacred in the expectation of the happy day.

With the Talmudists these sentiments of popular enthusiasm, this mystic heroism underwent a transformation. The doctors taught the restoration of the Jewish empire; in order that Jerusalem might be born anew from its ruins, they wanted to preserve the people of Israel pure, to prevent them from mixing with other people, to inculcate on them the idea that they were everywhere in exile, amidst enemies that held them captive. They said to their disciples: "Do not cultivate strange lands, soon you will cultivate your own; do not attach yourself to any land, for thus will you be unfaithful to the memory of your native land; do not submit to any king, for you have no master but the Lord of the Holy Land, Jehovah; do not scatter amongst the nations, you will forfeit your salvation and you will not see the light of the day of resurrection; remain such as you left your house; the hour will come and you will see again the hills of your ancestors, and those hills will then be the centre of the world, which will be subject to your power."

Thus all those complex sentiments which had in olden days served to build up the hegemony of Israel, to maintain its character as a nation, to develop a high and powerful originality, all those virtues and vices which gave it the spirit and countenance necessary to preserve a nation; which enabled it to attain greatness and later to defend its independence with desperate valour worthy of admiration; all that, after the Jews had ceased to be a State, combined to shut them up in the most complete, the most absolute isolation.

This isolation has been their strength, in the opinion of some apologists. If they mean to say that owing to it the Jews have survived, so much is true; if the conditions are considered, however, under which the Jews have preserved their identity as a people, it is obvious that this isolation has been their weakness, and that they have survived up to modern times, as a race of pariahs, persecuted, often martyred. Moreover, it is not only to their seclusion that they owe this surprising persistence. Their extraordinary solidarity, due to their misfortunes, and mutual support count for very much; and even in our day, when they take part in public life in some countries, having abandoned their sectarian dogmas, this very solidarity prevents them from dissolving and disappearing as a people, by conferring upon them certain benefits to which they are by no means indifferent.

This solicitude for worldly goods, which is a marked feature of the Hebrew character, has not been without effect upon the conduct of the Jews, especially since they left Palestine; by directing them along certain avenues, to the exclusion of all others, this feature of their character has drawn upon them the most violent animosities. The soul of the Jew is twofold : it is both mystic and positive. His mysticism has come down from the theophanies of the desert to the metaphysical dreaming of the kabbala; his positivism, or rather his rationalism, manifests itself in the sentences of the Ecclesiastes as well as the legislative enactments of the rabbis and the dogmatic controversies of the theologians. Still if mysticism leads to a Philo or Spinoza, rationalism leads to the usurer, the weigher of gold; it creates the greedy trader. It is true that at times these two states of the mind are found in just opposition, and the Israelite, as it occurred in the middle ages, can split his life into two parts : one devoted to meditation on the Absolute, the other to business.

Of the Jewish love for gold, there can be no question here. Though it may have grown so abnormal with this race as to have become well-nigh the only motive of their actions, though it may have engendered a violent and exasperated antisemitism, yet it cannot be classed among the general causes of antisemitism. It was, on the contrary, the effect of those very causes, and we shall see that it is partly the exclusiveness, the persistent patriotism, and pride of Israel, that has driven it to become the hated usurer of the whole world.

In fact, all the causes we have just enumerated, if they be general, are not the only ones. I have called them general, because they depend upon one constant element : the Jew. Still the Jew is only one of the factors of antisemitism; he provokes it by his presence, but he is not the only one that determines it. The nations among whom the Israelites have lived, their manners, their customs, their religion, the philosophy even of the nations in whose midst Israel has developed determine the particular character of antisemitism, which changes with time and place.

We shall trace these modifications and variations of antisemitism through the course of ages down to our epoch; and we shall examine whether, in some countries at least, the general causes I have attempted to deduce are still operating, or whether the reasons for modern antisemitism must not be sought elsewhere.

ANTI-JUDAISM IN ANTIQUITY

MODERN antisemites who are in quest of sires for themselves, un-hesitatingly trace the first demonstrations against the Jews back to the days of ancient Egypt. For that purpose they are particularly pleased to refer to Genesis, xliii, 32, where it is said : "The Egyptians might not eat bread with the Hebrews; for that it is an abomination unto the Egyptians." They also rely upon a few verses of the Exodus, among them the following : "Behold, the people of the children of Israel are more and mightier than we; come on, let us deal wisely with them, lest they multiply." (Exodus, i, 9, 10.)

It is certain that the sons of Jacob who came to the land of Goshen under the Shepherd Pharaoh Aphobis, were treated by the Egyptians with the same contempt as their brothers, the Hyksos, referred to in hieroglyphic texts as *lepers,* called also "plague" and "pest" in some inscriptions.[15] They arrived at that very epoch when a very strong national sentiment manifested itself against the Asiatic invaders, hated for their cruelty; this sentiment soon led to the war of independence, which resulted in the final victory of Ahmos I., and the enslavement of the Hebrews. However, unless one is a violent anti-Jew, it is impossible to perceive in those remote disturbances anything beyond a mere incident in a struggle between conquerors and conquered.

There is no antisemitism until the Jews, having abandoned their native land, settle as immigrants in foreign countries and come into contact with natives or older settlers, whose customs, race and religion are different from those of the Hebrews.

Accordingly, the history of Haman and Mordecai may be taken as the beginning of antisemitism, and the antisemites have not failed so to do. This view is, perhaps, more correct. Though the historical reality of the book of Esther can scarcely be relied upon, still it is worthy of note that its author puts into the mouth of Haman some of the complaints, which, at a later period, are uttered by Tacitus and other Latin writers. "And Haman said unto the king, Ahasuerus : there is a certain people scattered abroad and dispersed among the people in all the provinces of thy kingdom; and their laws are diverse from all people; neither keep they the king's laws." (Esther, iii, 8.)

The pamphleteers of the middle ages, of the sixteenth and seventeenth centuries, and of our own time, say nothing else; and if the history of Haman is apocryphal, which is highly probable, still it cannot be denied that the author of the Book of Esther has very ably brought out some of the causes, which for many centuries exposed the Jews to the hatred of nations.

Yet we must go to the period of Jewish expansion abroad, to be enabled to observe with certainty that hostility against them, which by a peculiar misuse of terms has in our days been called antisemitism.

Some traditions refer the entrance of the Jews into the ancient world to the epoch of the first captivity. While Nabu-Kudur-Ussur led away to Babylonia a portion of the Jewish people, many of the Israelites, to escape from the conqueror, fled to Egypt, to Tripoli, and reached the Greek colonies. Tradition brings back to the same period the arrival of the Jews in China and India.

Historically, however, the wanderings of the Jews across the globe commence in the fourth century before our era. About 331 B.C. Alexander transported some Jews to Alexandria, Ptolemy sent some of them to Cyrenaica, and about the same time Seleucus led some of them to Antioch. When Jesus was born Jewish colonies flourished everywhere, and it was among them that Christianity recruited its first adherents. There were Jews in Egypt, in Phoenicia, in Syria, in Coele-Syria, in Pamphylia, in Cilicia, and as far as Bithynia. In Europe they had settled in Thessalia, Boeotia, Macedonia, Attica and Peloponnesus. They were to be found in the Great Isles, on Euboea, on Crete, on Cyprus, and at Rome. "It is not easy to find a place on earth," says Strabo, "which has not received that race."

Why were the Jews hated in all those countries, in all those cities? Because they never entered any city as citizens, but always as a privileged class. Though having left Palestine, they wanted above all to remain Jews, and their native country was still Jerusalem, *i.e.,* the only city where God might be worshipped and sacrifices offered in His Temple. They formed everywhere republics, as it were, united with Judea and Jerusalem, and from every place they remitted monies to the high priest in payment of a special tax for the maintenance of the Temple—the didrachm.

Moreover, they separated themselves from other inhabitants by their rites and their customs; they considered the soil of foreign nations impure and sought to constitute themselves in every city into a sort of a sacred territory. They lived apart, in special quarters, secluded among themselves, isolated, governing themselves by virtue of privileges which were jealously guarded by them, and excited the envy of their neighbours. They intermarried amongst themselves and entertained no strangers, for fear of pollution. The mystery with which they surrounded themselves excited curiosity as well as aversion. Their rites appeared strange and gave occasion for ridicule; being unknown, they were misrepresented and slandered.

At Alexandria they were quite numerous. According to Philo,[16] Alexandria was divided into five wards. Two were inhabited by the Jews. The privileges accorded to them by Caesar were engraved on a column and guarded by them as a precious treasure. They had their own Senate with exclusive jurisdiction in Jewish affairs, and they were judged by an ethnarch. They were ship-owners, traders, farmers, most of them wealthy; the sumptuousness of their monuments and synagogues bore witness to it. The Ptolemies made them farmers of the revenues; this was one of the causes of popular hatred against them. Besides, they had a monopoly of navigation on the Nile, of the grain trade and of provisioning Alexandria, and they extended their trade to all the provinces along the Mediterranean coast. They accumulated great fortunes; this gave rise to the *invidia auri Judaici*. The growing resentment against these foreign cornerers, constituting a nation within a nation, led to popular disturbances; the Jews were frequently assaulted, and Germanicu, among others, had great trouble protecting them.

The Egyptians took revenge upon them by deriding their religious customs, their abhorrence of pork. They once paraded in the city a fool, Carabas by name, adorned with a papyrus diadem, decked in a royal gown, and they saluted him as king of the Jews. Under Philadelphus, one of the first Ptolemies, Manetho, the high-priest of the Temple at Heliopolis, lent his authority to the popular hatred; he considered the Jews descendants of the Hyksos usurpers, and said that that leprous tribe had been expelled for sacrilege and impiousness. Those fables were repeated by Chæremon and Lysimachus. It was not only popular animosity, however, that persecuted the Jews; they had also against them the Stoics and the Sophists. The Jews, by their proselytism, interfered with the Stoics; there was a rivalry for influence between them, and, notwithstanding their common belief in divine unity, there was opposition between them. The Stoics charged the Jews with irreligiousness, judging by the sayings of Posidonius and Apollonius Molo; they had a very scant knowledge of the Jewish religion. The Jews, they said, refuse to worship the gods; they do not consent to bow even before the divinity of the emperor. They have in their sanctuary the head of an ass and render homage to it; they are cannibals; every year they fatten a man and sacrifice him in a grove, after which they divide among themselves his flesh and swear on it to hate strangers. "The Jews, says Apollonius Molo, are enemies of all mankind; they have invented nothing useful, and they are brutal." To this Posidonius adds : "They are the worst of all men."

Not less than the Stoics did the Sophists detest the Jews. But the causes of their hatred were not religious, but, I should say, rather literary. From Ptolemy Philadelphus, until the middle of the third century, the Alexandrian Jews, with the intent of sustaining and strengthening their propaganda, gave themselves to forging all texts which were capable of lending support to their cause. The verses of Aeschylus, of Sophocles, of Euripides, the pretended oracles of Orpheus, preserved in Aristobulus and the *Stromata* of Clement of Alexandria were thus made to glorify the one God and the Sabbath. Historians were falsified or credited with the authorship of books they had never written. It is thus that a History of the Jews was published under the name of Hecataeus of Abdera. The most important of these inventions was the Sibylline oracles, a fabrication of the Alexandrian Jews, which prophesied the future advent of the reign of the one God. They found imitators, however, for since the Sibyl had begun to speak, in the second century before Christ, the first Christians also made her speak. The Jews would appropriate to themselves even the Greek literature and philosophy. In a commentary on the Pentateuch, which has been preserved for us by Eusebius,[17] Aristobulus attempted to show that Plato and Aristotle had found their metaphysical and ethical ideas in an old Greek translation of the Pentateuch. The Greeks were greatly incensed at such treatment of their literature and philosophy, and out of revenge they circulated the slanderous stories of Manetho, adapting them to those of the Bible, to the great fury of the Jews; thus the confusion of languages was identified with the myth of Zeus robbing the animals of their common language. The Sophists, wounded by the conduct of the Jews, would speak against them in their teaching. One among them, Apion, wrote a *Treatise against the Jews.* This Apion was a peculiar individual, a liar and babbler, to a degree uncommon even among rhetors, and full of vanity, which earned him from Tiberius the nickname *"Cymbalum mundi."* His stories were famous; he claimed to have called out, by means of magic herbs, the shade of Homer, says Pliny.

Apion repeated in his *Treatise against the Jews* the stories of Manetho, which had been previously restated by Chaeremon and Lysimachus, and supplemented them by quoting from Posidonius and Apollonius Molo. According to him, Moses was "nothing but a seducer and wizard," and his laws contained "nothing but what is bad and dangerous."[18]

As to the Sabbath, the name was derived, he said, from a disease, a sort of an ulcer, with which the Jews were afflicted, and which the Egyptians called *sabbatosim,* i.e., disease of the groins.

Philo and Josephus undertook the defence of the Jews and fought the Sophists and Apion. In *Contra Apionem,* Josephus is very severe on his adversary. "Apion," says he, "is as stupid as an ass and as imprudent as a dog, which is one of the gods of his nation." Philo, on the other hand, prefers to attack the Sophists in general, and if he mentions Apion at all, in his *Legatio ad Caium,* it is merely because Apion was sent to Rome to prefer charges against the Jews before Caligula.

In his *Treatise on Agriculture* he draws a very black picture of the Sophists, and insinuates that Moses has compared them to hogs. Nevertheless, in his other writings, he advises his co-religionists not to irritate them, so as to avoid all provocation to disturbances, but to await patiently their chastisement, which will come on the day the Jewish Empire, the empire of salvation, will be established on earth.

Philo's injunctions were not heeded; the exasperation on both sides often led to violent riots and massacres of Jews; the latter, however, valiantly defended themselves.[19]

At Rome the Jews had a powerful and wealthy colony as early as the first year of the Christian era. If Valerius Maximus may be trusted, they first came to the city about 139 B.C., during the consulate of Popilius Loenus and Cajas Calpwinius.[20]

Certain it is that, in 160 B.C., an embassy from Judas Maccabee arrived in Rome to negotiate an alliance with the Republic against the Syrians; other embassies followed, in 143 and 139.[21]

The settlement of the Jews at Rome probably dates from that time. Under Pompey they came in numbers, and as early as 58 B.C., they had quite a settlement. Turbulent and formidable, they were an important factor in politics. Caesar availed himself of their support during the civil wars and lavished favours upon them; he even granted them exemption from military service. Under Augustus the distribution of free bread was postponed for them whenever it fell due on Saturday. The Emperor gave them permission to collect the didrachm which was sent to Palestine, and he ordered the sacrifice of one or two lambs to be offered in his behalf at the Temple of Jerusalem for all time to come. When Tiberius became emperor, there were at Rome 20,000 Jews, who were organized in colleges and *sodalitates*.

Except the Jews of prominent families, like the Herods and the Agrippas, who mixed in public life, the Jewish masses lived in retirement. The majority resided in the dirtiest and busiest quarter of the city, the Transtiberinus. They were to be seen near the Via Portuensis, the Emporium and the Great Circus, in the Campus Martius, and in Suburra, beyond the Capenian Gate, on the banks of the Egerian Creek, and near the sacred grove. They were engaged in retail trade and the sale of second-hand goods; those at the Capenian Gate were fortune tellers. The Jew of the Ghetto is already there.

At Rome the same causes were at work as at Alexandria. There, also, the excessive privileges of the Jews, the wealth of some of them, as well as their unheard-of luxury and ostentation, excited popular hatred. This resentment was aggravated by deeper and more important reasons of a religious character; it may even be maintained, strange as it may seem, that the motive of Roman anti-Judaism was religious.

The Roman religion resembled in nothing the admirable and profoundly symbolic polytheism of the Greeks. It was ritual rather than mythical; it consisted of customs closely connected with the doings of everyday life, as well as with all sorts of public acts. Rome was one body with its gods; its greatness was bound, as it were, with the rigorous observance of the practices of their national religion; its glory depended upon the piety of its citizens, and it seems that the Roman must have had, like the Jew, that notion of a covenant between the deities and himself, which was to be scrupulously lived up to by both parties. Somehow or other, the Roman was always in the presence of his gods; he left his hearth, where they abode, only to find them again in the Forum, on the public highways, in the Senate, even in the fields, where they kept watch over the power of Rome. At all times and on all occasions sacrifices were offered; the warriors and the diplomats were guided by auguries, and all authority, civil as well as military, partook of the priesthood, for the officer could not perform his duties unless he knew the rites and observances of the cult.

It was this cult that for centuries sustained the Republic, and its commandments were faithfully obeyed; when they were changed, when the traditions became adulterated, when the rules were violated, Rome saw its glory fade, and its agony commenced.

Thus the Roman religion preserved itself for a long time without change. True, Rome was familiar with foreign cults; she saw the worshipers of Isis and Osiris, those of the great Mother and those of Sabazius; still, though admitting them into her Pantheon, she gave them no place in her national religion. All these Orientals were tolerated; the citizens were allowed to practice their superstitions, provided they were harmless; but when Rome perceived that a new faith was subversive of the Roman spirit, she was pitiless, as in the case of the conspiracy of the Bacchantes, or the expulsion of Egyptian priests. Rome guarded herself against the foreign spirit; she feared affiliation with religious societies; she was afraid even of Greek philosophers, and the Senate, in 161, upon the report of the praetor Marcus Pomponius, barred them from entering the city.

From this, one may understand the feeling of the Romans toward the Jews. Greeks, Asiatics, Egyptians, Germans, or Gauls, while bringing with them their rites and beliefs, made no objection to bowing before Mars of the Palatine, or even before Jupiter Latiaris. They conformed within certain limits, to the rules of the city, to its religious customs; at all events, they showed no opposition. Not so the Jews. They brought with them a religion as rigid, as ritualistic, as intolerant, as the Roman religion. Their worship of Yahweh excluded all other worship; thus they shocked their fellow citizens by refusing to swear to the eagles, whereas the eagle was the deity of the legion. As their religious faith was blended with the observance of certain social laws, the adoption of this faith was pregnant with a change of the social order. Therefore the Romans were worried by its establishment in their midst, for the Jews were eager to make proselytes.

The proselytic spirit of the Jews is attested by all the historians, and Philo justly says : "Our customs win over and convert the barbarians and the Hellenes, the continent and the isles, the Orient and the Occident, Europe and Asia, the whole world, from end to end."

The ancient nations, at their decline, were deeply attracted by Judaism, by its dogma of divine unity, by its morals; many of the poor people were attracted by the privileges accorded to the Jews. These proselytes were divided into two great classes : those who accepted the circumcision and thereby entered into the Jewish community, thus becoming strangers to their families, and those who, without complying with the requisites for admission to the community, nevertheless gathered around it.

These conversions, generally by suasion and at times by force, as when the rich Jews converted their slaves, were bound to create a reaction. It was this chief cause, together with the secondary causes previously referred to, viz., the wealth of the Jews, their political influence, their privileged condition, that led to anti-Judaic demonstrations at Rome. The majority of Roman and Greek writers from Cicero on bear witness to this state of mind.

Cicero, who was a disciple of Apollonius Molo, inherited his teacher's prejudices; he found the Jews in his way : they were with the popular party against the party of the Senate, to which he belonged. He feared them, and we can see from some passages of *Pro Flacco,* that he hardly dared to speak of them, so numerous were they around him and in the public place. Nevertheless, one day he burst forth. "Their barbarous superstitions must be fought," says he; he accuses them of being a nation "given to suspicion and slander," and proceeds by saying that they "show contempt for the splendour of the Roman power,"[22] They were to be feared, according to him—those men who, detaching themselves from Rome, turned their eyes towards the far away city, that Jerusalem, and supported it by denaries which they drew from the Republic. Moreover, he reproached them for winning citizens over to the Sabbatarian rites.

It is this last charge that recurs most frequently in the writings of the polemists, the poets and the historians. The Jewish religion, which charmed those who had penetrated its essence, was repulsive to others who had a scant knowledge of it and regarded it as a heap of absurd and dismal rites. The Jews are nothing but a superstitious nation, says Persius;[23] their Sabbath is a lugubrious day, adds Ovid;[24] they worship the hog and the ass, affirms Petronius.[25]

Tacitus, well informed as he is, repeats, with regard to Judaism, the fables of Manetho and Posidonius. The Jews, says he, are descended from lepers, they honour the head of an ass, they have infamous rites. He further specifies his charges, which, one would say, are those of modern French Nationalists: "All those who embrace their faith," says he, "undergo circumcision, and the first instruction they receive is to despise the gods, to forswear their country, to forget father, mother and children." And he warms up by saying: "The Jews consider as profane all that is held sacred with us."[26] Suetonius and Juvenal repeat the same thing; the principal charge reads: "They have a particular cult and particular laws; they despise the Roman laws."[27] This is likewise the complaint of Pliny: "They despise the gods."[28]

Seneca has the same grudge, still with the philosopher other motives supervene. There was a rivalry between Seneca, the Stoic, and the Jews, the same as there had been between the Stoics and the Jews at Alexandria. He quarrelled less with their contempt of the gods than with their proselytism which thwarted the spread of the doctrine of the Stoics. He thus gives expression to his displeasure: "The Romans," says he regretfully, "have adopted the Sabbath."[29] And, further speaking of the Jews, he says in conclusion: "This abominable nation has succeeded in spreading its usages throughout the whole world; the conquered have given their laws to the conquerors."[30] Seneca's view was in accord with the attitude of both the Republic and the Empire, by which measures were adopted from time to time to check Jewish proselytism. Under Tiberius, in the year 22, a senatus-consult was directed against the Egyptian and Judaic superstitions and four thousand Jews, says Tacitus, were deported to Sardinia. Caligula subjected them to vexatious persecution; he encouraged the doings of Flaccus in Egypt, and Flaccus, sustained by the Emperor, robbed the Jews of the privileges granted to them by Caesar; he took away from them their synagogue and directed that they might be treated as inhabitants of a captured city. Domitian imposed a special tax upon Jews and those who led a Judaic life, hoping by the levy of the tax to stop coversions, and Antoninus Pius prohibited the Jews from circumcising others than their sons.

Anti-Judaism manifested itself not only at Rome and Alexandria, but wherever there were Jews : at Antioch, where great massacres occurred; in Lybia, where, under Vespasian, the governor Catullus stirred up the populace against them; in Ionia, where, under Augustus, the Greek cities, by an understanding among themselves, forced the Jews either to renounce their faith or to bear the entire burden of public expenditures.

Yet it is impossible to speak of the persecution of the Jews without speaking of the persecution of the Christians. For a long time Jews and Christians, these hostile brothers, were included in the same contempt, and the same causes which made the Jews hateful made the Christians hateful as well. The disciples of the Nazarene brought into the ancient world the same deadly principles. If the Jews taught the people to leave their gods, to abandon husband, father, child and wife, and to come to Jehovah, Jesus also said : "I have not come to unite, but to separate." The Christians, like the Jews, refused to bow to the eagle; like the Jews they would not lie prostrate before idols. Like the Jews, the Christians knew another country than Rome; like the Jews, they would be oblivious of their civic, rather than their religious duties.

Thus, during the first years of the Christian era, the Synagogue and the ancient Church were despised alike. Simultaneously with the Jews "a certain *chrestus*"[31] and his followers were driven from Rome. Each side endeavoured to convince the people that it ought not to be mistaken for the other, and no sooner did Christianity make itself heard than it rejected, in its turn, the descendants of Abraham.

THREE

ANTI-JUDAISM IN CHRISTIAN ANTIQUITY FROM THE CHURCH OF CONSTANTINE

THE Church is the daughter of the Synagogue; she owes her early development to the Synagogue; she grew in the shade of the Temple, and from her first infant cry she opposed her mother, which was quite natural, for they were divided by a wide divergence of opinion.

In the first centuries of the Christian era, during the apostolic age, Christian communities sprang forth from Jewish communities, like a swarm of bees escaping from a beehive; they settled on the same soil.

Jesus was not yet born when the Jews had built their prayer-houses in the cities of the Orient and the Occident; their expansion to Asia Minor, Egypt, Cyrenaica, Rome, Greece and Spain has already been noted. By their unceasing proselytism, by their preaching, by the moral influence they exercised over the nations amidst whom they lived, they paved the way for Christianity.

This immense class of proselytes won over by the Jews, this God-fearing multitude, was ready to receive the broader and more humanitarian teachings of Jesus, those teachings which the universal Church, from its very inception, undertook to adulterate and to turn away from their true meaning. These converts whose numbers steadily increased during the first century before Christ, were free from the national prejudices of Israel; they Judaized, but their eyes were not turned toward Jerusalem, and, one may say, the fervid patriotism of the Jews rather checked the conversions. The Apostles, or at least some of them, completely separated the precepts of the Jewish faith from the narrow idea of nationality; they built upon the foundation of Jewish work accomplished before and thus won for themselves the souls of those who had received the Jewish seed.

The Apostles preached in the synagogues. In the cities, where they arrived, they went straight to the prayer-houses and there made their propaganda and found their first helpers; later a Christian community was founded, side by side with the Jewish community, and the original Jewish nucleus was increased by all those whom they had convinced among the Gentiles.

Without the existence of Jewish colonies Christianity would have encountered much greater obstacles; it would have had greater difficulties in establishing itself. As has been stated, the Jews in ancient society enjoyed considerable privileges; they had protective charters assuring them an independent political and judicial organization and freedom of worship. These privileges facilitated the development of the Christian churches. For a long time the associations of the Christians were not distinguished by the authorities from Jewish associations, the Roman government taking no cognizance of the division between the two religions. Christianity was treated as a Jewish sect, thus benefiting by the same advantages; it was not only tolerated, but, in an indirect way, protected by the imperial governors.

Thus, on the one hand, unwillingly, the Jews were unconscious auxiliaries of Christianity while, on the other hand, they were its enemies, for which there were numerous reasons. It is known that Jesus and his teachings enlisted their first following among the Galilean provincials who were despised by the Jerusalemites for having yielded more than others to foreign influences. "Can there any good thing come out of Nazareth?" they said. These humble folks of Galilee, though much attached to the Judaic rites and customs, in which respect they were perhaps stricter than the Jerusalemites, were ignorant of the Law and were therefore despised by the haughty doctors of Judea. This scorn likewise followed the first disciples of Jesus, some of whom, besides, belonged to the disreputable classes, such as *e.g.*, the publicans.

Nevertheless, while the origin of the primitive Christians brought upon them the scorn of the Jews, it was not enough to excite their hatred; graver reasons were required for that, foremost among them was Jewish patriotism.

The birth and early development of Christianity coincided with the time when the Jewish nation attempted to shake off the yoke of Rome. Offended in their religious feelings, ill-treated by the Roman administration, the Jews felt a yearning for liberty, which grew with their hatred of Rome. Bands of zealots and assassins traversed the mountains of Judea, entering the villages and wreaking vengeance upon Rome by striking those of their brethren who bowed to the imperial authority. Plainly, these zealots and assassins who attacked the Sadducees for mere complacency towards the Roman procurators, could not spare the disciples of Him to whom the words were attributed, "Render unto Caesar the things which are Caesar's."

Absorbed in the expectation of the coming Messianic reign, the Jewish Christians of those days were "men without a country"; the thought of free Judea no longer made their hearts throb, though some, like the seer of the Apocalypse, had a horror of Rome, still they had no passion for captive Jerusalem, which the zealots strove to liberate; they were unpatriotic.

When all Galilee rose in response to the appeal of John of Gischala, they held aloof, and when the Jerusalemites triumphed over Cestius Gallus, the Jewish Christians, indifferent to the outcome of this supreme struggle, fled from Jerusalem, crossed the Jordan and sought refuge at Pella. In the last battles which Bar Giora, John of Gischala and their faithful gave to the Roman power, to the trained legions of Vespasian and Titus, the disciples of Jesus took no part; and when Zion was reduced to ashes, burying under its ruins the nation of Israel, no Christian met his death amidst the destruction.

One may well understand what could have been the treatment accorded, in those days of exaltation, before, during and after the insurrection, to the Jewish and Gentile Christians, who, with St. Paul, counselled submission to the power of Rome. The patriotic indignation roused by the nascent Church was seconded by the wrath of the rabbis against Christian proselytism.

Originally the relations between the Jewish Christians and the Jews were fairly cordial. The followers of the Apostles, as well as the Apostles themselves, recognized the sanctity of the ancient law; they observed the rites of Judaism and as yet had not placed the worship of Jesus side by side with that of the one God. The development of the dogma of the divinity of Christ made a breach between the Church and the Synagogue. Judaism could not admit of the deification of a man; to recognize any one as the son of God was blasphemy; and as the Jewish Christians had not severed their connections with the Jewish community, they were disciplined. This accounts for the flagellation of the Apostles and the new converts, the stoning of Stephen and the beheading of the Apostle James.

After the capture of Jerusalem, after that storm which left Judea depopulated, the best of her sons having perished in battle, or in the circus where they were delivered to the beasts, or in the lead mines of Egypt, during this third captivity called by the Jews the Roman exile, the relations between the Jews and Jewish Christians became still more strained. Their country being dead, Israel gathered around their doctors. Jabne, where the Sanhedrin reconvened, replaced Zion without extinguishing its memory, and the conquered attached themselves still more closely to the Law which the sages commented upon.

Thenceforth, those who assailed that Law, which had become the most cherished heritage of the Jew, were to be treated as enemies worse than the Romans. The doctors accordingly fought the Christian doctrine which was making proselytes amidst their flock. "The Gospels must be burned—says Rabbi Tarphon—for paganism is not as dangerous to the Jewish faith as the Jewish Christian sects. I should rather seek refuge in a pagan temple than in an assembly of Jewish Christians." He was not the only one who thought so, and all the rabbis comprehended the danger threatening Judaism from Jewish Christianity.

Some modern interpreters of the Talmud have gone to the rabbinical discussions and decisions of that epoch for weapons against the Jews, accusing them of blind hatred against anything that did not bear the mark of Israel; they do not seem, however, to have carried into their researches the requisite scientific spirit and good faith.

Originally, all Talmudical inhibitions contemplated the Jewish Christians alone. The *Tanaim* wanted to preserve the faithful from Christian contamination; for this purpose the Gospels were likened to books on witchcraft, and Samuel Junior, by order of the patriarch Gamaliel, inserted in the daily prayers a curse against the Jewish Christians, *Birkat Haminim,* which has furnished the foundation for the charge that the Jews curse Jesus thrice a day.

While the Jews thus sought to separate themselves from the Christians, the Church, swayed by a great religious movement, was forced to cast away Judaism. To conquer the world, to become a universal creed, Christianity had to rid itself of Jewish particularism, to break the narrow chains of the ancient law, so as to be able to spread the new one. This was the work of St. Paul, the true founder of the Church, who opposed to the exclusiveness of the Jewish-Christian doctrine the principle of catholicity.

As is well known, the struggle between these two tendencies in the nascent Christianity, which were symbolized by Peter and Paul, was long and bitter. The whole apostolic service of Paul was a long battle against the Judaizing. On the day when the Apostle declared that in order to come to Jesus one need not pass through the Synagogue nor accept the sign of the old covenant, the circumcision, on that very day all ties which bound the Christian Church to its mother were torn and the nations of the world were won over by Jesus.

The resistance of the Judaizing who wanted to belong to Jesus and at the same time to observe the Sabbath and the Passover, was in vain; their prejudice against the conversion of the Gentiles was of no avail. After Paul's journey to Asia Minor the cause of catholicism was won. The Apostle was braced up by an army, and that army arrayed against the Jewish spirit the Hellenic, Antioch against Jerusalem.

The great bulk of the Jewish Christians tore themselves away from the narrow doctrine of the little community of Jerusalem; the ruin of the holy city led them to doubt the efficacy of the ancient law. It was good for the further development of the Church. Ebionism met its death. If Christianity had followed the Jerusalemites it would have remained a small Jewish sect. Having rid itself of the Ebionites and the Jewish Christians and cut loose from its mother, Christianity allowed the nations to come to it without forfeiting their individuality.

To safeguard its supremacy, the Church had to fight the Jewish spirit in two forms. The first was that noted above, the Judaic positivism, hostile to anthropomorphism and deification of heroes. Nevertheless this positivism has maintained its existence throughout the ages so that a history of the Jewish current in the Christian Church could be written, beginning with early Ebionism down to Protestantism, including among others the Unitarians and Arians.

The second form is the mystic form represented by the Alexandria and Asiatic gnosis. The Alexandrian Jews, as known, were influenced by Platonism and Pythagorism; Philo himself was the forerunner of Plotinus and Porphyry in this renovation of the metaphysical spirit. Aided by Hellenic doctrines the Jews interpreted the Bible and scrutinized the mysteries contained therein, construing them into allegories and further developing them.

Proceeding from monotheism and the conception of a personal God as their religious point of departure, the Jews of Alexandria were bound to come metaphysically to pantheism, to the idea of a divine substance, to the doctrine of intermediaries between man and the Absolute, *i.e.*, to emanations, to the Eons of Valentinus and the Sephiroths of Kabbala. To this Jewish fund were super-added the contributions of Chaldean, Persian and Egyptian religions, which coexisted at Alexandria; at that time were elaborated those extraordinary Gnostic theogonies, so multifarious, so varied, so madly mystical.

When Christianity was born, the gnosis was already in existence; the Gospels brought new elements into it; it speculated on the life and words of Jesus, as it had speculated on the Old Testament, and when the Apostles, in their early preaching, addressed themselves to the Gentiles, they were confronted with the Gnostics, and primarily the Jewish Gnostics. Peter met them at Samaria in the person of Simon the Magician; Paul faced them at Colosse, at Ephesus, at Antioch, wherever he came with his Gospel, and possibly he fought Cerinthus; John himself fought them, and, in the Epistles of the Apocalypse he opposed the Nicolaites who were "of the Synagogue of Satan."

After having escaped the danger of crystallizing into a barren Jewish community, the Church was thus exposed to the new danger of Gnosticism, which, if triumphant, would have resulted in splitting it up into small sects and breaking its unity.

All preachers of the Christian religion had to contend against this gnosis; traces of that fight are found in the Epistles of Paul to the Colossians and Ephesians, in the pastoral letters, in the second Epistle of Peter, in the Epistle of Jude and in the Apocalypse. They did not confine themselves to persecuting the Jewish spirit in the gnosis; as soon as the Pauline spirit had triumphed over Peter, they declared war to the Judaizing tendencies within the Church, as well as to the Jews themselves.

We find all these sentiments reflected in the writings of the Apostle Fathers, with a growing desire to separate Christianity from Judaism; and with the development of the dogma of the divinity of Jesus, the Jews became the abominable people of Deicides, which they had not been originally. The Pauline traditions resound in the beginning of the second century in the seven letters of Ignatius of Antioch addressed to the churches of Rome, Magnesia, Philadelphia, Ephesus, Smyrna and Tralles and to the Bishop Polycarp.

Still in face of these hostile demonstrations the Jews were not inactive and proved very dangerous adversaries. It was under the fire of their criticism that the dogma was constructed; it was they who, by their subtle exegetics, by their firm logic, forced the teachers of Christianity to give precision to their arguments. Their hostility worried the theologians; though having severed themselves from Judaism, they wanted to win over the Jews to their side; they believed that the triumph of Jesus would only be assured on the day when Israel would recognize the power of the Son of God; indeed, this belief has survived under different forms throughout the ages. It would seem as though the Church were not satisfied of the legitimacy of its faith until the day when the people of whom its God had come were converted to the Galilean.

This work was taken up by the apologists of Christianity, and their apologetic prepossession was mixed with violent enmity. Thus the *Letter to Diognetus,* which has been preserved for us in the work of St. Justin, and was written to refute the errors of the adversaries of the Christians, may be considered as one of the first anti-Jewish writings. The unknown author of this brief epistle, in his vigorous attack upon the Millenarian ideas, speaks of the Jewish rites as superstitions. The motives are not the same as those which actuated the unknown author of the *Testament of the Twelve Patriarchs,* for he wanted, and so he declared, to convert the Jews and convince them of the excellence of the word of Christ.

The most thorough of the apologists of that epoch is assuredly Justin, the philosopher. His *Dialogue with Tryphon* will remain a model of this kind of dialogical polemics, of which we have another sample from the same epoch in the *Altercation of Jason and Papiscus,* from the pen of the Greek Ariston of Pella; the latter dialogue was reproduced in the fifth century by Evagrius, in his *Altercation of Simon and Theophilus.* Justin, a native of Samaria, and well acquainted with the Judeans, puts all the objections of the Jewish exegetes into the mouth of Tryphon, meant to represent Rabbi Tarphon, who vigorously fought against the apostolic evangelization. The author atempts to persuade him that the New Testament is in accord with the Old, and to reconcile monotheism with the theory of Messiah as the Word incarnate. At the same time, replying to Tryphon's reproach that the Christians have abandoned the Mosaic law, he maintains that it was merely a preparatory law. Justin attacked the Judaizing tendencies in both forms, viz., Jewish Christianity on the one hand, and, on the other, Alexandrinism, which would admit the Word only as a temporary irradiation of the One Being. He closes with the warning: "Blaspheme not the Son of God; listen not to the Pharisees; ridicule not the King of Israel, as you are doing daily." The irony of the Jews he met with sarcasm directed against the rabbis: "Instead of expounding the meaning of the prophecies your teachers indulge in tomfoolery; they are anxious to ascertain why male camels are referred to in this or that passage, or why a certain quantity of flour is required for your oblations. They are worried to know why an alpha is added to the original name of Abraham. This is the subject of their studies. As to things essential, worthy of meditation, they dare not speak of them to you, they do not attempt to explain them, and they prohibit you from listening to our interpretation."

The last complaint is important, it indicates the character of the struggle for the conquest of souls in which Judaism was defeated. The second century is one of the most momentous epochs in the history of the Church. The dogma, still uncertain in the first century, is then formulated and defined; Jesus advances toward divinity and attains it, and his metaphysics, his worship, his conception, are blended with Judeo-Alexandrian doctrines, with Philo's theories of the Word of God, the Chaldean *memra* and the Greek *logos*. The Word is born, it becomes identified with the Galilean; in Justin's apologetics and the fourth Gospel, we see the work completed. Christianity has become Alexandrian, and its most ardent upholders, its defenders, even its orators, are at that hour the Christian philosophers of the Alexandrian school: Justin, the author of the fourth Gospel, and Clement.

While this dogmatic transformation was going on, the idea of a universal church gained strength. Bonds of union were formed between the small Christian communities, detached from Jewish congregations; the more their numbers increased the stronger became the ties, and this conception of unity and catholicity kept pace with the growing expansion of Christianity.

This expansion could not proceed undisturbed. Christian preaching addressed itself to all the Jewries of Asia Minor, Egypt,

Cyrenaica and Italy, wherever there was an unorthodox element among them, the Hellenized Jews whom the Christian teachers sought to win over to their side. The propagandists likewise spoke to the anxious masses who had already lent their ears to the Jewish word. The Jews witnessed the failure of their influence and, perhaps, of their hopes; at all events, they saw their beliefs, their faith, attacked by the neophytes; the feeling of the Jews against the Christians was as bitter as that of the Christians when they saw the obstacles which the Jewish preachers put in their way. Furious hatred was mutual, and the parties were not content with Platonic hatred. The Christian congregations, unlike the Jewish communities, were not recognized by the law; they were considered enemies of law and a danger to the Empire. From this there was but one step to violence; this accounts for the periods of suffering the Church had to go through. The Church, in those evil days, could not count upon its rival, the Synagogue, for assistance; in some places where the struggle between the Jews and the Christians had reached an acute stage the Jews, recognized by Roman legislation and possessed of vested rights, would join the citizens of the towns in dragging the Christians before the court. In Antioch, for example, where the enmity between those two sects was most bitter, in all probability, the Jews, like the pagans, demanded the trial and execution of Polycarp. They are said to have fed with great eagerness the stake upon which the bishop was burned.

Still, not everywhere was the strife marked with such bloody manifestations. The controversy was always very lively, yet it must be said it was not conducted with equal weapons. The Bible was their common arsenal, but the Christian teachers had but a scant knowledge of it. They did not know Hebrew and used the Septuagint version, which they interpreted very freely, often relying, in support of their dogma, upon passages interpolated into the Septuagint by falsifiers for the good of the cause. The Greek-speaking Jews did not hesitate to do the same, so that the Septuagint, a bad translation as it was, full of absurdities, became available for any purpose.

These controversies, which continued through long centuries, were not always courteous. Simultaneously with touching legends concerning Jesus, scandalous stories were invented. To humiliate their enemies, the Jews attacked him of whom the former made their God, and to the deification of Jesus they opposed the stories of the soldier Pantherus, of abandoned Mary; these were taken up by philosophers hostile to Christianity, and Origen refuted them in his *Contra Celsum,* meeting abuse with abuse.

Amidst these battles was born a theological anti-Judaism, purely ideological, which consisted in rejecting as bad or worthless anything coming from Israel. This sentiment is evidenced by Tertullian's *De Adversus Iudaeos.* In that work the fiery African attacked circumcision, which, he said, brought no salvation, but was a simple sign for distinguishing Israel; when Messiah would come he would substitute spiritual for bodily circumcision; he attacked the Sabbath, the temporal Sabbath, to which he opposed the eternal Sabbath.

But this special anti-Judaism, which we find again in *Octavius,* by Minucius Felix; in *De Catholicae Ecclesiae Unitate,* by Cyprian of Carthage; in *Instructiones Adversus Gentium Deos,* by the poet Commodian, and in *Divinae Institutiones,* by Lactantius, was mixed with the desire to convince the Jews of the truth of the Christian religion, of the soundness of its beliefs, its dogmas and principles; hence the ambition to make proselytes among them. This anti-Judaism crossed with the efforts which the Church was making to arrive at universality, and during the first three centuries remained purely theoretical. We shall further see how, since Constantine and the triumph of the Church, this anti-Judaism was transformed and more precisely defined.

FOUR

ANTISEMITISM FROM CONSTANTINE TO THE EIGHTH CENTURY

FOR three centuries the Church had to contend against those with whom the greatness of Rome was inseparable from the secular worship of the Gods. Still, the resistance of the civil authorities, of the priests and philosophers, could not arrest the march of the Church; persecutions, hatred, hostility enhanced its power of propaganda; it addressed itself to those whose spirit was troubled, whose conscience was vacillating, and to them it brought an ideal and that moral satisfaction which they lacked. Moreover, at that hour when the Roman Empire was rending all over, when Rome, having abdicated all power and authority, received its Caesars from the hands of the legions, and competitors for the purple bobbed up in every nook of the provinces, the Catholic Church offered to that expiring world the unity it was seeking.

Yet, while offering intellectual unity to the world, the Church at the same time was ruining its institutions, customs and manners. In fact, at Rome, as well as in the Empire, all public functions were at once civil and religious, the magistrate, the procurator, the *dux* being invested with priestly functions; no public act was performed without rites; the government was, in a manner, theocratic; this ultimately came to be symbolized in the worship of the Emperor. All those who wanted to withdraw from that worship were held to be enemies of Caesar and the Empire; they were considered bad citizens. This sentiment explains the Roman dislike of Oriental religions and of the Jews; it explains the measures adopted against the worshippers of Yahweh, and still more the severity shown towards the worshippers of Mithra, of Sabazius and particularly towards the Christians, for the latter were not foreigners like the Jews, but rebel citizens.

The triumph of Christianity was brought about by political considerations, and so, to make its victory and domination lasting, it was obliged to adopt many of the ceremonial observances of ancient Rome. When the Christians had increased in numbers, and formed a considerable party, they were saved and could see the dawn of victory glimmer, for now a pretender to the throne could find support among them and use their services to solidify his authority. So it happened with Constantine, and Constantius, perhaps, foresaw it when he commanded the Gallic legions. The victorious church succeeded to Rome. She inherited its haughtiness, its exclusiveness, its pride, and almost without any transition period the persecuted turned persecutrix, wielding the power by which she had been fought, holding the consular fasces and hatchet and commanding the legionaries.

While Jesus was taking possession of the superb city and his universal reign was commencing, Judaism was in agony in Palestine; the teachers of Tiberias were powerless to hold the young Judeans and the "illustrious, most glorious, right reverend" patriarch had but the shadow of authority. The flourishing Jewish schools were in Babylonia; the centre of Israel's intellectual life was transferred thither; still wherever Christianity endeavoured to extend its influence it had to reckon and to contend with the influence of Judaism; though since the close of the third century the latter was of little importance, at least directly. Indeed, at that time the Judaizing heresies were nearly extinct. The Nazarenes, those circumcised Christians attached to the old law, who are mentioned by St. Jerome and St. Epiphanius, were reduced to a handful of meek believers, who had found refuge at Berea (Alep), at Kokabe in Batanea, and at Pella, in the Decapolis. They spoke the Syro-Chaldaic language; a remnant of the primitive Church of Jerusalem, they no longer exerted any influence, swamped as they were amidst Greek-speaking churches.

Still, though Ebionism was dying out, Judaizing continued; the Christians attended the synagogues, celebrated the Jewish holidays, and the contentions over the Passover were still on. A large faction in the churches of the Orient insisted upon celebrating the Passover at the same time as the Jews. It required the action of the Nicæan Council to free Christianity of this last and weak bond by which it had still been tied to its cradle. After the Synod all was over between the Church and the Temple, officially, and from the orthodox standpoint, at least; it required, however, the action of further councils to prevent the faithful from conforming to the old usage, and it was not until 341 A.D., when the Council of Antioch had excommunicated the Quartodecimans that unity of the celebration of the Easter was effected.

Since the Church had become armed, anti-Judaism underwent a transformation. Purely theological in the beginning, confined to arguments and controversies, it defined itself and became harsher, more severe and aggressive. Beside writings, laws appeared; the enactment of laws resulted in popular manifestations. The writings themselves underwent a change. Throughout the centuries of persecution, apologetics had flourished, and a vast literature had come into being, born of the need felt by the Christians to convince their adversaries. They addressed themselves now to the Jews, now to the pagans, now to the emperors, and all of them, Justin, Athenagoras, Tatian, Aristo of Pella, Melito, endeavoured to prove to Caesar that their doctrines were not dangerous to the public weal; that even without sacrificing to the gods, they could be loyal subjects, as obedient as the pagans and morally superior. They argued with the Jews that it was they, the Christians, that were the only faithful to tradition, for they fulfilled the prophecies and the least details of their dogmas were foreseen and announced by the Scriptures. Triumphant Christianity was no longer in need of apologists; Caesar had been converted and Cyril of Alexandria, the author of a book against Julian the Apostate, was the last of the apologists. As regards Israel, the Christians persisted, even to our own day, in demonstrating to them their stubbornness; it was done in a less insidious and less convincing manner; they spoke as masters, and from the middle of the fifth century, apologetics proper ceased, reappearing only much later considerably modified and transformed.

They no longer tried to win over the Jews to Christ; indeed, a few years sufficed to show to the theologians the futility of their efforts, and the effect of their reasoning, based most frequently upon a fantastic exegesis or a few absurdities of the Alexandrian translation of the Bible, was lost on these stubborn men, who listened only to their own teachers and clung the stronger to their faith the more it was despised. To arguments was added insult; the Jew was regarded less as a possible Christian than as an unrepenting deicide. They denounced those men, whose persistence was so shocking and whose very presence marred the complete triumph of the Church. Pains were taken to forget the Jewish origin of Jesus and the Apostles; to forget that Christianity had grown in the shade of the Synagogue. This oblivion perpetuated itself, and today who in all Christendom would acknowledge that he bows to a poor Jew and a humble Jewess of Galilee?

The Fathers, the bishops, the priests, who had to contend against the Jews treated them very badly. Hosius in Spain; Pope Sylvester; Paul, bishop of Constantine; Eusebius of Cæsarea,[32] call them "a perverse, dangerous and criminal sect."

Some, like Gregory of Nyssa,[33] remain on dogmatic ground, and merely reproach the Jews for being infidels, who refuse to accept the testimony of Moses and the prophets on the Trinity and Incarnation. St. Augustine[34] is more vehement. Irritated by the objections of the Talmudists he brands them as falsifiers, and declares that one need seek no religion in the blindness of the Jews, and that Judaism may serve only as a term of comparison to demonstrate the beauty of Christianity. St. Ambrose[35] attacked them from another side; he took up anew the charges of the ancient world, those which had been used against the first Christians, and accused the Jews of despising the laws of Rome. St. Jerome[36] claimed that an impure spirit had seized the Jews. Having learned Hebrew in the schools of the rabbis, he said, referring doubtless to the curses pronounced against the Mineans and distorting their meaning: "The Jews must be hated, for they daily insult Jesus Christ in their synagogues"; and St. Cyril of Jerusalem[37] abused the Jewish patriarchs, claiming that they were a low race.

We find all these theological and polemical attacks combined in the six sermons delivered at Antioch, by St. John Chrysostom[38] against the Jews; an examination of those homilies will give us an understanding of the methods of discussion, as well as the reciprocal attitude of Christians and Jews and their mutual relations.

The Jews, says Chrysostom in the first of his sermons, are ignoramuses, who lack all understanding of their own law, and are consequently impious. They are wretches, dogs, bull-headed; their people are like a herd of brutes, like wild beasts. They have driven Christ away, therefore they are capable of evil only. Their synagogues may be likened to playhouses, they are dens of brigands, the abode of Satan. Being obliged to admit that the Jews are not ignorant of the Father, he adds that this is not enough, since they have crucified the Son and reject the Holy Ghost, and that their souls are the abode of the devil. Therefore they must be mistrusted; the *Jewish disease* must be guarded against.

In the second sermon these diatribes are resumed; Chrysostom appears in it much worried over the influence exerted by the Jews. "Our sheep," he exclaims, "are surrounded by Jewish wolves," and he reiterates the warning : Avoid them; avoid their impiety; it is not significant controversies that separate us from them, but the death of Christ. If you think that Judaism is true, leave the Church; if not, quit Judaism.

The other four sermons are chiefly theological. Availing himself of the invectives of the prophets, Chrysostom calls the Jews thieves, impure, debauchees, rapacious, misers, crafty, oppressors of the poor; they have filled the measure of their crimes by immolating Jesus. He does not content himself with all that. He advances arguments upon controversies which must have been very lively at Antioch. He defends the Church; he shows that Israel is dispersed in consequence of the death of Christ; he draws from the prophets and the stories of the Bible proofs of the divinity of Jesus, and he recommends to his flock to stay away from the sermons of those Jews who call the cross an abomination and whose religion is null and useless to those who know the true faith. In short, says he in conclusion, it is absurd to consort with men who have treated God with such indignity and at the same time to worship the Crucified.

These homilies of Chrysostom are characteristic and valuable. One finds there already the policy which the Christian preachers were to pursue throughout the ages to follow; that mixture of argument and apostrophizing, of suasion and abuse, which has remained peculiar to anti-Jewish preaching. Especially worthy of notice is the part of the clergy in the development of anti-Judaism —originally religious anti-Judaism, for social anti-Judaism arose much later in Christian society. These sermons portray, in a live picture, the relations between Judaism and Christianity in the fourth century; these relations continued for a long time, until about the ninth century. The Jews had not arrived yet at that exclusive conception of their individuality and their nationality which was the work of the Talmudists. Their proselytic ardour was not dead; they were not conscious of the fact that they had forever lost their moral power over the world, and they struggled on. They persuaded pagans and Christians to Judaize, and they found followers; if need be they would make converts by force; they did not hestitate to circumcise their slaves. They were the only foes the

Church had to face, for paganism was quietly passing away, leaving in the souls but legendary survivals, which have not entirely died out even to this day. If paganism, through its last philosophers and poets, still opposed the diffusion of Christianity, it no longer sought, since the fourth century, to regain those whom Jesus held by his bonds. The Jews, however, had not given up; they deemed themselves in possession of the true religion, upon as good a title as the Christians, and in the eyes of the people their assertion had the attraction flowing from unflinching convictions.

In the morning of its triumph the Church as yet did not hold that universal ascendancy which it gained later; it was still weak, though powerful; but those who directed it aspired to universality, and they could not help considering the Jews as their worst adversaries; they had to strain themselves to the utmost to weaken Jewish propaganda and proselytism. In this the Fathers followed a secular tradition; upon this battle ground they are unanimous, and there are legions of theologians, historians and writers who think and write of the Jews the same as Chrysostom : Epiphanius, Diodorus of Tarsus, Theodore of Mopsuestia, Theodoret of Cyprus, Cosmas Indicopleustes, Athanasius the Sinaite, Synesius, among the Greeks; Hilarius of Poitiers, Prudentius, Paulas Orosius, Sulpicius Severus, Gennadius, Venantius Fortunatus, Isidore of Seville, among the Latins.

However, after the edict of Milan, anti-Judaism could no longer confine itself to oral or written controversies; it was no longer a quarrel between two sects equally detested or despised. Before his conversion, Constantine, who originally declined to grant any exclusive privileges to Christians, accorded, by the edict of tolerance, to everyone the right to observe the religion of his choice. The Jews were thus put on an equal footing with the Christians; the pagan pontiffs, the priests of Jesus, the patriarchs and teachers of Israel enjoyed the same favour and were exempt from municipal taxes. But in 323, after the defeat and death of Licinius, who had reigned in the Orient, Constantine, the victor and lord over the Empire, supported by all the Christians of his states, showed them marked preference. He made them his great dignitaries, his councillors, his generals, and thenceforth the Church had the imperial power at its disposal to build up its dominion. The first use it made of this authority was to persecute those who were hostile to the Church; it found Constantine quite obedient to its wishes. On the one hand, the emperor prohibited divination and sacrifices, closed the temples, ordered the gold and silver statues of the gods to be melted for the embellishment of the churches; on the other hand, he consented to repress Jewish proselytism and revived an ancient Roman law which prohibited the Jews from circumcising their slaves; at the same time he deprived them of many of their former privileges and barred them from Jerusalem, except on the anniversary of the destruction of the Temple, and that upon payment of a special tax in silver. Thus, by aggravating the burdens which were oppressing the Jews, Constantine favoured Christian proselytism, and the preachers were not slow to represent to the Jews the advantages baptism would bring.

Still, in spite of his hostility to the Jews, perhaps factitious, since the authenticity of the letter written in a violent language and attributed to him by Eusebius[39] cannot be vouched for, he took pains to protect them against the attacks of their own renegades. Under his successors, no such reservation was made. The Church was now all-powerful with the emperors. Catholicism became the established religion, the Christian worship was the official worship, the importance of the bishops increased from day to day, as well as their influence. They inculcated upon the minds of the emperors those sentiments with which they were inspired themselves, and while their anti-Judaism manifested itself in writings, imperial anti-Judaism found expression in statutes. These laws, inspired by the clergy, were directed not only against the Jews, but against Christian heretics as well. Indeed, during the fourth century, so fertile in heresies, the orthodox themselves were at times disturbed when heretical theologians led the emperors.

Of these laws, all of which were enacted from the fourth to the seventh century, the majority are directed against Jewish proselytism. The penal statutes directed against those who circumcise Christians are reaffirmed;[40] the offence is made punishable by exile for life and confiscation of property. The Jews are prohibited from owning Christian slaves;[41] they are not allowed to marry Christians; such unions are treated like criminal fornication.[42] Other laws encourage Christian propaganda and proselytism among the Jews, either directly—by protecting the apostates[43] and enjoining Jews from disinheriting their converted sons and grandsons[44]—or indirectly, by vexatious legislation against Jews. Their privileges were curtailed. It was decreed that the moneys which were sent by the Israelites to Palestine should be paid into the imperial treasury;[45] they were debarred from holding public office;[46] they were assessed with hard and oppressive curial taxes;[47] they were practically deprived of their special tribunals.[48] The vexations were not confined to that; the Jews were harassed even in the observance of their religion; the law undertook to regulate the manner of observing the Sabbath;[49] they were ordered not to celebrate their Passover before Easter, and Justinian went as far as to prohibit them from reciting the daily prayer, the *Schema*, which proclaimed one God, as against the Trinity.

Still, notwithstanding the favourable disposition of Emperor Constantine, the Church was not given a free hand in everything. While restricting the religious liberties of the pagans and the Jews, he was obliged to act with caution; the worshippers of the gods were still numerous under his reign, and he dared not provoke dangerous disturbances. The Jews benefited to some extent by this hesitation. With Constantius everything changed. Constantine, who was baptized only on his deathbed by Eusebius of Nicomedia, was a sceptic and a politician, who used Christianity as a tool; Constantius was an orthodox, as fanatical and intolerant as the clergy and the monks of his day. With him, the Church became dominant, and wielded its power for revenge; it seems the Church was eager to make its erstwhile persecutors pay dearly for all it had suffered at their hands. No sooner was it armed than it forgot its most elementary principles, and directed the secular arm against its adversaries. The pagans and the Jews were persecuted with utmost severity; those who offered sacrifices to Zeus, as well as those who worshipped Jehovah, were maltreated : anti-Judaism went together with anti-paganism.

The Jewish teachers of Judea were exiled, they were threatened with death if they persisted in giving instruction, they were compelled to flee from Palestine, while in other provinces of the empire they were denied the rights of Roman citizenship. While the Roman legions, on expedition against King Shabur II, of Persia, were camping in Judea, the Jews were treated like inhabitants of a conquered country. They were heavily taxed; they were forced to bake bread for the soldiers on Sabbath and on holidays.

In the cities, monks and bishops denounced pagans and Jews, inciting against them the Christian populace and leading fanatical mobs in assaults upon temples and synagogues. Under Theodosius I, and under Arcadius, synagogues were burned at Rome and at Callinicus, in Mesopotamia. Under Theodosius II, at Alexandria, St. Cyril stirred up the mob, hermits invaded the city, massacred all the Jews and pagans they met, assassinated Hypathia, plundered synagogues, set the libraries on fire, defying the efforts of the prefect Orestes whom the emperor later disavowed. At Imnestar, near Antioch, Simon, the ascetic, acts likewise, and under Zeno similar scenes are enacted at Antioch. A fury of destruction takes possession of the Christians; one might say, they wish to destroy all traces of the old world to prepare the sweet reign of Christ.

Still the Jews did not behave passively in the face of their enemies, they had not, as yet, acquired that stubborn and touching resignation which became their characteristic later.

To the vehement discourses of the priests they replied by discourses, to acts they responded by acts; to Christian proselytism they opposed their own proselytism and vowed execration on their apostates. Violent sermons were preached in the synagogues. Jewish preachers thundered against Edom, *i.e.,* against Rome, the Rome of the Caesars which had become the Rome of Jesus, and which was now ravishing the faith of the Jews after having ravished their nationality. They did not content themselves with rhetorical common-places, they excited their brethren to revolt. While Gallus, Constantius's nephew, governed the Oriental provinces, Isaac of Sepphoris raised the Judeans, being aided in his undertaking by a fearless man, Natrona, whom the Romans called Patricius. The Jews took up arms, but they were severely repressed by Gallus and his general, Ursicinus. Women, children, and old men were butchered, Tiberias and Lydda were half destroyed, Sepphoris was razed to the ground and the catacombs of Tiberias were filled with fugitives who were hiding for months to escape detection and death.

Under the reign of Phocas the Jews of Antioch, tired of persecutions, outrages and massacres, one day rushed upon the Christians, assassinated the patriarch Anastasius the Sinaite, and took possession of the city. Phocas sent against them an army with Kotys in command, the Jews at first repelled the imperial legions, but unable to hold out against large enforcements brought to Antioch, they were subdued and massacred, maimed, or banished. Their submission, however, was merely apparent; they were awaiting an opportunity to renew the struggle; the opportunity soon presented itself. When Chosru II, king of Persia, marched against the Byzantine empire, to avenge his son-in-law, Mauritius, whose throne had been usurped by Phocas, the Jews joined the king. Sharbarza invaded Asia Minor, disregarding the peace proposals of Heraclius, who had just dethroned Phocas, and he saw the Jewish warriors of Galilee flock under his banners. Benjamin of Tiberias was the soul of the revolt; he armed and led the rebels. The Jews wanted to reconquer Palestine and restore it to that purity which to them had been polluted by the Christian cult. They burned the churches, sacked Jerusalem, destroyed the convents, raising on their way all their co-religionists, and joined by the Israelites of Damascus, Southern Palestine, and the Isle of Cyprus, they besieged Tyre, but were forced to raise the siege. For fourteen years they were masters of Palestine, and the Christians of Palestine were in great numbers converted to Judaism. Heraclius drew them away from the Persians, who had not lived up to their promise to surrender to their allies the holy city of Jerusalem; he reached an understanding with Benjamin of Tiberias, promising to the Jews impunity and other advantages; but when the emperor reconquered his provinces from Chosru, he ordered, at the instigation of monks and the Patriarch Modestus, to massacre those with whom he had treated. When Julian the Apostate, after repealing the restrictive laws of Constantine and Constantius against the Jews, wanted to reconstruct the Temple of Jerusalem, the foreign Jewish communities remained deaf to the imperial appeal; they had become estranged from their national cause, at least directly. With all the Jews of that time, the restoration of the Kingdom of Judah was intimately bound with the advent of Messiah and they could not expect it from a crowned philosopher; they had but to await the heavenly king who had been promised them; this sentiment persisted throughout the ages. With the death of the last patriarch Gamaliel VI, the phantom of royalty and of a Jewish nationality passed away and there was left to Israel but the chief of exile, the exilarch of Babylonia, who disappeared in the eleventh century.

In Persia and Babylonia, the Jews lived since their captivity; after the ruin of Jerusalem many more sought refuge in that admirable and fertile country, where they were given land to farm on and lived happily under the benevolent rule of the Arsacidæ. They founded schools at Sora, Nachardea and Pumbaditha, and made numerous proselytes. But in the middle of the third century the dynasty of the Arsacidæ, who were very unpopular, fell with Artaban, and Ardashir founded the dynasty of the Sassanides. It was a national and religious movement. The Neo-Persians or Guebres execrated the Hellenizing Arsacidæ who had abandoned the fire worship. The triumph of Ardashir was the triumph of the Magi, who raged against the Hellenizing, the Christians of Edessa and the Jews, for the anti-Judaism of the Magi was combined with anti-Christianity; so the hostile brothers were persecuted simultaneously, still the Jews, more feared for their numbers and their strength, suffered more in consequence, in those troublous days. However, those persecutions were never of long duration. After suffering oppression at the end of the third century from Shabur II, who led away 70,000 Jewish prisoners from Armenia to Ispahan, the Israelites were for many years left undisturbed; but in the sixth and the seventh century under Yezdigerd II, under Pheroces, and under Kobad, restrictive measures were adopted at the instigation of the Magi. The Jews were prohibited from celebrating the Sabbath; their schools were closed, the Jewish tribunals were abolished. During the reign of Kobad, Mazdak, the Magus, was the originator of these persecutions. Mazdak, the founder of the sect of Zendiks, preached communism and deprived the Jews and Christians of their wives and property. Under the leadership of the Exilarch Mar Zutra II, the Jews rebelled, and, according to Persian chronicles, they defeated the partisans of the Magus and founded a state, whose capital was Mahuza, a city inhabited by Persian converts to Judaism. This state existed for seven years until Mar Zutra was defeated and killed.

Since then the Jews, in Persia, witnessed alternately peace and trouble; happy under Chosroes Nushirvan and Chosru II, oppressed under Hormisdas IV, they ultimately tired of their precarious situation, and, in concert with the Christians of the Sassanide kingdom aided Omar to capture the throne of Persia, thus contributing to the triumph of Mohammed and the Arabs.

Still the Jews had little to rejoice at under the Mussulman yoke. Their first settlement in Arabia, disregarding the legends which trace it as far back as Joshua or Saul, must date from the time of the captivity, or of the destruction of the first Temple. The original nucleus was swelled by fugitives from Judea, who reached Arabia at the time Palestine was conquered by the Romans. In

the beginning of the Christian era there were in Arabia four
Jewish tribes, whose centre was Medina.

The Jews accomplished a moral and intellectual conquest of the
Arabs, whom they converted to Judaism; at least they made them
adopt its rites. The kinship between the two peoples made it easy,
the more so that, in Yemen, the Jews had in their turn adopted
Arabian customs, which differed but little from the early Jewish
customs. They were farmers, shepherds and warriors, at times
freebooters and poets. Divided into small groups, fighting among
themselves and taking part in the quarels which divided the Arab
tribes, they at the same time founded schools at Yathrib, built
temples and propagated their religion as far as the Himyarites with
whom their traders were in regular intercourse. In the sixth century, under the reign of Zorah-Dhu-Nowas, all Yemen was Jewish.
With the conversion of one Arab tribe of Nedjran to Christianity,
difficulties began; they were, however, of short duration, for
Christian progaganda was cut short in Arabia by Mohammed.
Mohammed was nursed by the Jewish spirit; fleeing from Mecca,
where his preaching had aroused against him the Arabs who were
true to old traditions, he sought refuge at Medina, the Jewish city,
and as the apostles found their first adherents among the Hellenic
proselytes, so he found his first disciples among the Judaizing
Arabs. Likewise, the same religious causes embittered Mohammed
and Paul to hatred. The Jews rebelled against the preaching of the
prophet, they heaped ridicule upon him, and Mohammed who had
until then been inclined to compromise with them, violently repu-
diated them and wrote the celebrated Sura of the Cow, in which
he unmercifully inveighed against them. When the prophet had
assembled an army of followers he no longer confined himself to
abuse, he marched against the Jewish tribes, vanquished them, and
decreed that "neither Jews nor Christians" should be accepted as
friends. The Jews rose and allied themselves to those Arabs who
rejected the new doctrines, but the extension of Mohammedanism
triumphed over them. By the time of Mohammed's death they had
been reduced to extreme weakness; Omar completed the work. He
drove out of Chaibar and Wadil Kora the last Jewish tribes, as
well as the Christians of Dedjran, for Christians and Jews alike
polluted the sacred soil of Islam.

Wherever Omar carried his arms, the Jews, oppressed by reason
of that very affinity which united them with the Arabs, favoured

the second calif, who took possession of Persia and Palestine. Omar enacted severe laws against the Jews, who had assisted his antagonist; he subjected them to restrictive legislation, prohibited the erection of new synagogues, forced them to wear dress of a particular colour, enjoined them from riding on horseback, and imposed upon them a personal and a land tax. Christians were treated likewise. Nevertheless the Jews enjoyed greater liberty under Arab rule than under Christian domination. On the one hand, the legislation of Omar was not rigorously enforced; on the other hand, aside from a few manifestations of fanaticism, the Mussulmanic mass, in spite of religious differences, showed a friendly disposition towards them. And later, with the expansion of Islam, the Arabs were hailed as liberators by all the Western Jews.

The condition of the Western Jews since the destruction of the fragile Roman empire and the rush of barbarians upon the old world, was subject to all the vicissitudes of the times. The Cæsars, those poor Cæsars who bore the names of Olybrius, Glycerius, Julius Nepos, and Romulus Augustulus, fell, but the Roman laws remained; and if for short periods they were not enforced against the Jews, they still remained in effect, and the German sovereigns could make use of them at pleasure.

From the fifth to the eighth century the fortunes of the Jews wholly depended upon religious causes which were external to them, and their history among those who were called barbarians is bound with the history of Arianism, its triumph and defeats. So long as the Arian doctrine predominated, the Jews lived in a state of relative welfare, for the clergy and even the heretical government were busy fighting against orthodoxy and little worried about the Israelites, who, to them, were not the enemies to be crushed. Theodoric, however, was an exception. No sooner was the Ostrogoth empire established than the king prohibited the erection of synagogues and endeavoured to convert the Jews.[50] He protected them, however, against popular outbreaks, and compelled the Roman Senate to rebuild the synagogues which had been set on fire by the Catholic mobs which rose against the Arian Theodoric.

Still in Italy, under the Byzantine dominion so harassing to them, or under the more indifferent Lombard rule, for the Arian and the pagan Lombards scarcely took notice of the existence of Israel—the Jews were guarded against the zeal of the lower clergy and their flocks by the benevolence of the pontifical authority, which, from the earliest days of its power, seems to have desired, with rare exceptions, to preserve the synagogue as a living testimony of its victory.

In Spain the condition of the Jews was quite different. From time immemorial they freely settled in the peninsula; their numbers increased under Vespasian, Titus and Hadrian, during the Judean wars and after the dispersion; they owned large fortunes, they were wealthy, powerful and respectable and exerted a great influence upon the population among whom they lived. The imprint received by the peoples of Spain from Judaism, endured for centuries, and that land was the last to witness once more the contest, with almost equal weapons, between the Jewish and the Christian spirit. More than once Spain came very near becoming Jewish, and to write the history of that country until the fifteenth century means to write the history of the Jews, for they were intimately connected in a most remarkable way, with its literature and intellectual, national, moral and economic development. The church, from its very establishment in Spain, contended against Jewish tendencies and proselytism, and it was only after a struggle of twelve centuries that it succeeded in completely extirpating them.

Until the sixth century the Spanish Jews lived in perfect happiness. They were as happy as in Babylonia, and they found a new mother country in Spain. The Roman laws did not reach them there and the ecclesiastical ordinances of the Council of Elvira, in the fourth century, which enjoined Christians from intercourse with them, remained a dead letter.

The Visigothic conquest did not change their condition and the Arian Visigoths confined themselves to persecuting the Catholics. The Jews enjoyed the same civil and political rights as the conquerors; moreover, the Jews joined their armies and the Pyrenean frontier was guarded by Jewish troops. With the conversion of King Reccared everything changed; the triumphant clergy heaped persecution and vexation upon the Jews, and from that hour (589 A.D.) their existence became precarious. They were gradually brought under severe and meddlesome laws which were drafted by the numerous councils, held during that period in Spain, and were enacted by the Visigoth kings. These successive laws are all combined in the edict promulgated, in 652, by Receswinth; they were re-enacted and aggravated by Erwig, who had them approved by the twelfth council of Toledo (680).[51] The Jews were prohibited from performing the right of circumcision and observing the dietary laws, from marrying relatives until the sixth generation, from reading books condemned by the Christian religion. They were not allowed to testify against Christians or to maintain an action in court against them, or to hold public office. These laws which had been enacted one by one, were not always enforced by the Visigoth lords, who were independent, in a way, but the clergy doubled their efforts to procure their strict enforcement. The object of the bishops and the dignitaries of the church was to bring about the conversion of the Jews and to kill the spirit of Judaism in Spain and the secular authority lent them its support. From time to time the Jews were put to the choice between banishment and baptism; from that epoch dates the origin of the class of *Marranos,* those Judaizing Christians who were later dispersed by the Inquisition. Until the eighth century the Spanish Jews lived in that state of uncertainty and distress, relying only upon the transitory good will of some kings like Swintila and Wamba. They were liberated only by Tarin, the Mohammadan conqueror, who destroyed the Visigothic empire with the aid of the exiled Jews joining his army and with the support of the Jews remaining in Spain. After the battle of Xeres and the defeat of Roderick (711), the Jews breathed again.

About the same epoch a better era dawned for them in France. They had established colonies in Gaul in the days of the Roman republic, or of Cæsar, and they prospered, benefiting by their privileges of Roman citizenship. The arrival of the Burgundians and Franks did not change their condition, and the invaders accorded them the same treatment as the Gauls. Their history was subject to the same fluctuations and rhythms as in Italy and Spain. Free under pagan or Arian dominion, they were persecuted as soon as orthodoxy became dominant. Sigismund, king of the Burgundians, after his conversion to Catholicism enacted laws against them which were confirmed by his successors.[52] The Franks, being ignorant of the very existence of the Jews, were wholly guided by the bishops, and after Clovis they naturally began to apply to the Jews the provisions of the Theodosian Code. These provisions were aggravated and complicated by ecclesiastical authority which left to the secular power the duty of enforcing and compelling the observance of its decrees. From the fifth to the eighth century that part of the canon law relating to the Jews was worked out in Gaul. The laws were formulated by the councils and approved by the edicts of the Merovingian kings.

The chief concern of the church, during those three centuries, seems to have been to separate the Jews from the Christians, to prevent Judaizing among the faithful and to check Israelite proselytism. This legislation which had, towards the eighth century, become extremely severe in dealing with the Jews and the Judaizing, was not enacted at one stroke; beginning with the council of Vannes, of the year 465, the synods first confined themselves to platonic injunctions. The clergy at that epoch had but very scant authority and could inflict no penalties; it was not before the sixth century that the support of the Frank chiefs enabled it to enact penal legislation, which originally applied only to clerical offenders against the decisions of the councils, but later was extended to laymen.

Nevertheless, one must not imagine the condition of the Jews at that epoch as very miserable. On the Jewish, as well as on the Christian side, one notices a mixture of tolerance and intolerance which is accounted for either by a mutual desire to make converts, or even to some extent by reciprocal religious good-will. The Jews took an interest in public life, the Christians ate at their tables; they shared in their joys and sorrows, as well as in factional fights. Thus they are seen, at Arles, to unite with the Visigothic party against the bishop Cæsarius,[53] and later to follow the funeral of the same bishop, crying : *Vae! vae!* They were the clients of great seignors (as witnessed by two letters of Sidonius Apollinaris),[54] and the latter helped them to evade the vexatious ordinances. In many regions the clergy visited them, a great many Christians went to the synagogues, and the Jews likewise attended Catholic services during the mass of the catechumens. They resisted, as far as possible, the numerous efforts to convert them, at times attended with violence, notwithstanding the recommendations of certain Popes,[55] and they boldly engaged in controversies with theologians who endeavoured to persuade them by the same means as the Fathers of former ages. We shall return to these controversies and writings when we shall come to study the anti-Jewish literature.

Thus, as shown above, during the first seven centuries of the Christian era, anti-Judaism proceeded exclusively from religious causes and was led only by the clergy. One must not be misled by popular excesses and legislative repression, for they were never spontaneous, but always inspired by bishops, priests, or monks. It was only since the eighth century that social causes supervened to religious causes, and it was only after the eighth century that real persecution commenced. It coincided with the universal spread of Catholicism, with the development of feudalism and also with the intellectual and moral change of the Jews, which was mostly due to the influence of the Talmudists and the exaggerated growth of exclusiveness among the Jews. We shall now proceed to examine this new transformation of anti-Judaism.

FIVE

ANTI-JUDAISM FROM THE EIGHTH CENTURY TO THE REFORMATION

THE church reaches its final constitution in the eighth century. The period of great doctrinal crises is at an end, dogma is settled and heresies will not cause it any trouble until the Reformation. Pontifical primacy strikes deep root, the organization of the clergy is henceforth solid, religion and liturgy are unified, discipline and canonic law are settled, ecclesiastic property increases, the tithe is established, the federal constitution of the Church—sub-divided into sufficiently autonomous circuits—disappears, the movement of centralization for the benefit of Rome is clearly outlined. This movement came to an end, when the Carolingians had established the temporal power of the popes, and the Latin church, strongly hierarchical before, became as centralized, in a comparatively short time, as the Roman empire of yore, which the church's universal authority had thus supplanted. Simultaneously Christianity spread further still and conquered the barbarians. The Anglo-Saxon missionaries had set the examples in Saint Boniface and Saint Willibrod; they had followers. The gospel was preached to the Alamans, the Frisians, the Saxons, the Scandinavians, the Bohemians and the Hungarians, the Russians and the Wends, the Pomeranians and the Prussians, the Lithuanians and the Finns. The work was accomplished at the end of the thirteenth century : Europe was christianized.

The Jews settled in the wake of Christianity as it kept spreading by degrees. In the ninth century, they came from France to Germany, got thence into Bohemia, into Hungary and into Poland, where they met another wave of Jews—those coming by way of the Caucasus and converting on their march several Tartar tribes. In the twelfth century they settled in England and Belgium, and everywhere they built their synagogues, they organized their communities at that decisive hour, when the nations were coming out from chaos, when states were being formed and consolidated. They

remained outside of these great agitations, amid which conquering
and conquered races were amalgamating and uniting one with the
other; and in the midst of these tumultuous combinations they
remained spectators, strangers and hostile to these fusions : an
eternal people witnessing the rise of new nations. However, their
role was surely of account at all times; they were one of the active
elements of ferment of these societies in the process of formation.

In some countries, as *e.g.,* in Spain, their history is in so high a
degree interlinked with that of the peninsula, that, without them
it is impossible to grasp and appreciate the development of the
Spanish people. But if they had influenced its constitution by the
numbers of their converts in that country, by the support they had
given in succession to the various masters in possession of its soil—
they did so by seeking to bring to themselves those among whom
they lived and not by letting themselves be absorbed. Still, the
history of the Spanish Marranos is exceptional. Everywhere, though,
as we shall see, the Jews played a part of economic agents; they
did not create a social state, but they assisted after a fashion in
establishing it, and yet they could not be treated with favour among
the organizations to whose formation they had lent aid. For this
there was a serious obstacle. All the states of the Middle Ages were
moulded by the church; in their essence, in their very being, they
were permeated with the ideas and doctrines of Catholicism; the
Christian religion gave the unity they lacked to the numerous
tribes which had gathered together into nations. As representatives
of contrary dogmas, the Jews could not but oppose the general
movement, both by their proselytism, and by their very presence
as well. As the church led this movement it was from the church
that anti-Judaism, theoretical and legislative, proceeded, anti-
Judaism which the governments and the peoples shared and which
other causes came to aggravate. The social and religious state of
affairs and the Jews themselves gave origin to these causes. But
they had remained ever subordinated to those essential reasons
which may be traced to the opposition, then secular already—
between the Christian spirit and the Jewish spirit, between the
universal, and so to say, international Catholic religion, and the
particularist and narrow Jewish faith.

Only towards the end of the eighth century the activity of the
Western Jews developed. Protected in Spain by the Khalifs, given
support by Charlemagne who let the Merovingian laws fall into

disuse, they extended their commerce which until then centred chiefly in the sale of slaves. For this they were, indeed, particularly favoured by circumstances. Their communities were in constant communication, they were united by the religious bond which tied them all to the theological centre of Babylonia whose dependencies they considered themselves up to the decline of the exilarchate. Thus they acquired very great facilities for exporting commerce, in which they amassed considerable fortunes, if we are to believe the diatribes of Dagobard,[56] and later those of Rigord,[57] which, with all their exaggeration of the property of the Jews must not, yet, be entirely rejected as unworthy of credence.[58] Indeed, with regard to this wealth of the Jews, especially in France and Spain, we possess the testimonies of chroniclers and the Jews themselves, several of whom reproached their coreligionists for devoting to worldly welfare much more time than to the worship of Jehovah. "Instead of calculating the numerical value of the name of God," says the Kabbalist Abulafia, "the Jews prefer to count their riches."

Parallel with the general advance we really see this preoccupation with wealth grow among the Jews and their practical activity concentrating on a special business : I mean the gold business. Here we must emphasize a point. It has often been said, and it is repeated still, that the Christian societies had forced the Jews into this position of creditor and usurer, which they have for a long time kept : this is the thesis of the philosemites. On the other hand the antisemites assert that the Jews, from time immemorial, had natural inclinations for commerce and finance, and that they but followed their normal disposition, and that nothing had ever been forced upon them. In these two assertions there is a portion of verity and a portion of error, or rather that there is room to comment on them, and especially to give them a hearing.

At the time of their national prosperity the Jews, like all other nations, for that matter, had a class of the rich, which proved itself as eager for gain and as hard to the lowly as the capitalists of all ages and all nations have proven. The antisemites, as well, who make use of the texts of Isaiah and Jeremiah, *e.g.,* to prove the constant eternal rapacity of the Jews, act very naively, and, thanks to the words of the prophets, can but establish—and puerile it is— the existence, in Israel, of possessors and poor. If they examined impartially the Judaic codes and precepts only, they would acknow-

ledge that legislation and morals prescribed never to charge interest
on debts.[59] Taking all in all, the Jews were, in Palestine, the least
mercantile of the Semites, in this regard much inferior to the
Phoenicians and Carthaginians. It was only under Solomon that
they entered into intercourse with the other nations. Even at that
time, it was a powerful corporation of Phoenicians that was engaged in the banking business at Jerusalem. However, the
geographical position of Palestine prevented its inhabitants from
devoting themselves to a very extensive and considerable traffic.
Nevertheless, during the first captivity and through the contact with
the Babylonians, a class of merchants had formed, and from it
came the first Jewish emigrants, who established their colonies in
Egypt, Cyrenaica and Asia Minor. In all cities that admitted them
they formed active communities, powerful and opulent, and, with
the final dispersion, important groups of emigrants joined the
original groups which facilitated their installation. To explain the
attitude of the Jews it is, accordingly, not necessary to fall back
upon a theory of the Arian genius and the Semitic genius. Indeed,
we well know the traditional Roman cupidity and the commercial
sense of the Greeks. The usury of the Roman *feneratores* had no
limit any more than had their bad faith; they were encouraged by
the very harsh laws against the debtors—a worthy daughter of that
law of the Twelve Tables which granted to the creditor the right
of cutting pieces of flesh from the live body of an insolvent borrower.
In Rome gold was absolute master, and Juvenal could speak of the
"sanctissima divitiarum maiestas."[60] As to the Greeks, they were the
cleverest and boldest of spectators; rivalling the Phoenicians in the
slave-trade, in piracy, they knew the use of letters of exchange and
maritime insurance, and, Solon having authorized usury, they never
did away with it.

    As a nation the Jews differed in nothing from other nations,
and if at first they were a nation of shepherds and agriculturists,
they came, by a natural course of evolution, to constitute other
classes among them. And devoting themselves to commerce, after
their dispersion, they followed a general law which is applicable to
all colonists. Indeed, with the exception of cases when he goes to
break virgin soil, the emigrant can be only an artisan or merchant,
as nothing but necessity or allurement of gain can force him to
leave his native soil. Therefore, the Jews coming into Western
cities acted in no way differently from the Dutch or English when

they established business offices. Nevertheless, they came soon enough to specialize in the money business, for which they have been so bitterly reproached ever since, and in the fourteenth century they constituted quite a coterie of changers and lenders : they had become the bankers of the world.

The Middle Ages considered gold and silver as tokens possessing imaginary value, varying at the will of the king, who could order its rate according to the dictations of his fancy. This notion was derived from Roman law, which refused to treat money as a merchandise. The church inherited these financial dogmas, combined them with the biblical prescriptions which forbade loan on interest, and was severe, from its very start, against the Christians and ecclesiastics even that followed the example of the *feneratores,* who advanced money at 24, 48 and even 60 per cent., when the legal rate of interest was 12 per cent. The canons of councils are quite explicit on this point; they follow the teaching of the Fathers, Saint Augustin, Saint Chrysostom, Saint Jerome; they forbid loans and are harsh against those clerics and laymen who engage in the usurer's business.

At the same time, in the twelfth and thirteenth centuries, the wage system was established, the bourgeoisie developed, grew rich and acquired privileges and franchises : capitalistic power was now born. Commerce having taken on a new form, the value of gold increased and the passion for money grew with the importance which the currency had acquired.

Indeed, on one hand were the rich, on the other—the peasants, landless, subject to the tithe and prestations; workingmen dominated over by the capitalist laws. To cap it all, perpetual wars, revolts, diseases and famines. Whenever the year was bad, the money gave out, the crop failed, an epidemic came, the peasant, the proletarian, and the small bourgeois were forced to resort to borrowing. Hence, by necessity there had to be borrowers. But the church had forbidden loan at interest, and capital does not choose to remain unproductive, but during the Middle Ages capital could only be either merchant or lender, as money could be made productive in no other way. As far as the ecclesiastical decisions had any influence, a great part of the Christian capitalists did not want to begin an open revolt against their authority; there was also formed a class of reprobates for whom the bourgeoisie and nobility often acted as silent partners. It consisted of Lombards, Caeorsins, to whom the princes, the lords granted the privileges of loaning on interest, gathering a part of the profits which were considerable, as the Lombards lent money at 10 per cent. a month; or of unscrupulous foreigners, like Tuscan emigrants settled in Istria who went in usury to such extremes that the community of Triest suspended, in 1350, all execution for debts for three years. This did not take away the ground from under the usurers, but as I have said they found obstacles which the church placed in the way of their operations (the council of Lyons of 1215 wanted to declare the wills of usurers void).

As for Jews, these obstacles did not exist. The church had no moral power over them, it could not forbid them, in the name of the doctrine and dogma, to engage in money exchanging and banking. Thus a religious conception of the functions of capital and interest, and a social system which ran counter to this conception, led the Jews of the Middle Ages to adopt a profession cried down but made necessary; and in reality they were not the cause of the abuses of usury, for which the social order itself was responsible. If they did not cultivate land, if they were not agriculturists, it is not because they possessed none, as has often been said; the restrictive laws relative to the property rights of the Jews came at a date posterior to their settlement. They own property, but had their domains cultivated by slaves, for their stubborn patriotism forbade them to break foreign soil. This patriotism, the notion which they attached to the sanctity of their Palestinian fatherland, the allusion which they kept alive in them of the restoration of that fatherland and this particular faith which made them consider themselves exiles who would one day again see the holy city—all this drove them above all other foreigners and colonists to take up commerce.

As merchants they were destined to become usurers, given the conditions which the codes had imposed upon them and the conditions they had imposed upon themselves. To escape persecution and annoyance they had to make themselves useful, even necessary, to their rulers, the noblemen upon whom they depended, to the church whose vassals they were. Now the nobleman, the Church—despite its anathemas—needed gold, and this gold they demanded from the Jews. During the Middle Ages gold became the great motive power, the supreme deity; alchemists spent their lives in search of the magistery which was to produce it, the idea of possessing it inflamed the minds, in its name all kinds of cruelties were committed, the thirst of riches laid hold of all souls; later on, for Cortez and Pizarro, the successors of Columbus, the conquest of America meant the conquest of gold. The Jews fell under the universal charm—the same under which the Templars had fallen—and for them it was particularly fatal, because of their state of mind and the civil status imposed upon them. In order to exist, they turned brokers in gold, but this the Christians sought as eagerly as they. More than that, under the constant menace of banishment, always acamp, forced to be nomads, the Jews had to guard against the terrible eventualities of exile. They had to transform their property so as to make it more convertible into money, that is, to give it a more movable form, and they were the most active in developing the money value, in considering it as a merchandise, hence the lending and—to recoup for periodic and unavoidable confiscations—the usury.

The creation of guilds—merchant and craft—guilds and their organization, in the thirteenth century, finally forced the Jews into the condition to which they had been led by the social conditions—general and special—under which they lived. All these organizations were, so to speak, religious organizations, brotherhoods which none joined but those who prostrated themselves before the standard of the patron saint. The ceremonies attendant upon the initiation into these bodies being Christian ceremonies, the Jews could not but be shut out from them : and so they were. A series of prohibitions successively shut them out of all industry and all commerce, except that in odds and ends and in old clothes. Those who escaped this disqualification did so by virtue of special privileges for which they oftenest paid too dearly.

However, this is not all; other more intimate causes were added to those I have just enumerated, and all joined in throwing the Jew more and more out of society, in shutting him up in the ghetto, in immobilizing him behind the counter where he was weighing gold.

An energetic, vivacious nation, of infinite pride, thinking themselves superior to the other nations, the Jews wished to become a power. They instinctively had a taste for domination, as they believed themselves superior to all others by their origin, their religion, their title of a "chosen race," which they had always ascribed to themselves. To exercise this kind of power the Jews had no choice of means. Gold gave them a power which all political and religious laws denied them, and it was the only one they could hope for. As possessors of gold they became the masters of their masters, they dominated over them, and this was the only way to deploy their energy and their activity.

Would they not have been able to display it in some other fashion? Yes, and they tried it, but there they had to fight their own spirit. For many long years they had worked in the intellectual line, devoted themselves to sciences, letters, philosophy. They were mathematicians and astronomers; they practised medicine, and, if the school of Montpellier was not founded by them, they surely helped in developing it; they had translated the works of Averroes and of the Arabic commentators of Aristotle; they had revealed the Greek philosophy to the Christian world, and their metaphysicians Ibn Gabirol and Maimonides had been among the teachers of the schoolmen.[61] Who stopped them in this advance? They themselves.

Their doctors endeavoured to confine Israel to the exclusive study of the law in order to preserve Israel from outside influences, pernicious, it was said, to the integrity of the law. Efforts to this effect had been made since the time of the Maccabees, when the Hellenizers constituted a great party in Palestine. Beaten at first, or, at least, hardly listened to, those who later acquired the name of obscurantists, kept at their task. When Jewish intolerance and bigotry grew in the twelfth century, when exclusiveness increased, the struggle between the partisans of profane science and their opponents became fiercer, it blazed up after the death of Maimonides and ended in the victory of the obscurantists.

In his works, particularly in the *Moreh Nebukhim* (*Guide of the Perplexed*)[62] Moses Maimonides attempted to reconcile faith and science. As a convinced Aristotelian, he wished to unite peripatetic philosophy with the Mosaic faith, and his speculations on the nature of the soul and its immortality found followers and ardent admirers as well as fierce detractors. As a matter of fact, especially in France and Spain, the Maimunists were led to neglect the ritual practices and petty ceremonies of worship : bold rationalists, they had allegoric interpretations for the biblical miracles, as the disciples of Philo before them, and thus they escaped the tyranny of religious precepts. They claimed the right of taking part in the intellectual movement of the time and mingling in the society in which they lived without giving up their beliefs. Their opponents clung to the purity of Israel, to the absolute integrity of its worship, its rites, and its beliefs; in philosophy and science they saw the most deadly enemies of Judaism and maintained that the Jews were destined to perish and scatter among the nations, if they did not recover their wits and did not reject everything that was not of the Holy Law.

In 1232, Rabbi Solomon of Montpellier issued an anathema against all those who would read the *Moreh Nebukhim* or would take up scientific and philosophic studies. This was the signal for the struggle. It was violent on both sides, and all weapons were resorted to. The fanatical rabbis appealed to the fanaticism of the Dominicans, they denounced the *Guide of the Perplexed* and had it burned by the inquisition. At the instigation of a German doctor, Asher Ben Yechiel, a synod of thirty rabbis met at Barcelona, with Ben Adret in the chair, and excommunicated all those who read books other than the Bible and the Talmud, when under twenty-five years.

A counter-excommunication was proclaimed by Jacob Tibbon, who, at the head of all Provencal rabbis, boldly defended condemned science. All was in vain : those wretched Jews, whom everybody tormented for their faith, persecuted their coreligionists more cruelly and severely than they had ever been persecuted. Those whom they accused of indifference had to undergo the worst punishments; the blasphemers had their tongues cut; Jewish women who had any relations with Christians were condemned to disfigurement : their noses were subjected to ablation. Despite this, Tibbon's followers persisted. It was due to them, that Jewish thought did not completely die out in Spain, France and Italy during the fourteenth and fifteenth centuries. Even such men as Moses of Narbonne and Levy de Bagnols, as Elias of Crete and Alemani, the teacher of Pico di Mirandola, as well as later Spinoza, were all isolated men. As for the mass of Jews, it had completely fallen under the power of the obscurantists. Hereafter it was separated from the world, its whole horizon was shut out; to nourish its spirit it had nothing but futile talmudic commentaries, idle and mediocre discussions on the Law.

Henceforth the Jew thought no longer. And what need had he of thinking since he possessed a minute, precise code, the work of casuist legists, which could give answer to any question that it was legitimate to ask? For believers were forbidden to inquire into problems which were not mentioned in this code—the Talmud.

The Jew found everything foreseen in the Talmud : the sentiments, the emotions, whatever they might be, were designated; prayers, formulas, all ready-made, supplied the means for expressing them. The book left room neither to reason nor to freedom, inasmuch as in instruction the legendary and gnomical portions were almost proscribed—to lay stress upon the law and ritual. True, by the tyranny they had exercised over their flock they developed in each the ingenuity and spirit of craftiness necessary to escape from the net which closed without pity; but they also increased the natural positivism of the Jews by presenting to them as their only idea the material and personal happiness, a happiness which one could attain on earth if one knew how to bind oneself to the thousand religious laws. To attain this selfish happiness, the Jew, whom the prescribed ceremonies rid of all care and trouble, was fatally led on to strive after gold, for under the existing social conditions which ruled him, as they ruled all the people of that epoch, gold alone could give him the gratification which his limited and narrow brain could conceive. He was prepared to be changer, lender, usurer, one who strives after the metal, at first for the pleasures it could afford and then afterwards for the sole happiness of possessing it; one who greedily seizes gold and avariciously immobilizes it. The Jew having become such, anti-Judaism became more complicated, social causes intermingled with religious causes; the combination of these causes explains the intensity and gravity of the persecutions which Israel had to undergo.

Indeed, the Lombards and Caeorsins, for instance, were the object of popular animosity; they were hated and despised but they were not victims of systematic persecutions. It was deemed abominable that Jews should have acquired wealth, especially because they were *Jews*. Against the Christian who cheated him, and was neither better nor worse than the Jew, the poor wretch when plundered felt less anger than against the Israelite reprobate, the enemy of God and man. When the deicide, even so the object of terror, had become the usurer, the collector of taxes, the merciless agent of the fisc—the terror increased; it became intermingled with hatred on the part of the oppressed and downtrodden. The simple minds did not seek the real causes of their distress; they only saw the proximate causes. For the Jew was the proximate cause of usury; by the heavy interest he charged he caused destitution, severe and hard misery; accordingly, it was upon the Jews that enmities fell. The suffering populace did not trouble themselves about responsibilities; they were neither economists nor reasoners; they only ascertained that a heavy hand weighed upon them : that was the hand of the Jew, and the people rushed upon him. They did not rush upon him alone; when at the limit of their endurance, they often attacked all the rich, indiscriminately killing Jews and Christians alike. In Gascony and southern France the *Pastoureaux* destroyed 120 Jewish communities, but the Jews were not their only victims; they invaded castles, they exterminated the nobles and the propertied. Only that among the Christians the propertied alone suffered violence at the hands of the rebels, the poor were spared; among the Jews the rich and the poor were exterminated indiscriminately, for, before any crime, they were guilty of being Jews.

At all events, the masses, restrained by authority and law rarely attacked the capitalists in general; to goad them on to revolt a terrible accumulation of miseries was necessary. But with reference to the Jews their ill-feeling was not restrained at all; on the contrary, it was encouraged. This was a means to divert attention, and every now and then kings, nobles or burghers offered their slaves a holocaust of Jews. This unfortunate Jew was utilized for two purposes during the Middle Ages. They employed him as a leech, let him swell up, fill himself with gold, then they made him clear; or, whenever popular hatred was too bitter, he was subjected to corporal punishment which was profitable to the Christian capitalists, who thus paid a tribute of propitiary blood to those whom they oppressed.

To give satisfaction to their wretched subjects, the kings would from time to time proscribe Jewish usury, would cancel debts; but oftenest they tolerated the Jews, encouraged them, being sure to derive benefit from them through confiscation or by taking their place as creditors. Nevertheless these measures were always but temporary, and governmental anti-Judaism was purely political. They banished the Jews either to mend their finances, or to elicit the gratitude of the small fry by partly relieving them of the heavy burden of debt; but they would soon recall the Jews, as they could find no better tax collectors. However, anti-Jewish legislation was, as we have said, most frequently forced upon the royal power by the church, either by the monks or the popes and synods. Even the regular clergy and the secular clergy acted upon different principles.

The monks addressed themselves to the people, with whom they were in constant touch. In the first place they preached against the deicides, but they represented these deicides as domineering, while they should have been bent forever under the yoke of Christendom. All these preachers gave expression to popular grievances. "If the Jews fill their granaries with fruit, their cellar with victuals, their bags with money and their chests with gold," said Pierre de Cluny :[63] "it is neither by tilling the earth, nor by serving in war, nor by practising any other useful and honourable trade, but by cheating the Christians and buying, at low price, from thieves the things which they have stolen." They thundered against the "infamous" nation "which lives by pillage," and while their invectives were prompted by zeal in proselytism, they posed especially as avengers, who had come to punish "the isolence, avarice and hard-heartedness" of the Jews. And they found a hearing. In Italy, John of Capistrano, "the scourge of the Hebrews," was stirring up the poor against the usury and obduracy of the Jews. He continued his work in Germany and Poland, leading gangs of poor wretches and desperadoes who exacted expiation for their sufferings from the Jewish communities. Bernardinus of Feltre followed his example, but he was haunted by more practical notions, among others by that of establishing mont-de-piétés to counteract the rapacity of the lenders. He travelled all over Italy and Tyrol, demanding the expulsion of the Hebrews, inciting insurrections and riots, causing the massacre of the Jews in Trent.

The kings, nobles and bishops did not encourage this campaign of the regulars. They protected the Jews from the monk Radulphe, in Germany; in Italy, they set themselves against the preachings of Bernardinus of Feltre, who accused the princes of having sold themselves to Yechiel of Pisa, the wealthiest Jew of the peninsula; in Poland, Pope Gregory XI stopped the crusade of Jan of Ryczywol. The rulers had every interest to suppress these partial uprisings; from experience they knew that when the bands of starvelings were through slaughtering the Jews, they would kill those who possessed too great wealth, those who enjoyed excessive privileges, or those lords, counts or barons, whose power weighed too heavily on the shoulders of tax-payers.

As for the Church, it kept to theological anti-Judaism, and, being essentially conservative, favouring the mighty and rich, it took care not to encourage the passions of the people. I speak of the official

Church, abounding in prebendaries; striving for unity and centralization, cherishing dreams of universal domination; the Church of the Synods, the law-making Church, and not the church of petty priests and monks which was stirred by the same passions as agitated the lowly. But if the church sometimes interfered in behalf of the Jews when they were the object of the mob's fury, it nursed this fury and supplied it with fuel by combating Judaism, even though combating it from different motives.

Faithful to its principles, it vainly persecuted the spirit of Judaism in all its forms. It could not get rid of it, as this Jewish spirit had inspired it in its earliest stages. It was impregnated with it as the beach-sands are impregnated with the sea-salt which rises to their surface, and despite its efforts from the second century on to rebuff its origin, to thrust far away all memory of its original foundation, it still preserved the marks of it. In seeking to realize its conception of Christian states directed and ruled over by the Papacy, the church strove to reduce all anti-Christian elements. Thus it inspired Europe's violent reaction against the Arabs, and the struggle of the European nationalities against Mahommedanism was a struggle at once political and religious.

Still the Moslem danger was external, but the internal dangers threatening the dogma proved quite as grave for the church. Formerly benign and confining itself to canonic penalties, hereafter it appealed to the secular powers, and the Vaudois, Albigenses, Beghards, Apostolic Brothers, Luciferians were treated with cruelty. The limit of this movement was reached in the inquisition which the Pope Innocent III. instituted in the thirteenth century. Henceforth, a special tribunal, backed by civil authority, obedient to its orders was to be the sole judge, and pitiless at that, of heresy.

The Jews could not be overlooked in this legislation. They were persecuted not as Jews—the church wished to preserve the Jews as a living testimony of its triumph—but because they instigated people to judaization, either directly or unconsciously, by the very fact of their existence. Had not their philosophers sent forth metaphysicians like Amaury de Béne and David de Dinan? What is more, were not certain heretics judaizing? The Pasagians of Upper Italy observed the Mosaic law; the Orleans heresy was a Jewish heresy; an Albigens sect maintained that the doctrine of the Jews was preferable to that of the Christians; the Hussites were supported by the Jews; accordingly, the Dominicans preached against the Hussites and the Jews, and the imperial army that advanced against Jan Ziska massacred the Jews on its way.

In Spain, where the mingling of Jews and Christians was considerable, the Inquisition was instituted by Gregory XI, who gave it its constitution, to survey the judaizing heretics and the Jews and Moors, who, though not subjects of the Church, were subject to the will of the Holy Office whenever "by their words or their writings they urged the Catholics to embrace their faith." More than that, the popes recalled the canonic decisions to the minds of the Kings of Spain, because the *fueros, i.e.,* Castillian customs which superseded the Visigothic laws, had granted equal rights to Jews, Christians and Moslems.

All these ecclesiastic measures reinforced the anti-Jewish sentiments of kings and nations; they were the prime causes; they upheld a special state of mind, which political motives emphasized with the kings; social motives—with the nations. Owing to it, anti-Judaism became general, and no class of society was free from it, for all classes were more or less guided by the Church or inspired by its teachings, all of them were or thought themselves harmed by the Jews. The nobility took offence at their riches; the proletarians, the artisans and peasants, in a word the small people, were provoked by their usury; as for the bourgeoisie, the merchant class, the dealers in money, it was in permanent rivalry with the Jews, and their constant competition engendered hatred. The modern contest between Christian and Jewish capital assumes shape in the fourteenth and fifteenth centuries, the Catholic bourgeois looks with calm eyes on the murder of Jews, which rids him of an often successful rival.

Thus everything concurred to make of the Jew an universal foe, and the only support that he found during this terrible period of several centuries was with the popes, who, while abetting the passions of which they made capital, still wanted to guard carefully this witness of the excellence of the Christian faith. If the Church preserved the Jews, it often was not without schooling and punishing them. The Church forbade giving them public positions that might confer upon them authority over Christians, it instigated the kings to adopt restrictive measures against them; it imposed upon them distinctive badges, the *rouelle* and hat; it shut them in those ghettoes, which the Jews had often accepted and even sought in their eagerness to separate themselves from the world, to live apart,

without mixing with the nations, to preserve intact their beliefs
and their race; so that in many points the edicts bidding the Jews
to remain confined in special quarters really but sanctioned an
already existing state of affairs. But the chief task of the Church
was to combat the Jewish religion dogmatically. However, controversies, numerous as they were, did not suffice for this; laws were
issued against the Jewish books. The reading of the *Mishna* in
synagogues had already been prohibited by Justinian; after him no
laws were passed against the Talmud, until the time of Saint Louis.
After the controversy between Nicholas Donin and Yechiel of Paris
(1240) Gregory IX ordered to burn the Talmud; this order was
repeated by Innocent IV (1244), Honorius IV (1286), John XXII
(1320) and the anti-pope Benedict XIII (1415). Moreover, the
Jewish prayers were expurgated and the erection of new synagogues
was forbidden.

The civil laws expounded the ecclesiastical decrees and were
inspired by them, as *e.g.*, the laws of Alfonso X of Castile, in the
code of *Siete Partidas*,[64] the dispositions of Saint Louis, those of
Phillip IV, those of the German emperors and the Polish kings.[65]
The Jews were forbidden to appear in public on certain days; a
personal toll was imposed upon them as if on cattle; they were
sometimes forbidden to marry without authorization.

To the laws one must add the customs—vexatious customs—like
that of Toulouse, which made the syndic of the Jews subject to
boxing on the ear. The mob insulted them during their holidays
and sabbaths; it profaned their cemeteries; on leaving the Mysteries
and Passion plays it would lay their houses waste.

Not content with vexing them, with expelling them, as did
Edward I in England (1287), Phillip IV and Charles VI in France
(1306 and 1394), Ferdinand the Catholic in Spain (1492), they
killed the Jews everywhere.

When on their way to liberate the Holy Tomb, the Crusaders
prepared themselves for the Holy War by the immolation of Jews;
whenever the black plague or a famine raged, the Jews were
sacrificed in holocaust to the angered divinity; whenever extortions,
misery, hunger, destitution maddened the people, they would
avenge themselves on the Jews, who were made victims of expiation.
"What's the use of going to fight the Mohammedans," cried Pierre
de Cluny,[66] "when we have among us the Jews, who are worse than
the Saracens?"

What was to be done against an epidemic unless to kill the Jews who conspired with the lepers to poison the wells? And so they were exterminated in York and London, in Spain at the instigation of St. Vincent Ferrer; in Italy, where John of Capistrano preached; in Poland, Bohemia, France, Moravia, Austria. They were burned in Strassburg, Mayence, Troyes. In Spain the Marranos mounted the scaffold by the thousands, elsewhere they were ripped open with pitchforks and scythes; they were beaten to death like dogs.

What crimes could have deserved such frightful punishments? How poignant must have been the afflictions of those beings! In those evil hours they cuddled one to the other and felt themselves brethren; the bond that joined them was fastened more tightly. To whom could they tell their plaints and their feeble joys, if not to themselves? From these general desolations, from these sobs was born an intense and suffering brotherhood. The ancient Jewish patriotism became still more exalted. These outcasts, maltreated all over Europe, and marching with bespattered faces, got it into their heads to feel Zion and its hills brought back to life, to conjure up —what a supreme and sweet consolation!—the beloved banks of the Jordan and the lake of Galilee; they arrived there through an intense solidarity.

Still, to understand exactly the position of the Jews during these Dark Ages, one must compare it with that of the people surrounding them. The persecutions of the Jews would go on now that their exclusive character would render them more sorrowful. In the Middle Ages the proletarians and the peasants were not much better off; after being shaken up by terrible upheavals, the Jews would enjoy periods of comparative tranquility, of which the serfs knew nothing. Steps were taken against them, but what steps were not taken against the Moriscoes, the Hussites, the Albigenses, the Pastoureaux, the Jacques, against the heretics and the outcasts? From the eleventh to the end of the sixteenth century, abominable years fell out, and the Jews suffered from it not a whit more than did those among whom they lived. They suffered for other reasons, and traces of it were left impressed in a different way. But as the manners had grown softer, hours of greater happiness for them were born. We shall see what changes the Reformation and the Renaissance were to bring about in their position.

SIX

ANTI-JUDAISM FROM THE TIME OF THE REFORMATION TO THE FRENCH REVOLUTION

WHEN the first breath of freedom swept over the world at the dawn of the sixteenth century, the Jews were but a nation of captives and slaves. Cooped up in the ghettoes, whose walls their own foolish hands helped only to make thicker, they were retired from human society, and, for the most part, lived in a state of lamentable and heartrending abjection. Their intellect had become atrophied, as they had themselves barred all the doors and shut all the windows through which air and light might have come to them.

The number of those who had escaped this abasement was very limited, and the Jews who succeeded in keeping a free brain and proud spirit were in the lowest minority. These were mostly physicians, as medicine is the only science permitted by the Talmud; at the same time there were philosophers occasionally, and we shall see the role they played in Italy during the Renaissance.

Toward the end of the fifteenth century, the Jew had become the serf of the Imperial Chamber in Germany; in France he was the king's serf, the serf of the lord, less even than a serf, for a serf could still own something, while a Jew in reality had no property; he was a thing rather than a person. The king and the lord, the bishop or the abbot, could dispose of all his belongings, *i.e.*, of all that seemed to belong to him, since for him the possibility of owning was purely fictitious. He was taxable at will; he was subjected to fixed imposts, without prejudice to confiscations, and while, on the one hand, the Church was making every effort to attract to it the Jew, on the other hand, the baron and church dignitaries kept him in his condition. If he turned to Christianity he lost his possessions in favour of the lord, who was anxious to make good the loss of the taxes which he could no longer levy on the convert, and thus it was to his interest to remain in the slaves' prison. He was looked upon as a beast, impure and useful at that, as lower than a dog or hog, to which the personal toll likened him, however; he was the one forever accursed, he upon whom it was lawful, even meritorious, to shower the blows which the Crucified had received in Pilate's pretorium.

The only country where the Jews could claim the dignity of human beings was closed to them at the opening of the sixteenth century. The capture of Granada and the conquest of the Moorish Kingdom had deprived the Jews of their last refuge. The whole of Spain became Christian on the day (January 2, 1492) when Ferdinand and Isabella entered the Mohammedan city. The holy war of the Spaniards against the infidels ended victoriously, and the Moors in existence were cruelly persecuted in spite of the security which had been granted them. The victory having aroused on the one hand fanaticism, and the national sentiment on the other, Spain, now free from the Moors, wished to get rid of the Jews, whom the Catholic king and queen expelled the very year of Boabdil's fall, while the Inquisition doubled the severities against the Marranos and the descendants of the Moriscoes.

Still, the time of great sorrows had passed for the Jews, notwithstanding that the circumstances to which they had been reduced were lamentable. They began to descend the hill which they had so laboriously climbed, and if they found as yet no complete security in their paths, they met with more humaneness, more pity. The manners soften at this epoch, the souls become less rude, people actually acquire the idea of a human being; this age when individualism increases, better understands the individuals; while personality develops, more tenderness is displayed towards the personality of the other.

The Jews felt the effects of this state of mind. They were despised all the same, but they were hated in a less violent way. It was still sought to attract them to Christianity, but that was by persuasion. They were banished from a good many cities and countries; they were driven from Cologne and Bohemia in the sixteenth century; the trade-bodies of Frankfort and Worms, led by Vincent Fettmilch, forced them to leave those cities; but as serfs of the Imperial Chamber, they were efficiently protected by their suzerain. If Leopold I sent them out of Vienna, if later on Maria Theresa expelled them from Moravia, these decrees of exile had but a temporary effect, their consequences were felt but for a short time; and when the Jews re-entered the cities by virtue of undoubted tolerance, they were not molested. The massacres of Franconia and Moravia, the funeral piles of Prague, were exceptions in the sixteenth century, and as for the extermination ordered in Poland by Chmielnicki, in the seventeenth century, they reached the Jews by ricochet only.

Hereafter there have been no systematic persecutions, except those kept up in Spain against the Jewish converts, and in Portugal when introduced by the Pope Clement VII, at the request of John III, and after the massacres of 1506. Even there the inquisition was entrusted to the Franciscans, who had shown themselves less cruel than the Spanish Dominicans.

Still the Jews did not change. Such as we have seen them right in the Middle Ages, we find them also at the moment of the the Reformation; morally and intellectually the mass of the Jews was perhaps even worse. But if they had not changed, those by their side had changed. People were less believing, and therefore less inclined to detest heretics. Averroism had prepared this decadence of faith, and the part played by the Jews in the spread of Averroism is well known; so that they thus had worked for their own benefit. The majority of Averroists were unbelievers, or more or less assailed the Christian religion. They were the direct ancestors of the men of the Renaissance. It is owing to them that the spirit of doubt, as well as the spirit of investigation, had worked itself out. The Florentine platonists, the Italian Aristotelians, the German humanists came from them; thanks to them Pomponazzo composed the treatises against the immortality of the soul; thanks to them, too, among the thinkers of the sixteenth century sprang up the theism which corresponded with the decadence of Catholicism.

Animated by such sentiments, the men of this period could not glow with religious indignation against the Jews. Other preoccupations engaged them, though, and they had to abate two powerful authorities—scholasticism and the supremacy of Rome. The struggles of the preceding century, the schisms of the West, the licence in the manners of the clergy, simony, the sale of benefices and indulgences, all these had weakened the Church and impaired the Papacy. There were protests rising against them on all sides. "The clergy must be made moral," said the Father of the Vienna Synod (1311). The movement of the Hussites, that of the Frerots, the Fraticellians, the Beghards, had already been a protest against the wealth and corruption of the Church; but the Papacy was incapable of reform, and the Reformation had to take place outside of and against it.

The Humanists were its promoters. Everything turned them away from Catholicism. The Greeks of Constantinople, fleeing from the Turks, had brought to them the treasures of the ancient literatures. By discovering a new world Columbus was to open for them unknown horizons. They were finding new reasons for combatting scholasticism, that old servant-maid of the Church. The humanists were becoming sceptics and pagans in Italy, but in Germany the emancipating movement which they helped to bring about was becoming more religious. To beat the scholastics the humanists of the empire became theologians, and went to the very sources in order to arm themselves better; they learned Hebrew, not as Pico di Mirandola and the Italians had done, in the way of a dilettante or out of love for knowledge, but in order to find therein arguments against their opponents.

During these years which ushered in the Reformation, the Jew turned educator, and taught the scholars Hebrew; he initiated them into the mysteries of the kabbala after having opened to them the doors of Arabic philosophy. Against Catholicism he equipped them with the formidable exegesis which the rabbis had cultivated and built up during centuries : the exegesis which protestantism, and later on rationalism, would make good use of. By a singular chance the Jews, who had consciously or unconsciously supplied humanism with weapons, had also given it the pretext for its first serious battle. The contest for or against the Talmud was the forerunner of the disputes over the Eucharist.

The struggle started at Cologne, the city of the inquisition and capital of the Dominicans. A converted Jew, Joseph Pfefferkorn, once more denounced the Talmud before the Christian world, and, with the aid of the great inquisitor, Hochstraten, obtained from the Emperor Maximilian an edict authorizing him to examine the contents of the Jewish books and destroy those which blasphemed the Bible and the Catholic faith. From this decision the Jews appealed to Maximilian, and succeded in having the power originally conferred upon Pfefferkorn transferred to the archbishop elector of Mayence. As his advisors the archbishop took the doctors, the humanists, and among them Reuchlin, who felt no unbounded sympathy for the Jews, having even attacked them once upon a time. But though he scorned the Jews in general, he was a hebraizer for all that, and as such was doubtless more interested in the Talmud than in the inquisitorial tribunal with its arrests. He, therefore, violently fought the projects of Pfefferkorn and the Dominicans, and not only declared that the books of the Israelites ought to be preserved, but even maintained that chairs of Hebrew ought to be created in the universities. Reuchlin was accused of having sold himself for the gold of the Jews. He replied with a terrible pamphlet, *The Mirror of the Eyes,* which was condemned to be burned.

But new times were approaching; the storm foreseen by everybody broke over the Church. Luther issued at Wittenberg his ninety-five theses, and Catholicism not only had to defend the position of its priests, but was also forced to fight for its essential tenets. For a moment the theologians forgot the Jews, they even forgot that the spreading movement took its roots in Hebrew sources. Nevertheless, the Reformation in Germany and England as well was one of those movements when Christianity acquired new force in Jewish sources. The Jewish spirit triumphed with Protestantism. In certain respects the Reformation was a return to the ancient Ebionism of the evangelic ages. A great portion of the protestant sects was semi-Jewish, the anti-trinitarian doctrines were later preached by the protestants, by Michel Servet and the two Socins of Sienna among others. Even in Transylvania anti-trinitarianism had flourish since the sixteenth century, and Seidelius had asserted the excellence of Judaism and of the Decalogue. The Gospels had been abandoned for the Old Testament and the Apocalypse. The influence exercised by these two books over the Lutherans, the Calvinists and especially the Reformers and the English revolutionists, is well known. This influence continued to the nineteenth century; it produced the Methodists, Pietists, and particularly the Millenaries, the men of the Fifth Monarchy, who in London dreamed with Venner of a republic and allied themselves with the Levellers of John Lilburne.

Moreover, Protestantism, at its inception in Germany, endeavoured to win over the Jews, and in this respect, the analogy between Luther and Mohammed is striking. Both had drawn their teachings from Hebrew sources, both wished to have the remains of Israel stamp with approval the new dogmas which they were formulating. But the Jews had always been the stubborn people of the Scriptures, the people with the hard nape, rebellious against injunctions, tenacious, fearlessly faithful to its God and its Law.

Luther's preaching proved vain, and the irascible monk issued a terrible pamphlet against the Jews.[67] "The Jews are brutes," he said; "their synagogues are pig-sties, they ought to be burned, for Moses would do it, if he came back to this world. They drag in mire the divine words, they live by evil and plunders, they are wicked beasts that ought to be driven out like mad dogs."

In spite of these violent outbursts and excitement, in spite of the numerous controversies, which had taken place between the protestants and Jews, the latter were not ill-treated in Germany; people had no spare time to busy themselves with them.

Overwhelmed with miseries, decimated by war, ruined, reduced to slavery, a prey to destitution and famine, the peasants of the sixteenth century no longer went for the Jewish money-lender or the Christian usurer, but they aimed higher; they attacked in the first place a whole class—of the rich—and then the social order as a whole. The revolt was general; at first it was the peasants of the Netherlands, then, and chiefly, those of Germany. All over the Empire they founded secret societies, the *Bundschuh*,[68] the Poor Conrad, the Evangelic Confederation. The peasants of Speyer and of the banks of the Rhine rose in 1503; the bands of Joss Fritz, in 1512; the peasants of Austria and Hungary, in 1515; those of Suabia, in 1524; those of Suabia, Alsace and the Palatinate, in 1525. All marched with the battle cry: "In Christ there is no longer master or slave." The tradesmen joined them; knights, like Goetz von Berlichingen, placed themselves at their head, and they massacred the nobles and set the castles and convents on fire. In this formidable movement which convulsed a part of Europe until 1535, everywhere leaving deep traces, the Jews had been neglected, they had ceased to be the scapegoat, and the poor wretches, famished and miserable, no longer fell upon them.

Were they as happy in the Catholic countries? Yes, for there, too, they ceased to be the chief and sole enemies of the Church, and it was no longer they that were feared. The relaxation of religious ideas brought in Italy a rapprochement between a certain class of Jews and the various classes of society. First, the humanists, the poets, visited the Jewish scholars, philosophers and physicians. This familiarity had begun in the fourteenth century, when Dante was seen to have for his friend the Jew Manoello, the cousin of the philosopher Giuda Romano; it continued in the fifteenth and the sixteenth centuries. Alemani was the teacher of Picodi Mirandola, Elias del Medigo publicly taught metaphysics in Padua and Florence, Leo the Hebrew published his platonic dialogues on love. The Jewish printers, like the scholar Soncino, were in constant touch with the literature of the period; his library was the centre of Hebrew publications, and he even rivalled Aldo by publishing Greek authors. Hercules Gonzago, bishop of Mantua and disciple of the Jew Pomponazzo of Bologna, accepted the dedication of Jacob Mantino, who had translated the *Compendium* of Averroes, while other princes encouraged Abraham de Balmes in his work of translation.[69] And not only the sceptical, even unbelieving faction, of the Hellenists and Latinists, worshippers of Zeus and Aphrodite more than of Jesus, were on good terms with the Jews, but the lord and the bourgeois were likewise. "There are," says the bishop Maiol, "persons, and often persons of quality, both men and women, who are so foolish and senseless as to take counsel with Jews over their most intimate affairs, to their own detriment. They (the Jews) are seen visiting the houses and palaces of the great ones, the dwellings of officers, councillors, secretaries, gentlemen, both in the city and country." People did not content themselves with receiving Jews, they went to their houses, and, what is more, attended their religious ceremonies. "There are among us," says again Maiol, "some who visit and superstitiously revere the synagagues"; and, addressing them, he exclaims : "You hear the Jews blow their trumpets on the days of their festivities, and you run with your families to look at them." Thus it went on during the seventeenth century. In Ferrara they went to hear the sermons of Judah Azael, and, in 1676, Innocent XI threatened with excomunication and a fine of fifteen ducats those who frequented the synagogues. After the terrible shock which had just disturbed the Church, they more than ever wished to guarantee security to the Catholic dogma. Julius III had the Talmud burned in Rome and Venice upon denunciation by Solomon Romano, a converted Jew; Paul IV condemned it again at the request of another convert, Vittorio Eliano; Pius V and Clement VIII did likewise.

During the dogmatic and theological reaction which followed the Reformation, the Roman Church, friendly to the Jews heretofore, came to be the only government, almost the only power, systematically to persecute Judaism. Paul IV revived the ancient canonic laws and had the Marranos burned; Pius V banished the

Jews from his domains, except from Rome and Ancona, after having issued his Constitution against the Jews, while the Spaniards, as they penetrated further into Italy, were driving them from Naples, Genoa and Milan.

The other sovereigns had not the same motives as the popes to attend to the Jews. And so, from the sixteenth century on, legislation against the Jews ceased. We find only the edict of Ferdinand I against Jewish usury—in Germany; a few decrees in Poland, and much later, the prohibitions of Louis XV and Louis XVI. Again to find anti-Jewish legislation, it will be necessary to study modern Russia, Rumania and Servia, which we shall shortly do.

Anti-Judaism consisted chiefly in molestations and outrages. The populace delighted in jeering the Jews, and the grandees often gave them a chance to do it. Leo X, that ostentatious pontiff, who was fond of buffoonery—he had at his side two monks to divert him with their pleasantries—would order races between Jews, and, being very shortsighted, would watch them, glass in hand, from the heights of his balconies. During the carnival in Rome the people would parody the burial of rabbis, and a Jew would be marched through the city streets, mounted backward on a donkey and holding the animal's tail in his hand. On the ghetto-gates a sow was carved, and they were often covered with obscene groups, in which rabbis were represented. The sow symbolized the synagogue—exactly as with the Israelites the Roman Church was designated by the Hebrew name for hog—and the Jews were constantly reminded of it; a painter once even related at Wagenseil how he had painted a sow on the door-leaf of the arch of a synagogue which he was engaged to adorn.

With the scholars, the learned and the theologians, anti-Judaism was becoming dogmatic and theoretical. True they wanted to bring the Jews back, but by soft measures. It was no longer a question of burning their books, but of translating them. It was said that now that the Christian faith had struck deep enough roots, there was no danger to believers from publishing Hebrew books, as had been done in the case of those of the Arians and other heretics. Thus it would be possible to know the polemic practices of the Israelites, and it would thus be possible successfully to combat them.

This study brought about a result quite different from that expected. By scrutinizing the Jewish spirit one came nearer to the

Jews, and thereby became more sympathizing with them. Men, like Richard Simon, e.g., who had prepared themselves for scientific exegesis, through talmudists and hebraizing researches, could not look with hatred upon those from whom they held their knowledge. Others were anxious to know when the Jews would be called to Christian communion. The seventeenth century was the most propitious time for the disputes over the recalling of the Jews. In France this question as to whether the Jews would be recalled at the end of the world or before it—divided Bossuet and the Figurists led by Duguet.[70] In England the Millenaries proclaimed the return of the Jews.[71] In Germany also this opinion had its advocates, such as Bengal, e.g. In France, not only did the convulsionaries of Saint-Menard proclaim the approaching entry of the Jews into the Church, but some were seen entertaining these dreams until our days, and in 1809 President Agier fixed upon 1849 as the year of the conversion of the Jews.

All over Europe the Jews enjoyed the greatest tranquillity during the eighteenth century. In Poland alone they fared badly for having once lived too well. They had been prosperous there up to the middle of the seventeenth century. Rich, powerful, they had lived on an equal footing with the Christians, treated as though of the people amid whom they lived; but they could not help giving themselves up to their usual commerce, their vices, their passion for gold. Dominated by the Talmudists they succeeded in producing nothing beyond commentators of the Talmud. They were tax collectors, spirit-distillers, usurers, seigneurial stewards. They were the noblemen's allies in their abominable work of oppression, and when the Cossacks of Ukraina and Little Russia had risen, under Chmielnicki, against Polish tyranny, the Jews, as accomplices of the lords, were the first to be massacred. It is said that over 100,000 of them were killed in ten years, but just as many Catholics and especially Jesuits, were killed as well.

Elsewhere they were very prosperous. Thus, in the Ottoman Empire, they were simply liable to the tax on foreigners and subject to no other restrictive regulations, but nowhere was their prosperity so great as in the Netherlands and England. Marranos fleeing the Spanish Inquisition had settled in the Netherlands in 1593, and thence settled a colony in Hamburg, then, later on, under Cromwell, one in England, whence they had been banished for centuries and whither Menasse-ben-Israel brought them back.

The Dutch, as practical and circumspect a people as the English, utilized the commercial genius of the Jews and turned it to their own enrichment. In France Henry II had authorized the Portuguese Jews to settle in Bordeaux, where, on the strength of the granted privileges, confirmed also by Henry III, Louis XIV, Louis XV, and Louis XVI, they acquired great wealth in maritime commerce.

In the other cities of France there were few of them, and, besides, those residing in Paris or elsewhere had settled there only because of the administrative tolerance. In Alsace alone there was a great agglomeration.

Their splendid condition provoked no violent demonstrations; now and then protests would be heard, they would say with Expilly : "With infinite grief one sees how such base people, who had been received in the capacity of slaves, possess costly furniture, lead a refined life, wear gold and silver on their garments, dress showily, perfume themselves, study instrumental and vocal music and ride horseback for mere diversion." At the same time, greater and greater toleration was shown them from day to day; the world was drawing nearer to them. Were they, in turn, drawing nearer to the world? No. They seemed more and more to attach themselves to their mystic patriotism; the further they went, the more the dreams of Kabbala haunted them, with ever renewed confidence they awaited the Messiah, and never had the pseudo-Messiahs been received with so much enthusiasm as they were in the seventeenth and eighteenth centuries. The Kabbalists exhausted arithmetical combinations to calculate the exact date of the coming of him, who was so longed for. Toward 1666, the date most commonly designated as the sacred date, all Jews of the Orient were raised by the preachings of Sabbatai Zevi. From Smyrna, where Sabbatai had proclaimed himself Messiah, the movement spread to the Netherlands, and England even, and everybody expected the restoration of Jerusalem and of the holy kingdom from the King of Kings, as Sabattai was called. The same enthusiasm was displayed in 1755 when Frank appeared in Podolia as the new Messiah.

These hopes which the illuminism of the Kabbalists entertained, helped to keep the Jews apart, but those who were not seduced by the speculations of dreamers, were weighed down by the yoke of the Talmud, a yoke at all events even ruder and more humiliating.

So far from decreasing, the Talmudic tyranny had even increased since the sixteenth century. At this time Joseph Caro had edited the *Shulchan Aruch,* a Talmudic code, which—according to the traditions inculcated by the rabbinists—set up as laws the opinions of the doctors. Up to our time the European Jews had lived under the execrable oppression of these practices.[72] The Polish Jews improved even upon Joseph Caro and refined the already enormous subtleties of the *Shulchan Aruch* by making additions thereto, and they introduced the method of *Pilpul* (pepper-grains) into their instruction.

Accordingly, as the world grew kinder to them, the Jews—at least the masses—retired into themselves, straitened their prison, bound themselves with tighter bonds. Their decrepitude was unheard of, their intellectual sinking was equalled only by their moral debasement; this nation seemed dead.

However, the reaction against the Talmud had proceeded from the Jews themselves. Mordecai Kolkos,[73] of Venice, had already published a book against the Mishna; in the seventeenth century, Uriel Acosta[74] violently fought the rabbis, and Spinoza[75] exhibited little affection for them. But anti-talmudism displayed itself particularly in the eighteenth century, at first among the mystics, such as, *e.g.,* the Zoharites, disciples of Franck, who declared themselves enemies of the doctors of the law. At any rate these opponents of the rabbinites were unable to extricate the Jews from their abjection. To begin this task, it was necessary for Moses Mendelssohn, a Jew and philosopher at the same time, to array the Bible against the Talmud. His German version (1779)—was a great revolution. It was the first blow dealt to the rabbinical authority. The Talmudists, too, who had once wished to kill Kolkos and Spinoza, violently attacked Mendelssohn, and prohibited, under penalty of excommunication, to read the Bible which he had translated.

These outbursts of rage were of no avail. Mendelssohn had followers: young men, his disciples, founded the periodical *Meassef,* which advocated the new Judaism, endeavoured to snatch the Jews from their ignorance and humiliation, and prepared their moral emancipation. As for political emancipation, the humanitarian philosophy of the eighteenth century was working hard to bring it about. Though Voltaire was an ardent Judoephobe, the ideas which he and the Encyclopaedists represented were not hostile to the Jews, as being ideas of liberty and universal equality. On the other hand, if the Jews really were isolated in the various states, they still had some points of contact with those surrounding them.

Capitalism had by this time developed among the nations; stock-jobbing and speculation were born; the Christian financiers applied themselves to them with a zeal, just as they had applied themselves to usury, just as they had, in the capacity of farmers-general, collected imposts and taxes. The Jews could, therefore, take their place among those whom "discounts were enriching at the public's expense, and who were masters of all possessions of the French of all classes," as already Saint Simon was saying.

The economic objections which were raised against their possible emancipation had no longer the same import as in the Middle Ages, when the church wanted to make the Jews the only representatives of the class of money-brokers. As for the political objections, that they formed a State within the State, that their presence as citizens could not be tolerated in a Christian society and was even injurious to it, they remained valid until the day when the French Revolution dealt its direct blow to the conception of a Christian State, And so Dohm, Mirabeau, Clermont-Tonnerre, the Abbot Grégoire were right with regard to Rewbel, Maury and the Prince de Broglie, and the Constituent Assembly obeyed the spirit which had guided it since its inception when it declared on September 27, 1791, that the Jews would enjoy in France the rights of actual citizens The Jews were on the threshold to society.

SEVEN

ANTI-JUDAIC LITERATURE AND THE PREJUDICES

WE have studied only the legal and the popular anti-Judaism from the eighth century to the French Revolution. We have seen how anti-Jewish legislation, at first canonic and later civil, was little by little instituted. We have shown how the populace had been partly prepared by the decrees of the popes, kings and republics, to hate and abuse the Jews, and how far this exasperation of the people, the massacres it committed, the insults and outrages it showered, had given the counter-blow to this legislation. We have shown that up to the fifteenth century, the accusations weighing over the Jews, had grown each year, so that they had reached their maximum at this period, and from then on went decreasing, that the codes had ceased to be applied rigorously, that customs had gradually fallen into disuse, that few, if at all, new laws were made, and that the Jew thus marched towards liberation.

However, there is a kind of anti-Judaism to which we have paid no special attention, and which we must hereafter examine. While the Church and the monarchies issued laws against the Jews, the theologians, philosophers, poets, and historians were writing about them. It is the role, the working and the importance of this anti-Judaism of the pen that we still have to examine.

Theological anti-Judaism, chronologically the first, naturally had apologetic ways at its inception; it could not be otherwise as Judaism was fought only to glorify the Christian faith and prove its excellence. As we have said, they ceased producing apologetic writings towards the end of the fourth century; the young church, in the intoxication of its triumph, did no longer think it necessary to prove its superiority, and as representatives of the apologetic manner, we find in the fifth century only the *Altercation of Simon and Theopilus* of Evagrivs,[76] in which the *Altercation of Jason and Papiscus* of Aristo of Pella was imitated and even plagiarized; after that one has to come to the seventh century to find the three books of Isidore of Seville directed against the Jews.[77]

When scholasticism was born, apologetics reappeared. They had two ends in view : they defended the Catholic dogmas and symbols, and they combated Judaism. They set themselves against that judaizing which the church, its doctors, philosophers and apologists had always feared, imagining the Jew as a sort of wolf that prowled around the sheep-fold in order to carry the sheep away from a happy life. These were the sentiments that guided, *e.g.*, Cedrenus[78] and Theophanes[79] when they wrote their *Contra Judaeos,* and Gilbert Crépin, abbot of Westminster, in his *Disputatio Judei cum Christiano de fide Christiana.*[80]

The form of these writings was little varied; they reproduced almost servilely the classic arguments of the Fathers of the Church, and their wording followed similar patterns. To analyze one of them means analyzing all. Thus, *e.g.*, Pierre de Blois's *Against the Perfidy of the Jews,*[81] enumerated through thirty chapters the testimonies which the Old Testament, and especially the prophets, contain in favour of the divine Trinity and Unity, of the Father and the Son, of the Holy Spirit, of the Messianism of Jesus Christ, of the Davidic descent of the Son of Man, and of his incarnation. He ended by proving, on the basis of the same authorities, that the Law had been transmitted to the Gentiles, that the Jews had been doomed to reprobation, but that the remnants of Israel would nevertheless one day be converted and saved.

Yet these writings, discussions, fictitious dialogues hardly, if at all, attained their object. They were consulted by clergymen only, and were thus directed at converts; rabbis read them in very rare cases; their own biblical exegesis and science being much superior to those of the good monks, these latter rarely were at an advantage. At all events they never convinced those whom they were to convince, and they could not effectively fight the Jews, as they did not know the talmudic and exegetic commentaries, from which the Jews drew their weapons and forces. Things changed in the thirteenth century. The works of Jewish philosophers had spread and exercised considerable influence on the scholasticism of the time; men like Alexandre de Hales had read Maimonides (Rabbi Moses) and Ibn Gebirol (Avicebron), and they bore the impress of the teachings exposed by the *Guide of the Perplexed* and the *Fountain of Life.* Curiosity was awakened, people wanted to know Jewish thought and dialectics, at first for philosophical motives, then to fight against the Jews with better success.

The dominican Raymond de Penaforte, confessor of James I, of Aragon, and a great converter of the Jews, bade the Dominicans to learn Hebrew and Arabic to be able better to persuade and battle with the Jews. He established schools for the instruction of monks in these two languages and was the pioneer of Hebrew and Arabic studies in Spain. He thus started a line of apologists who were no longer contented with collecting the passages of the Old Testament that foreshadowed the Trinity or prophesied the Messiah, but who endeavoured to refute the rabbinical books and Talmudic assertions.

The best known among all these theological lampoons are those published by the dominican Raymund Martin, "a man as remarkable for his knowledge of Hebrew and Arabic writings as for that of Latin works."[82] These squibs bear characteristic enough titles : *Capistrum Judaeorum* (*Muzzle of the Jews*) and *Pugio Fidei* (*Dagger of the Faith*).[83] The second had the greatest circulation. "It is well," Raymund Martin said therein, "that the Christians take in hand the sword of their enemies, the Jews, to strike them with it?"

During the thirteenth and fourteenth centuries the *Pugio Fidei* was quite in vogue among the monks, especially the Dominicans, ardent defenders of the faith. It was studied, consulted, plagiarized. The number of writings which were inspired by Raymund Martin and for which the *Pugio Fidei* served as the prototype and even mould, was considerable. Among others those of Porchet Salvaticus,[84] Pierre de Barcelona,[85] and Pietro Galatini[86] may be named.

Still even Martin's knowledge was not perfect, and as we shall presently see, the rabbis very often worsted their opponents in their controversies. The anti-Jews needed better weapons : the Franciscan, Nicholas de Lyra, supplied them. He had made a careful study of rabbinical literature, and his hebraic attainments, their extent, variety and solidity led to the belief that he was of Jewish origin, which is of little probability. At all events, he was the precursor of modern exegesis, which is the daughter of Jewish thought and whose rationalism is purely Jewish; he was the ancestor of Richard Simon. Nicholas de Lyra declared that the literal explanation of the text of the Scriptures should form the foundation of ecclesiastic science, and that the text and its meaning once established four meanings should be derived therefrom : the literal, allegoric, moral and anagogic.[87] Nicholas de Lyra expounded his researches in the *Postilla* and the *Moralitates,* collected and recast later into a larger work. Hereafter this was the arsenal to draw upon in the polemics against the Jews, as well as for the defence of the Gospels against the Jewish attacks, for Nicholas de Lyra had refuted, in his *De Messia,* the criticisms passed on the Old Testament by the Jews. Numerous editions of Nicholas de Lyra's works appeared, commentaries, notes and additions thereto were made, and in the matter of exegesis even Luther was his pupil.

But praiseworthy as it was to combat the Jews, it was still more meritorious to convince them, and most of the polemist monks did not forget that the conversion of Judah was one of the aims of the church. While the councils took steps to convert the Jews, the writers, on their part, endeavoured to be convincing, several of them, the more practical, went so far as to seek ground for reconciliation. So, *e.g.,* by making certain concessions—he was even ready to accept circumcision—Nicholas de Lyra wanted to unite all religions into one, with the Trinity as its principal dogma. The ancient *"obstinatio Judaeorum"* which maintained divine unity resisted these attempts, and the overtures of the Christians were generally received with disfavour. However, conversions were not infrequent, and I mean not only those brought about by violence, but also those obtained by persuasion. These converted Jews played a very great role in the anti-Jewish literature as well as in the history of the persecutions. Toward their coreligionists they proved themselves the most cruel, unjust and treacherous of adversaries. This is generally characteristic of converts, and the Arabs converted to Christianity or Christians turned to Islam witness that this rule allows of very few exceptions.

A host of sentiments united in maintaining this bilious disposition among the apostates. Above all they wished to give proof of their sincerity : they felt that a sort of suspicion surrounded them at entering into the Christian world, and the affectation of piety which they proclaimed did not seem sufficient to them to dispel the suspicions.

Nothing did they fear so much as the accusation of lukewarmness or sympathy with their former brethren, and the way in which the Inquisition treated those it deemed relapsers, was not calculated to diminish the fears entertained by the proselytes. Accordingly, they simulated an excess of zeal which in many, if not all, upheld a

genuine faith. Some of them, convinced of having found salvation
in their conversion, made even efforts to win over their coreligionists to the Christian faith; among these the church found several
of its most fearless and eagerly listened to converters.[88] Some even
informed against the Jews that they had abandoned the rigours of
the ecclesiastical and civil laws. About 1475, for instance, Peter
Schwartz and Hans Bayol, both converted Jews, instigated the
inhabitants of Ratisbon to sack the Ghetto; in Spain, Paul de
Santa-Maria instigated Henry III of Castile to take measures
against the Jews. This Paul de Santa-Maria, previously known
under the name of Solomon Levi of Burgos, was not an ordinary
personality. A very pious, very learned rabbi, he abjured at the
age of forty, after the massacres of 1391, and was baptized along
with his brother and four of his sons. He studied theology at Paris,
was ordained priest, became bishop of Cartagena and afterwards
chancellor of Castile. He published an *Examination of the Holy
Writ*—a dialogue between the infidel Saül and the convert Paul—
and issued an edition of Nicholas de Lyra's *Postilla,* supplemented
by his *Additiones* and glosses. He did not stop at that in his activity.
He is generally found the instigator in all the persecutions which
befell the Jews of his time, and he hunted the synagogue with a
ferocious hatred; and yet in his works he confined himself to
theological polemics.[89]

But the Talmud was the great antagonist of the converts, and
one that had to withstand most of their wrath. They constantly
denounced it before the inquisitors, the king, the emperor, the
pope. The Talmud was the execrable book, the receptacle of the
most hideous abuses of Jesus, the Trinity and the Christians;
against it Pedro de la Caballeria wrote his *Wrath of Christ Against
the Jews,*[90] Pfefferkorn, his *Enemy of the Jews,*[91] in which he con-
gratulated himself upon "having withdrawn from the dirty and
pestilential mire of the Jews," and Jerome of Santa Fé, his
Hebreomastyx.[92] The Catholic theologians followed the example of
the converts, most frequently they had about the Talmud no other
notions beyond those given them by the converts.

Usually auto-da-fés followed these denunciations of the Talmud,
but they were, as a rule, preceded by a disputation. This custom
of disputations goes back to deep antiquity. We know that already
the Hebrew doctors held disputations with the apostles. On several
occasions rabbis and monks were seen contending in eloquence in

the presence of the Emperors of Rome and Byzantium in order to convince their audience of the excellence of their cause, and the Chazar King made up his mind to embrace Judaism only after a discussion, in which a Jew, a Christian and a Mohammedan took part, so, at least, the legend relates.[93] These discussions were, however, rarely public, the church feared their consequences; it feared Jewish subtlety, clever at finding objections which embarrassed the defenders of the Catholic faith and troubled the believer. There remained in use only private discussions between ecclesiastical dignitaries and Talmudists, and few auditors were admitted to these meetings, except under rare and important circumstances, in which cases a legal sanction followed the dispute. In these queer disputes, in which one side acted as judge at the same time, the Jews were, in general, the stronger. Their more concise dialectics, their more genuine knowledge, their more serious and subtle exegesis, gave them an easy advantage. In spite of this, or rather, because of this, the Jews were very prudent in their assertions, they appeared in the most courteous light, and heeded those melancholy words of Moses Cohen of Tordesillas, addressed to his brethren : "Never let your zeal carry you away to the point of uttering stinging words, for the Christians hold the power and may silence the truth with fist-blows." These counsels were followed, but in spite of the precautions taken, at the end of the argument the Jew, who was always wrong in the end, was beaten to death.

However, the informers were usually commanded to sustain their charges. In 1239, a converted Jew, Nicholas Donin, of La Rochelle, brought before the pope, Gregory IX, a charge against the Talmud. Gregory ordered the copies of the book to be seized and an inquest made. Bulls were sent out to the bishops of France, England, Castile and Aragon. Eudes de Chateauroux, chancellor of the University of Paris, directed the investigation in France, the only country where the bulls had produced an effect. The disputation was ordered, and took place in 1240, between the informer, Nicholas Donin, and four rabbis : Yechiel of Paris, Jehuda ben David Melun, Samuel ben Solomon, and Moses of Coucy. The discussion was long, but Donin's skill finally divided the rabbis; the Talmud was condemned and burned a few years later.

In 1263, Raymond de Penaforte arranged at the Aragonian court a dispute between the rabbis, Nachmani of Girone (Bonastruc de Porta), and the Dominican, Pablo Christiani, a converted Jew and a zealous converter. This time Nachmani was victorious after a four-day disputation on the coming of Messiah, on the divinity of Jesus, and the Talmud. The king himself accorded him an audience, received him very cordially and loaded him with presents. But such victories were exceptional, as the Jewish books were most frequently condemned by the judges beforehand, whatever the skill of their defenders.

These controversies increased in number in Spain during the fourteenth and fifteenth centuries. Thus the convert Alfonso of Valladolid had a dispute with his former coreligionists at Valladolid; John of Valladolid, another convert, had a dispute with Moses Cohen de Tordesillas on the proofs of the Christian faith contained in the Old Testament, but was defeated in the contest; Shem-Tob ben Isaac Shaprut had at Pampeluna a controversy on the original sin and redemption, with the cardinal Pedro de Luna, later anti-pope Benedict XIII. Many more might be mentioned, all of them proving what amount of trouble the Jews were giving the church and how eagerly conversion was desired and solicited. Still all these disputes were courteous up to the moment the Inquisition was introduced.

But alongside of the Jew, considered the enemy of Jesus and the foe of Christianity, there was the Jew, the usurer, the money-dealer, he upon whom fell a part of the hatred of the oppressed and the poor, he whom the rising bourgeoisie was beginning to envy and hate. I have pictured that Jew at work, how he had come to the exclusive pursuit of gold, and how he became the object of popular passions as a sort of victim of expiation, the scape-goat for all the sins of a society that was no better than he. If the populace oftenest killed the deicide, it also fell upon the clipper of ducats; its anti-Judaism was not religious only, but social as well. The case was similar with anti-Judaism of the pen. If certain bishops and ecclesiastical writers confined themselves to defending the symbols of their faith against Jewish exegesis, if they fought against this Jewish spirit—the terror of the church that was, nevertheless, deeply impregnated with this spirit—others followed the example of the Fathers who had thundered against Jewish rapacity and the rapacity of the rich in general. To the theological treatises issued by them they added addresses to the court intended to combat the leaders on pawned articles, those who lived by usury. Dagobard,[94] Amolon,[95] Rigord,[96] Pierre de Cluny,[97] Simon Maiol[98] were these anti-Jews. They were among those whom the wealth of the Jews revolted more than their ungodliness, who were more scandalized by their luxury than by their blasphemies. No doubt, for them the Jews were the most hateful adversaries of the truth, the worst of the unbelievers;[99] they are the enemies of God and Jesus Christ; they call the apostles apostates; they scoff at the Bible of the Septuagint;[100] in their daily prayers they curse the Saviour under the name of the Nazarene; they build new synagogues as if to insult the Christian religion; they Judaize the believers, they preach the Sabbath to them and they persuade them to take a rest on Sabbath. But, besides, the Jews oppress the people; they hoard up wealth that is the fruit of usury and plunder;[101] they hold the Christians in servitude; they possess enormous treasures in the cities which had received them, *e.g.*, in Paris and Lyons; they commit larceny, they acquire money by evil methods; "everything passes through their hands, they insinuate themselves into houses and gain confidence; by their usury they draw the sap, the blood and the natural vigour of the Christians."[102] They sell counterfeit jewels, they receive stolen goods, they coin base money, cannot be trusted, collect their debts twice over. In brief, "there is no wickedness in the world which the Jews are not guilty of, so that they seem to aim at nothing but the Christians' ruin."[103]

To this picture of the *perfidia Judaeorum,* the anti-Jews, like Maiol or Luther,[104] added abundant abuse, and soon anti-Judaism became purely polemic. The theological and social considerations now occupy but a limited place in the books of Alonzo da Spina,[105] especially Pierre de Lancre[106] and Francisco de Torrejoncillo.[107] The *Sentinel Against the Jews,* a pamphlet by the last named, is particularly curious. Written in Spain at the beginning of the seventeenth century, it was aimed at the Marranos, who, it was said, invaded all the civil and religious offices. It consisted of fourteen books and showed that the Jews were presumptuous and liars, that they were traitors, that they were despised and dejected, that those favouring them came to an evil end, that neither they nor their work could be trusted, that they were turbulent, self-conceited, seditious, that the church preserved them only that in their midst might be born their Messiah the anti-Christ, who will be vanquished to allow Israel to recognize his error. At any rate Francisco de Torrejoncillo may be considered amiable if one compares his pamphlet with a singular little work of the same epoch bearing the title, *Book of the Alboraique*.[108] The Alboraique was Mohamet's mount, a queer animal, neither horse, nor mule, nor ox, nor donkey; to this singular animal the author of the squib likens the new Christians, the Marranos, who are Alboraiques as being neither Jews nor Christians.

Had all the polemists limited themselves to allegorical comparisons, not much harm would have come to the Jews. But some did not hesitate to relate the most extraordinary things about these accursed ones, and the anti-Jewish polemic literature enregistered all the popular prejudices, even made them worse; it originated new ones and perpetuated them in all instances. The wildest stories about the Jews were circulated; they were represented with monstrous features; the most abominable deformities, the blackest vices, the most heinous crimes, the most despicable habits were attributed to them. They have, so it was declared, the figure of a he-goat, they have horns and a caudal appendage,[109] they are subject to quinsy, to scrofula, to blood-flux, stinking infirmities which make them lower their heads,[110] they have haemorrhoids, bloody sores on their hands, they cannot spit; at night their tongue is overrun with worms. The belief in these diseases peculiar to the Jews had come from Spain, in the fourteenth century; later on they were arranged in lists, the oldest of which belongs to 1634. In these lists, to each of the twelve tribes its special disease is assigned.

Thus can be explained some other anti-Jewish prejudices; but though it is evident that the likening of the Israelites to the evil spirit caused the he-goat figure and horns on their foreheads to be attributed them, still many of these beliefs remain inexplicable. They all arise, in part, from the fact that the retired life of the Jews, their venerable habit of keeping aloof, not to mingle with those surrounding them—ever served to excite excessively the popular imagination.

As to the Templars, concerning whom so many similar abominations had been spread, they, above all others, can be likened unto the Jews. Like the latter, they were hated for their pride, their ostentation, their wealth in the midst of general misery, their eagerness for gain, their shameless use of means of acquisition, their making usurious contracts. They were hated because they advanced money on chattels and fiefs on condition that these fiefs and chattels remained theirs in case of the borrower's death; because the Templars' Order possessed a greater part of the French territory in the thirteenth century and formed a commonwealth within the state, the Templars having and recognizing no master but God.[111] We see then that the same causes produce the same results, create the same animosities, give rise to the same beliefs.

Were not the Templars said to "burn and roast the children they begat by young girls, and to sacrifice to and anoint their idols with the fat taken off";[112] were not the Cagots said to make use of Christian blood? Does not the charge of ritual murder weigh over the Jews as it had weighed over those wretches, the lepers, whom the Middle Ages treated as the Jew's brethren, thus taking up again the assertions of Manetho, repeated by Chaeremon, Lysimachus, Posidonius, Apollonius Molo and Apion, just as it had weighed over the sorcerers, who were also likened to the Jews? But we shall come back to this question when we speak of the modern antisemites.

What was the attitude of the Jews in the face of all these attacks and abuses which the theologians and polemists directed at them? They vigorously defended themselves. They opposed exegesis to exegesis; they opposed their logic to their opponents' arguments; they answered insults and calumnies with calumnies and insults; which is but normal, natural, inevitable, but all the same these insults fatally rebounded against them. If the anti-Jewish literature is enormous, the defensive literature of the Jews, as well as their anti-Christian literature—for the Jews oftentimes took up the offensive—is quite considerable.

The first controversial work belonging to the Israelite literature of the Middle Ages, was the *Book of the Lord's Wars,* written in 1170, by Jacob ben Ruben.[113] It was made up of twelve chapters, or gateways, proving that Messiah had not yet come, which, however, for the exegetic rhetoricians, was just as easy as, if not easier than to prove the opposite. But it was not enough to prove that Jesus was not the awaited Messiah; it was equally necessary to prove the superiority of the Jewish religion to those who were establishing, irrefutably, the superiority of the Christian religion, and this was easy for both sides, as each drew from the Bible what suited it. The Talmudists made use of the New Testament even to confirm their Judaic dogmas. This was done by Moses Cohen de Tordesillas, in his *Support of the Faith,* while Shem-Tob ben Isaac Shaprut resumed, in the form of a dialogue between a Unitarian and a Trinitarian, the ideas propounded by Jacob ben Ruben.[114]

In imitation of the ecclesiastical writers and inquisitors, the rabbis wrote books for the use of those who were challenged in disputes. A kind of *vade mecum*, these books pointed out the vulnerable sides of the Christian dogmas; and if, on the one hand, there were publications like "Judaism Defeated with Its Own Weapons," on the other hand were composed works like "Christianity Defeated with Its Own Arms," *i.e.,* with those found in the New Testament. In anti-Christian literature the Gospels played the part of the Talmud in anti-Jewish literature. Beginning with the eleventh or twelfth century they were often assailed, and numerous discussions took place between rabbinites and theologians. These discussions were sometimes gathered in collections, where they were presented in a light favourable to Jewish dialectics. Presently these collections came to be used as manuals; among them were the ancient *Nizzachon (Victory)* of Rabbi Mattathiah; *Nizzachon* of Lipman de Mülhausen; the one by Joseph Kimhi; the *Strengthening of the Faith,* by Isaac Troki,[115] and the *Book of Joseph the Zealot.*[116] Still this was not sufficient for the fervour of the Jews. Having prepared the minds for future debates, having assailed the Catholic doctrines, not in oratorical tournaments only, but in apologies as well, they wrote abusive pamphlets, like that famous *Toldot Jesho,* the life of the Galilean which goes back to the second or third century, and which Celsius possibly was acquainted with.[117] This *Toldot Jesho* was published by Raymund Martin, Luther translated it into German; Wagenseil and the Dutchman Huldrich also published it. It contained the story of Pantherus the soldier and the legends representing Jesus as a magician. After defending the Bible and Monotheism the Jews turned upon those who were their most dangerous enemies—the converted. If they had refuted Raymund Martin and Nicholas de Lyra,[118] they refuted with still greater energy Jerome de Santa Fé, the Santa Fé whom his former coreligionists called Megaddef, i.e., blasphemer. At Jerome they were incensed. Don Vidal ibn Labi, Isaac ben Nathan Kalonymos,[119] Solomon Duran,[120] several others, wrote to give the lie to the "calumniator." The same was done by Isaac Pulgar against Alfonso of Valladolid,[121] by Joshua ben Joseph Lorqui and Profiat Duran.[122]

In the seventeenth century anti-Judaism took on another form. The theologians were succeeded by erudites, scholars, exegetes. Anti-Judaism became milder and more scientific; it was represented by hebraizers, often of great attainments, like Wagenseil,[123] Bartolocci,[124] Voetius,[125] Joseph de Voisin,[126] etc. These men studied Jewish literature and manners in a more serious way. Thus Wagenseil denied ritual murder;[127] though saying that the Talmud contained "blasphemies, impostures and absurdities," Buxtorf declared that it also contained things of value for the historian and philosopher.[128] Yet the same ideas persisted which had inspired the authors of the preceding centuries. The object was always to prove the truth of the Christian faith and dogmas on the basis of the Old Testament; the anxiety to convert the Jews ever haunted the souls, the recall of Israel was spoken of, means of bringing them back were proposed;[129] the apostates invoked the Zohar and Mishna in favour of Jesus,[130] and the polemic literature was still in bloom under Eisenmenger, whose *Judaism Unveiled*[131] has inspired many contemporary antisemites; under Schudt,[132] later under Voltaire. It is true that literary anti-Judaism, particularly that of combative tendencies and pamphleteers, is varied but little. Most of the anti-Jewish writers imitate one another, without scruple; they plagiarize without even taking the trouble to verify the assertions of their predecessors. One book of the kind is responsible for similar others : Alonzo da Spina draws his inspiration from *Batallas de Dios,* by Alfonso of Valladolid; Porchet Salvaticus, Pietro Galatini, Pierre de Barcelona republish, under different names, Raymund Martin's *Sword of the Faith;* Paul Fagius and Sebastian Münster[133] help themselves to the *Book of the Faith*.

In spite of this, and independently of the dissimilarities I have noted, anti-Judaism, from the seventeenth century on, is in all respects quite different from the anti-Judaism of the preceding centuries. The social side gets gradually the upperhand of the religious side, though this latter continues to exist. The question is asked, not whether the Jews are wrong in being usurers, or merchants, or deicides, but whether, as Schudt[134] says, the Jews ought to be tolerated in a State or not, whether it is lawful to admit Jews into a Christian commonwealth, as John Dury[135] inquires, about 1655, in a pamphlet directed against Cromwell's protégé, Menasseh ben Israel. This is the social standpoint which we shall see developing henceforth in literary anti-Judaism; a part of modern antisemitism will rest on the theory of a Christian State and its integrity, and in this wise it will be connected with the ancient anti-Judaism.

EIGHT

MODERN LEGAL ANTI-JUDAISM

AFTER preliminary discussions, as a result of which any decision on the emancipation of the Jews was adjourned, the Constituent Assembly voted, on September 27, 1791, on a motion by Duport, and thanks to Regnault de Saint-Jean-d'Angély's intervention, the admission of the Jews to the rank of citizens. This decree had been ready for a long time, prepared as it was through the work of the commission assembled by Louis XVI, with Malesherbes in the chair; prepared by the writings of Lessing and Dohm, of Mirabeau and Grégoire. It was the logical outcome of the efforts made for some time by the Jews and the philosophers; in Germany Mendelssohn had been its promoter and most active advocate, and in Berlin Mirabeau drew his inspiration at the side of Dohm in the salons of Henriette de Lemos.

A certain class of Jews had, however, already been emancipated. In Germany the court Jews (*Hofjuden*) had obtained commercial privileges; even titles of nobility were being conferred upon them for money. In France the Portuguese Marranos returned to Judaism, enjoyed great liberties and prospered under the supervision of their syndics at Bordeaux, very indifferent nevertheless to the fate of their unfortunate brethren, though very influential : one of them, Gradis, failed to secure a nomination as deputy to the States-General. In Alsace even, several Jews obtained important favours, as, *e.g.*, Cerf Berr, purveyor to the armies of Louis XV, who granted him naturalization and the title of Marquis de Tombelaine.

Thanks to all these privileges, there sprang into existence a class of rich Jews which came into contact with the christian society; open-minded, subtle, intelligent, refined, of extreme intellectualism, it had given up, like so many Christians, the letter of religion or of the faith even, and retained nothing but a mystic idealism which, for good or ill, went hand in hand with a liberal rationalism. The fusion between this group of Jews and the elite led by Lessing, was brought about above all in Berlin, a young city and centre of a kingdom which was rising to fame, an easy-going city, with little tradition. Young Germany gathered at the houses of Henrietta de Lemos and Rachel von Varnhagen; with the Jews, German Romanticism ended in impregnating itself with Spinozaism; Schleiermacher and Humboldt were seen visiting there, and it may be said that if the Constituent Assembly decreed the emancipation of the Jews, it was in Germany that it had been prepared.

At any rate, the number of these Jews qualified to mingle with the nations, was extremely limited, the more so because the majority of them—like Mendelsson's daughters, like Boerne and Heine later on—ended by converting, and thus no longer existed as Israelites. As for the mass of Jews, it was in quite different circumstances.

The decree of 1791 freed these pariahs from a secular servitude; it broke the fetters with which the laws had bound them; it wrested them from all kinds of ghettos where they had been imprisoned; from, as it were, cattle it made them human beings. But if it was within its power to restore them to liberty, if it was possible for it to undo within one day the legislative work of centuries, it could not annul their moral effect, and it was especially impotent to break the chains which the Jews had forged themselves. The Jews were emancipated legally, but not so morally; they kept their manners, customs and prejudices—prejudices which their fellow citizens of other confessions kept, too. They were happy at having escaped their humiliation, but they looked around with diffidence and suspected even their liberators.

For centuries they had looked with disgust and terror at this world which was rejecting them; they had suffered from it, but they still more feared to lose their personality and faith from contact with it. More than one old Jew must have looked with anxiety at the new existence which opened before him; I should not even be surprised if there were some in whose eyes the liberation appeared a misfortune or abomination.

As the decree of emancipation did not change the Judaic self, the way in which this self manifested itself was not changed either. Economically the Jews remained what they were—be it understood that I speak of the majority—unproductive, *i.e.*, brokers, money-lenders, usurers, and they could not be otherwise, given their habits and conditions under which they had lived. With the excep-

tion of an insignificant minority among them, they had no other
aptitudes, and even nowadays a great many Jews are in the same
plight. They did not fail to apply these aptitudes, and during this
period of unrest and disorder they found occasion to apply them
more than ever. In France they availed themselves of events, and
the events were favourable for them. In Alsace, for instance, they
acted as auxiliaries to the peasants, whom they lent the funds
necessary for the purchase of national property. Already before
the revolution they were the home-bred usurers in this province,
and the objects of hatred and contempt,[136] after the Revolution,
the very peasants who had erstwhile forged quittances[137] to escape
from the clutches of their creditors, now appealed to them. Thanks
to the Alsatian Jews, the new ownership continued, but they meant
to draw profit from it with a plentiful, usurious hand. The debtors
raised a protest; they pretended they would be ruined if no aid
were forthcoming, and in this they exaggerated, as they, who previous to 1795 had nothing, had eighteen years later acquired
60,000,000 francs' worth of estates on which they owed the Jews
9,500,000 francs. Nevertheless, Napoleon lent ear to them, and suspended, during one year, judicial decisions in behalf of the Jewish
usurers of the Upper Rhine, the Lower Rhine, and the Rhine
provinces. His work did not stop at that. In the preambles of the
decree of suspension of May 30, 1806, he showed that he did not
consider the repressive measures sufficient, but wanted the source
of the evil done away with.

"These circumstances," said he, "caused us at the same time to
consider how urgent it was to revive among those subjects of our
country who profess the Jewish religion, the sentiments of civic
morals, which have unfortunately been deadened with a great
number of them through the state of humiliation in which they
have languished too long, and which is not our intention to maintain and renew."

To revive or rather to give birth to these sentiments, he wanted
to bend the Jewish religion to suit his discipline, to hierarchize it
as he had hierarchized the rest of the nation, to make it conform to
the general plan. When first consul he had neglected to take up
the question of the Jewish religion, and so he wanted to make
amends for this failure by convoking an Assembly of Notable Jews
for the purpose of "considering the means of improving the condition of the Jewish nation and spreading the taste for the useful

arts and professions among its members," and of organizing Judaism administratively. A list of questions was sent out among prominent Jews and when the answers had come in, the Emperor called together a Great Sanhedrin vested with the power of bestowing a religious authority upon the responses of the first assembly. The Sanhedrin declared that the Mosaic law contained obligatory religious provisions, and political provisions; the latter concerned the people of Israel when an autonomous nation, and had, therefore, lost their meaning since the Jews had scattered among the nations; it also forbade to make, in the future, any distinctions between Jews and Christians in the matter of loans, and entirely prohibited usury.

These declarations showed that the prominent Jews belonging for the most part to the minority I have mentioned, knew to adapt themselves to the new state of affairs, but could in no way make any presumption upon the dispositions of the mass. It required the candour of Napoleon the legist to believe that a synod could enjoin love for the neighbour, or forbid usury which the social conditions facilitated. The imperial prohibition for Jews against providing substitutes for military service—this for the purpose of making them better realize the grandeur of their civic duties—was bound to have the same effect as the prescriptions of the synod.[138] The case was the same with the decree of March 17, 1808, forbidding the Jews to engage in commerce without a personal licence issued by the prefect, or to take mortgages without authorization; besides, Jews were forbidden to settle in Alsace and the Rhine provinces, and the Alsatian Jews were forbidden to enter other *departments* unless to engage in agriculture.[139] These decrees issued for ten years, did not turn a single Jew into a farmer, and if any of them became chauvinists, the obligation of serving in the army had something to do with it. These were the last restrictive laws in France; the legal assimilation was consummated in 1830, when Lafitte had the Jewish creed incorporated in the budget. This meant the final downfall of the "Christian State," though the lay state was not, as yet, completely established. The last trace of the ancient distinctions between Jews and Christians disappeared with the abolition of the oath *More Judaico*, in 1839. Nor was the moral assimilation complete.

So far we have been speaking of the emancipation of the French Jews, it remains to examine the influence it had on the

Jews of Europe. From the moment of the foundation of the
Batavian Republic, in 1796, the National Assembly gave the Jews
in the Netherlands the rights of citizenship, and their position
regulated later by Louis Bonaparte was settled in a decisive way
by William I, in 1815. As a matter of fact, the Dutch Jews enjoyed
important privileges and quite a deal of liberty since the sixteenth
century : the Revolution was but the decisive cause of their total
liberation. In Italy and Germany emancipation was brought to the
Jews by the armies of the Republic and the Empire. Napoleon
became the hero and god of Israel, the awaited liberator, he whose
mighty hand was breaking the barriers of the Ghetto. He entered
all cities greeted by the acclamations of the Jews—witness the way
in which Heinrich Heine extolled him—who felt that their cause
was linked with the triumph of the eagles. And for this reason the
Jews were the first to feel the effects of the Napoleonic reaction. A
return to anti-Judaism went hand in hand with the exaltation of
patriotism. The emancipation was a French act; it was, therefore,
necessary to prove it bad, besides, it was a revolutionary act, and
there was a reaction against the Revolution and the ideas of
equality. While the Christian State was being re-established, the
Jews were being banished. In Germany in particular this antique
religious conception of the State again came to life with a new
splendour, and in Germany, especially, anti-Judaism manifested
itself more acutely, but the revival of anti-Jewish legislation was
general. In Italy legislation had been resumed in 1770; in Germany
the Vienna Congress abolished all imperial provisions for Jews,
leaving them only the rights granted by the lawful German governments. As a result of the decisions of the Congress, the cities and
communities showed themselves harsh toward the Jews. Lubeck
and Bremen expelled them; like Rome, Frankfort shut them up
anew in their ancient quarters.[140] Naturally, popular movements
followed suit of the legal measures. At this moment of overheated
patriotism, any restriction of the rights of strangers met with
approval; for the Jews were as ever *the* strangers *par excellence,*
who best represented noxious strangers, and so, about 1820, *i.e.,*
the moment when this state of minds reached its paroxysm, the
mob fell, in many places, upon the Jews and badly maltreated
them, even if it did not massacre them.

The thirty years following the disappearance of Napoleon did
not witness any great progress for the Jews. In England where they

were, as a matter of fact, treated liberally enough, they were, nevertheless, always considered dissidents, and, like the Catholics, were subject to certain obligations. Little by little only did they see their condition modified, and the history of their emancipation is an episode in the struggle between the House of Commons and the House of the Lords. Not before 1860 were they completely assimilated with the other English citizens.

In Austria they had been partly emancipated by the Toleration edict of Joseph II (1785), but had to undergo the same reaction; the Revolution was too fatal for the Austrian House, that the latter should even put up with this well-nigh equality of the Jews which a democratic and philosophic sovereign had granted. Only in 1848 the Austrian Jews became citizens.[141] At the same time their emancipation was achieved in Germany,[142] Greece, Sweden, and Denmark. Once more they owed their independence to the revolutionary spirit which once again came from France. However, we shall see that they were not strangers to the great movement which agitated all Europe; in some countries, notably in Germany, they aided in preparing it, and they were the advocates of liberty. They also were among the first to benefit thereby, as legal anti-Judaism may be said to have come to an end in the Occident after 1848. Little by little the last obstacles fell, and the last restrictions were abolished. The fall of the temporal power of the Popes, in 1870, did away with the last occidental Ghetto, and the Jews now could become citizens even in St. Peter's city.

Since then anti-Judaism has transformed, it has become purely literary, it has come to be but an opinion, and this opinion has no longer had its effect on laws. But before examining this anti-semitism of the pen which in certain countries existed until 1870, side by side with restrictive regulations, we must speak of the Christian States of Eastern Europe, where the anti-Judaism is even now legal and persecutionary, *i.e.,* of Roumania and Russia.

The Jews have lived in Roumania,[143] *i.e.,* the Moldau-Valachian lands, since the fourteenth century, but they came there in numbers at the beginning of this century only, and are about 300,000 in all, as a result of Hungarian and Russian emigration. For many long years they lived undisturbed. They naturally depended upon the boyars who hold the power in this country, and they leased the sale of spirits from these noblemen, who held the monopoly therefore. As they were indispensable to the noblemen as tax-collectors, fiscal

agents and all sorts of middlemen, the nobles were rather inclined
to grant them privileges, and they only had the excess of popular
superstitions or passions. The official persecutions of the Jews began
only in 1856, when Roumania adopted the representative system
and the power thus fell into the hands of the bourgeois class.
Thenceforth restrictive measures grew more serious. The Jews
could not obtain any rank, they were deprived of the right of
permanent domicile in country places, they were forbidden to hold
real estate—except in cities—or lands, or vineyards. They were
prohibited to take estates on lease, to keep hotels and taverns outside
of cities, to retail spirits, to have Christian domestics, to build new
synagogues. Some of these decisions were passed arbitrarily by
certain municipalities; in other villages, on the contrary, the Jews
were tolerated. This state of affairs lasted till 1867. At this time
the minister Jean Bratiano published a circular in which he recalled
to mind the fact that the Jews had no right to live in rural communities, or to take there property on lease. As a result of this
circular the Jews were expelled from the villages they inhabited,
they were condemned like vagabonds, and the expulsions continued
till 1877; they were generally called forth by the uprisings in
Bucharest, Yassy, Galatz, Tecucin, as well as in other places, and
during these uprisings cemeteries were profaned and synagogues
burned.

What were, what are still the causes of this special legislation,
and of this animosity of the Roumanians towards the Jews? They
are not exclusively religious, and despite the persistence of ancestral
prejudices, it is not a case of a confessional war. The Roumanian
Jews constituted, especially at the moment of the formation of
Roumania, agglomerations completely isolated from the bulk of
the population in the Moldau-Valachian lands. They wore a
special garb, lived in quarters set apart in order to escape con-
taminations, and spoke a Judaeo-German jargon, which rounded
off their marks of distinction. They lived under the domination of
their rabbis, narrow-minded, limited, ignorant Talmudists, from
whom they received in Jewish schools—*heder*—an education
which was conducive to their intellectual abasement and their
degradation.

They were the victims of this isolation which was due to their
guides, the rabbinists. The patriotic passions were particularly
aroused in this land, which was being born, was acquiring a

nationality and striving for unity. There has been a pan-Roumanism, just like pan-Germanism or pan-Slavism. There were discussions on the Roumanian race, on its integrity, its purity, the danger threatening it from adulteration. Associations were formed to counteract foreign encroachment, and Jewish encroachment in particular. Schoolmasters, university professors were the soul of these societies; just as in Germany, they were the most active antisemites. They asserted that the Jewish education crippled the brains of those receiving it, that it rendered them unfit for social life, which was but too correct, and yet they were going to shut the Jews out completely from obtaining the education given to Christians, exactly the one that would lift them from their degradation.

But the college-bred were not the sole antisemites in Roumania, and there were economic causes beside patriotic causes. As I have said, antisemitism was born with the advent of the bourgeoisie, because this bourgeois class, composed of merchants and manufacturers, came into competition with the Jews who displayed their activity exclusively in commerce and industry, when not in usury. The bourgeoisie had every interest in the passage of protective laws, which, though nominally directed at strangers and not at the Jews, principally aimed at placing obstacles to the expansion of their formidable rivals. It achieved its point by skilfully fomenting disturbances which gave their representatives in Parliament a chance to propose new regulations. Thus these diverse causes of antisemitism may be reduced to a single one—national protectionism—and very clever it is, as simultaneously with denying the Jews all civic rights on the ground that they are strangers, it forces them into military service, which again is a contradiction, as none but a citizen can form a part of a *national army*.

Harder still, more miserable than in Roumania, is the condition of the Jews in Russia. Their history in that country, where they arrived in the third century B.C. and founded colonies in Crimea, has been that of the Jews of all Europe. They were banished in the twelfth century never to be recalled. Nevertheless, at present Russia counts 4,500,000 Jews, and to say, as the antisemites maintain, that the Jews have invaded it is nonsense, for Russia has acquired them by seizing White Russia in 1769 and later on the Polish provinces and Crimea, which contained a great number of Jews. At the moment of this conquest it was out of the question to apply the ukase of 1742 which banished the Jews once more. On the one hand, it was not an easy thing to drive out several million individuals into the neighbouring states; on the other, commerce, industry, and particularly the treasury, would have fared ill from such wholesale expulsion. Catherine II then granted the Jews equal rights with her Russian subjects, but the Senate ukases of 1786, 1791 and 1794 curtailed these privileges and confined the Israelites within White Russia and Crimea—thenceforth constituting the *Jewish territory—and Poland*. Only in certain cases and under special conditions were they allowed to leave the limits of this territorial Ghetto.

In Russia all modern antisemitism, which is official antisemitism *par excellence,* consists in keeping the Jews from escaping the Senate ukases just spoken of. Russia has resigned herself to her Jews, but she wants to leave them where she found them. Still there were favourable or rather less unfavourable times for the Jews. Alexander I permitted them in 1808 to settle in the crown lands on condition of engaging there in agriculture; Nicholas I gave them permission to travel when their business required it, they were allowed to attend the universities; and under Alexander II their position improved still further.[144]

After the death of Alexander II the autocratic reaction became monstrous in Russia : an abominable reawakening of absolutism was the answer to the bomb of the nihilists. The national orthodox spirit was overexcited, the liberal and revolutionary movement was charged to foreign influences, and the Jews were made the scapegoats, in order to divert the people from the nihilistic propaganda; hence the massacres of 1881 and 1882, during which the mob burned Jewish houses, robbed and killed the Jews, saying : "Our daddy, the Tsar, wants it."

After these disturbances General Ignatyeff promulgated the "May Laws" of 1882. They read as follows :

1. As a temporary measure and until the general revision of the laws regulating their status, Jews are forbidden to settle hereafter outside of cities and towns. Exception is made with regard to Jewish villages already in existence where the Jews are engaged in agriculture.

2. Until further order all contracts for the mortgaging or renting of real estate situated outside of cities and towns to a Jew, shall be of no effect. Equally void is any power of attorney granted to a

Jew for the administration or disposition of property of the above-indicated nature.

3. Jews are forbidden to do business on Sundays and Christian holidays; the laws compelling Christians to close their places of business on those days will be applied to Jewish places of business.

4. The above measures are applicable only in the governments situated within the Jewish pale of settlement.

These laws were enacted *as a temporary measure*. Accordingly, a commission presided over by Count Pahlen met in 1883 to settle finally the Jewish question. The conclusions of this commission were quite liberal in spirit; it recommended that certain civil rights be given to the Jews. Owing to the influence of Pobyedonostseff, the Procurator of the Holy Synod, the report of the Pahlen Commission was buried, and the *May Laws* have remained in force. Since that time, and especially from 1890 on, the persecutions redoubled. The "pale" was narrowed by forbidding the Jews to enter certain fortified places, and by creating a frontier belt where the Jews could not reside. The ukase of 1865 of Alexander II, allowing "skilled" artisans to choose a domicile throughout the empire was abrogated. Thus nearly 3,000,000 Jews were crowded into the cities of the pale of settlement, while a million was spread over Poland, and 500,000 privileged—merchants of the first rank, financiers and students—all over Russia.

Other measures, besides this systematic crowding, were taken against the Jews. They were shut out of certain occupations and certain professions; those sheltered in hospitals as invalids were sent away; employees of railroads and steamship companies were dismissed; the number of those who could enter universities, colleges and high schools was limited; they were barred from becoming attorneys, physicians, engineers, or at least their opportunities for entering these professions were restricted; even their own schools were closed to them, they are not admitted even to hospitals, they are burdened with special taxes on their rents, inheritances, the animals they kill for meat, the candles they light on Friday evenings, the skull-caps they wear during religious ceremonies, even when these are of a private nature.

Besides these official taxes imposed by the government, the Jews are under the exploitation of the Russian administration and police, the basest, the most corrupt and venal in all Europe. Half the income of the middle class Jews, says Weber and Kempster, and

Harold Frederic, goes to the police. Every Jew in easy circumstances is the victim of constant extortion. As for those (and they
are the majority), who are too poor to be able to pay, they are
subjected to the most loathsome, most inhuman treatment, forced
to bow to all the whims of brutal policemen who domineer and
martyrize them, as they martyrize also the nihilists and the suspects
of liberalism whom the horrible autocracy of the Tsar places in
their power.[145]

We shall not deal with the frauds with which Jewish business
men are charged, as exactly these business men occupy a privileged
position; as for the lawlessness of a part of the miserable mass,
those of whom it is made up "would not have food if they did not
rob," and so they are in the same position with a great number of
orthodox Russians whom the social and economic condition of
Russia forces to resort to unscrupulous methods, in order to make
a living.

What are then the real causes of antisemitism? They are political
and religious. Antisemitism is by no means a popular movement in
Russia; it is purely official. The Russian people, laden with misery,
crushed under taxes, groaning under the most atrocious of
tyrannies, embittered by administrative violence and governmental
abuse of power, burdened with suffering and humiliation is in an
unbearable condition. Generally resigned, they are liable to yield to
passions; their uprisings and revolts are formidable; antisemitic
riots are the proper thing to divert popular anger, and that is why
the government encouraged them and often provoked them. As to
the peasants and workingmen, they fell upon the Jews because, they
said, "the Jew and the nobleman are of a pair, only it is easy to
thrash the Jew."[146] Thus is explained the plundering of rich Jewish
merchants, of wealthy money-lenders, often of poor Jewish workmen, and it is heart-rending to see these disinherited fall upon one
another instead of uniting against the oppressive tsarism.

The possibility of a union between these two camps of misery is,
perhaps, foreseen by those whose interest it is to engender and
keep their antagonism and who actually saw the rioters burn many
Christian houses during the riots of 1881 and 1882. After Alexander
II's death it became urgent to blot out of the moujik's and proletarians' memories the nihilists' attempts at liberation. The revolution was more than ever the frightful hydra and dragon, against
which Holy Russia was to be protected. To accomplish it a return

to orthodox ideas was thought necessary. All evil, it was said, comes from the foreign, the heretical, that which pollutes the sacred soil.

The religious origin of the official antisemitism has often been denied; yet it cannot be denied, and the Russians will yet probably give up even Panslavism in order to arrive at religious unity, a unity which to some of them, at least, seems indispensable for the unity of the State. The national and the religious question are but one in Russia, the Tsar being simultaneously the temporal and spiritual head, Caesar and Pope; but to faith more importance is attached than to race, and the proof is that a Jew who is willing to be converted is not persecuted. On the contrary, the Jew is encouraged to embrace orthodoxy.

Thus we may say that in eastern *Europe* where the actual condition of the Jews fairly well represents what had been their condition in the Middle Ages, the causes of antisemitism are twofold : social causes, and religious causes combined with patriotic ones. It now remains for us to see what are the causes that maintain antisemitism in the countries where it has become antisemitism of the pen instead of legal antisemitism, and, first of all, to examine this transformation and the phenomena to which it has given rise.

MODERN ANTISEMITISM
AND ITS LITERATURE

THE emancipated Jews scattered among the nations just like
strangers, and, as we have seen, it could not be otherwise, since for
centuries they formed a nation among the nations, a special people
preserving its characteristics thanks to the strict and precise ritual,
as well as owing to the legislation which kept it apart and tended
to perpetuate it. As conquerors, not as guests did they come into
modern societies. They were like a penned-in flock; suddenly the
barriers fell and they rushed upon the field opened to them. They
were not warriors, what is more, the moment was not favourable
to an expedition of a small band, but they made the only conquest
for which they were armed, the economic conquest for which they
had been preparing for some many long years. They were a race
of merchants and money-dealers, perhaps degraded by mercantile
practice, but, thanks to this very practice, equipped with qualities
which were becoming preponderant in the new economic system.
And so it was easy for them to take to commerce and finances, and,
it must be repeated, they could not act otherwise. Crowded together, oppressed for centuries, ever curbed in their soarings, they
had acquired a formidable power of expansion, and this power
could find application in certain channels only; their efforts were
limited, but their nature was not changed, and it was not changed
on the day of their liberation either, and they marched ahead on
the road which was familiar to them. However, the state of affairs
was particularly favourable to them. At this period of great over-
throws and reconstructions, when nations were being modified,
new principles established, new social, moral and metaphysical
conceptions wrought out, they were the only ones to be free. They
were without any attachments to those surrounding them; they had
no ancient patrimony to defend, the heritage which the former
society was leaving to nascent society was not theirs; the thousand
ancestral ties which linked the citizens of the modern state with

the past, could not influence their conduct, their intellectuality, their morality; their spirit had no shackles.

I have shown that their liberation could not change them, that a number of them regretted their past of isolation, and even if they did endeavour to remain themselves, if they did not assimilate, they marvellously adapted themselves, by the very force of their special tendencies, to the economic conditions which had affected the nations since the beginning of the nineteenth century.

The French Revolution was above all an economic revolution. If it is considered as the termination of a struggle between classes, it must be viewed as the consummation of a struggle between two forms of capital, viz : real property and personal property, or landed capital, and industrial and speculative capital. With the supremacy of the nobility the supremacy of landed capital disappeared, too, and the supremacy of the bourgeoisie brought on the supremacy of industrial and speculative capital. The emancipation of the Jew is linked with the growth of the prevalence of industrial capital. So long as landed capital retained the political power, the Jew was deprived of any right; the Jew was liberated on the day when political power passed to industrial capital, and that proved fatal. The bourgeoisie needed help in the struggle it undertook; the Jew was for it a valuable ally, whom it was its interest to emancipate. Since the days of the Revolution, Jew and bourgeois marched hand in hand, together they sustained Napoleon at the moment when dictatorship became necessary to defend the privileges gained by the Third Estate, and when the imperial tyranny became too heavy and oppressive for capitalism the bourgeois and the Jew, united and preluded the fall of the Empire by forestalling provisions at the time of the Russian campaign and helped to bring about the final disaster by calling forth slumps at the exchange and buying the disloyalty of marshals.

At the beginning of the great industrial development, after 1815, when canal, mine, and insurance companies were formed, the Jews were among the most active in promoting combination of capital. Moreover, they were the most skilful, because the spirit of combination had for centuries been their only support. But they were not content to aid in bringing about in this practical way the triumph of industrialism, they gave their aid in a theoretical way, also. They gathered around Saint-Simon, the philosopher of the bourgeoisie; they worked at diffusing and developing his teaching.

Saint-Simon had said :[147] "The manufacturers must be entrusted with the administration of the temporal power," and "the last step that remains for industry to make is to obtain the direction of the State and the chief problem of our time is to secure to industry a majority in our parliaments." He had added :[148] "The industrial class must occupy the first rank, because it is the most important of all; because it can do without all the others, while none other can do without it; because it exists by its own forces, by its personal labours. The other classes must work for it, because they are its creatures and because it sustains their existence; in a word, as everything is made by industry, everything must be made for it." The Jews helped to realize the Saint-Simonian dream; they proved themselves the most trustworthy allies of the bourgeoisie, inasmuch as in working for it they worked for themselves and, in all Europe, they were in the front rank of the liberal movement, which from 1815 till 1848 succeeded in establishing the domination of bourgeois capitalism.

This role of the Jews did not escape the class of landed capitalists, and we shall see that therein lay one of the causes of the anti-Judaism of the conservatives, but to the Jews it was not worth so much as the recognition of the bourgeoisie. When the latter had firmly established its power, when it became restful and secure, it discovered that its ally, the Jew, was its formidable competitor, and it reacted against it. Thus the conservative parties, made up, as a rule, of capitalist agriculturers, became anti-Jewish in their fight against industrial and speculative capitalism, represented chiefly by the Jew, and industrial and speculative capitalism became anti-Jewish in its turn, on account of Jewish competition. Anti-Judaism, which had been religious at first, became economic, or, rather, the religious causes, which had once been dominant in anti-Judaism, were subordinated to economic and social causes.

This transformation, which corresponded with the change in the role played by the Jews, was not the only one. Once a matter of sentiment, the hostility towards the Jews became one of reason. The Christians of yesterday hated the deicides instinctively, and they never attempted to justify their animosity : they showed it. The antisemites of to-day conceived a desire to explain their hatred, *i.e.*, they wanted to dignify it : anti-Judaism moulted into antisemitism. How was this antisemitism manifested? It had no other way of expression but through the printing press. Official antisemitism was dead in the West, or it was dying; as a result anti-Jewish legislation, too, was disappearing; there remained theoretical antisemitism, it was an opinion, a theory, but the anti-semites had a very distinct object in view. Up to the time of the Revolution literary anti-Judaism sustained legal anti-Judaism, since the Revolution and the emancipation of the Jews, literary antisemitism has striven to restore legal anti-Judaism in the countries where it no longer exists. It has not, as yet, achieved that, and we have to study only the manifestations of the antisemitism of the pen, manifestations, some of which represent the opinion of the many, for, if literary antisemities have supplied reasons to the unconscious antisemites, they were produced by them; they attempted to explain what the flock felt, manifested, and if they have at times ascribed strange and improbable motives, they often but echoed the sentiments of their inspirers. What were these senti-ments? We shall see if we examine the antisemitic literature, and at the same time we shall disentangle the manifold causes of con-temporary antisemitism.

Except in the case of some of them, it is impossible to classify the antisemitic works under too narrow categories, as each of them often presented manifold tendencies. Still they each have a domin-ant idea, in accordance with which their classification may be settled, always remembering that a work approaching a definite type does not belong solely and exclusively to it. We shall, then, subdivide antisemitism into Christian, Socialist, economic, ethno-logical and national, metaphysical, revolutionary and anti-Christian antisemitism.

Christian Socialist antisemitism was generated by the per-manency of religious prejudices. If the Jews had not changed on entering into society, the sentiments felt toward them for so many long years would not have disappeared either. The Jews owed their emancipation to a philosophical movement coinciding with an economic movement and not to the abolition of secular prejudices against them. Those who thought the Christian State the only State possible looked with disfavour upon the intrusion of the Jews, and anti-Talmudism was the first manifestation of this hostility. The Talmud which was justly considered the religious stronghold of the Jews was assailed and a host of polemists devoted themselves to proving how much the teachings of the Talmud were opposed to the teachings of the Gospel. Against the

book they resumed all the complaints of the controversialists of
yore, those enumerated by the Jewish apostates in debates, and
repeated in the thirteenth century by Raymund Martin, those
raised by Pfefferkorn and later on by Eisenmenger. Not even the
method or the make-up was changed; the same moulds were made
use of; in writing pamphlets the same traditions were followed as
those of the dominican inquisitors, and not a whit more of critical
acumen was put to use in the study of the Talmudic "deep."
Nevertheless, concerning the Jew, his dogmas, his race, the Christian
antisemites of our time have the same notions as the Jews of the
Middle Ages had. The Jew preoccupies and haunts them, they see
him everywhere, they trace everything back to him, they have the
same conception of history as had Bossuet. For the bishop, Judea
was the centre of the world; all events, disasters and joys, conquests
and downfalls, as well as the foundings of empires had for its
primary, mysterious and ineffable cause the whims of a God faithful to the Bene-Israel, and this people, wanderer, founder of
kingdoms and captive, in turn, had continually directed mankind
toward its only goal : the coming of Christ. Ben Hadad and
Sennacherib, Cyrus and Alexander, seem to exist only because
Judah exists, and because Judah must now be exalted and then
humiliated, until the hour when he will enjoin upon the world the
law which must come from him. But what Bossuet had conceived
for the purpose of unheard of glorification, the Christian antisemites
renew that with quite opposite ends in view. For them the Jewish
race, the scourge of the nations, scattered over the earth, accounts
for the misfortunes and blessings of the alien nations in whose
midst it had settled, and the history of the Hebrews once more becomes the history of monarchies and republics. Scourged or
tolerated, banished or admitted, they, by the very fact of these
political vicissitudes, account for the glory of the states or even
their decadence. To tell the story of Israel, is to tell the story of
France, or Germany, or Spain. This is what the Christian antisemites see, and their antisemitism is thus purely theological, it
is the antisemitism of the Fathers, that of Chrysostom, Saint
Augustin, Saint Jerome. Before the birth of Jesus, the Jewish people
was the chosen people, the beloved son of God; since the time it
had disowned the Saviour, since it had become a deicide, it had
become the fallen people *par excellence,* and having before brought
the world's salvation, it now causes its ruin.

Whatever their affinities and kinship with the anti-Jews of the Middle Ages, the anti-Talmudists, at all events, take a little different point of view. Formerly, the blasphemies against the Christian religion were chiefly sought in the Talmud, or arguments in support of the divinity of Jesus Christ were sought there; hereafter this book's enemies hunt it especially as an anti-social, pernicious and destructive work. The Talmud, according to them, makes the Jew an enemy of all nations, but if some of them, like des Mousseaux and Chiarini are guided, like the theologians of yore, above all by the desire to bring Israel back to the bosom of the church,[149] others, like Doctor Rohling,[150] are rather inclined to suppress him and they declare him forever incapable to be of any good. Quite the contrary; since, they say, not only are his teachings incompatible with the principles of Christian governments, but because he even seeks to ruin these governments in order to draw profit therefrom.

It is easy to understand that after the upsettings caused by the French Revolution, the conservatives felt called upon to hold the Jews responsible for the destruction of the ancient regime. When they cast a glance around them after the storm had passed away, one of the things that must have given them the greatest surprise, was surely the position of the Jew. But yesterday the Jew was nothing, he had no right, no power, and now he was shining in the front rank; not only was he rich, but he could even be a doctor and govern the land, as he paid his tax. Him particularly did the social change favour. Accordingly, the Christian antisemites did not stop at being incensed at the Jews' speculations over national property or the military supply, but applied to them the old juridical saying : *fecisti qui prodes* ("those hast done it who profitest thereby.") If the Jew indeed had profited by the Revolution in this respect, if he had derived from it so great a benefit, it means that he had prepared them, or rather, to say, he had helped along with all his forces.

Nevertheless it was necessary to explain how this despised and hated Jew, considered a thing, had obtained the power of accomplishing such deeds, how he had prepared so formidable a might. Here comes in a theory, or rather a philosophy of history familiar to the Catholic polemists. According to these historians, the French Revolution whose counter blow has been universal, and which has transformed the institutions of Western Europe, was but the capping of a secular conspiracy. Those who attribute it to the philosophical movement of the eighteenth century, to the excesses of monarchical governments, to a fatal economic change, to the decrepitude of a class, the enfeeblement of a form of capital, to the inevitable evolution of the ideas of authority and State, to the enlargement of the idea of an individual—all those are grievously in error, according to the historians I am speaking about. They are blind people who do not see the truth : the Revolution was the work of one or several sects, whose establishment goes back to great antiquity, sects brought out by the same desire and the same principle : the desire for domination and the principle of destruction.

The Genesis of this conception of history is easy to find. It took its origin under the Terror itself. The part taken by the Masonic lodges, by the Illumines, the Red-Crosses, the Martinists, etc., in the Revolution, had vividly struck certain minds which were carried away to exaggerate the influence and role of these societies. A thing which particularly astonished these superficial observers, was the international character of the Revolution of 1789 and the simultaneousness of the movements it called forth. They contrasted its general effect with the local effect of the previous Revolutions, which had agitated, as, *e.g.*, in England, only the countries where they took place, and, in order to account for this difference they attributed the work of centuries to a European association with representatives in the midst of all nations, rather than to admit that the same stage of civilization and similar intellectual, social, moral and economic causes, could have simultaneously produced the same effects. The very members of these lodges, of these societies, helped in spreading this belief.[151] They, too, exaggerated their importance, they not only asserted to have worked, during the eighteenth century, for the changes then in the process of preparation—which was true—but they even claimed to have been their distant initiators. This, however, is not the place to debate this question; suffice it to have stated the existence of these theories : we are going to show how they came to the assistance of the Christian antisemites.

The first writers to set forth these ideas confined themselves to stating the existence of "a peculiar nation which was born and had grown in darkness, amidst all civilized nations, for the purpose of subjecting all of them to its rule,"[152] as, *e.g.*, the cavalier de Malet, brother of the conspiring general, wanted to prove in a book, little-known and very poor at that. Men like P. Barruel, in his *Memoirs on Jacobinism*,[153] like Eckert in his works on Free Masonry,[154] like Dom Deschamps,[155] like Claudio Jannet, like Crétineau Joly,[156] have developed and systematized this theory, they have even endeavoured to prove its reality and though they did not attain their aim, they have at least gathered all the elements necessary to undertake so curious a history as that of secret societies. In all their works, they were led to examine what had been the position of the Jews in these groups and sects, and, struck by the analogies presented by the mystagogic rites of Masonry as compared with certain Judaic and Kabbalistic traditions,[157] misled by the Hebrew pomp which characterizes the initiation in these lodges, they arrived at the conclusion that the Jews had always been the inspirers, guides and masters of Free Masonry, nay, more than that, they had been its founders, and that they, with its aid, persistently aimed at the destruction of the church, from the very time of its foundation.

They went further in this path, they wanted to prove that the Jews had preserved their national constitution, that they were still ruled by princes, the *Nassi*, who led them to the conquest of the world, and that these enemies of mankind possessed a formidable organization and tactics. Gougenot des Mousseaux,[158] Rupert,[159] de Saint André,[160] the abbot Chabeauty,[161] have supported these assertions. As for Edouard Drumont, the whole pseudo-historic portion of his books, when not borrowed from father Loriquet, is nothing but a clumsy and uncritical plagiarism of Barruel, Gougenot, of Dom Deschamps and Crétineau Joly.[162]

Whatever the case may be, with Drumont, as with pastor Stoecker, Christian antisemitism transforms or rather it borrows new weapons from several sociologists. Though Drumont fights the Jew's anti-clericalism, though Stoecker, in his anxiety to win the name of a second Luther, rises against the Jewish religion as destructive of the Christian State, other preoccupations engage them; they attack Jewish wealth and attribute to Jews the economic transformation which is the work of the 19th century. They still persecute in the Jew, the enemy of Jesus, the murderer of a God, but they aim particularly at the financier, and therein they join hands with those who preach economic antisemitism.

This antisemitism has manifested itself since the beginning of Jewish financiering and industrialism. If we find only traces of it in Fourier[163] and Proudhon, who confined themselves to stating only the role of the Jew as middle-man, stock-jobber and non-producer,[164] it gave life to men like Toussenel[165] and Capefigue;[166] it inspired such books as *The Jews Kings of the Epoch* and the *History of Great Financial Operations*; and later on, in Germany, the pamphlets of Otto Glagau against the Jewish bankers and brokers.[167] However, I have already pointed out the origin of this antisemitism, how, on the one hand, the landed capitalists held the Jew accountable for the predominance of industrial and financial capitalism, so hateful to them, how, on the other hand, the bourgeoisie, stocked with privileges, turned against the Jew, its erstwhile ally, henceforth its competitor and a foreign competitor at that; for to his position as a non-assimilated stranger the Jew owes the excessive animosity shown him, and thus economic anti-semitism is bound up with ethnologic and national antisemitism.

This last form of antisemitism is modern, it was born in Germany, and from the Germans the French antisemites have derived their theory.

This doctrine of races, which Renan advocated in France[168] was wrought out in Germany under the influence of the Hegelian doctrines. It gained the ascendancy in 1840 and particularly in 1848, not only because German policy pressed it into service, but because it was in accord with the nationalist and patriotic move-ment that produced nations, and with that striving for unity which characterized all European nations.

The state, so they said, must be national; the nation must be one, and must include all the individuals speaking the national language and belonging to the same race. More than that, it is of importance that this national State reduce all the heterogeneous elements, *i.e.*, the foreigners. For the Jew, not being an Aryan, has not the same moral, social and intellectual conceptions as the Aryan; he is irreducible, and therefore he must be eliminated, or else he will ruin the nations that have received him, and some among the nationalist and ethnologic antisemites assert that the work has already been accomplished.

These notions, resumed since then by von Treitschke[169] and Adolph Wagner in Germany, by Schoenerer in Austria, Pattai in Hungary and, at a much later date, by Drumont in France,[170] were reduced, for the first time, to a system by W. Marr, in a pamphlet which had a certain echo in France : *The Victory of Judaism over Germanism*.[171] In it Marr declared Germany the prey of a conquering race, the Jews, a race possessing everything and wanting to Judaize Germany, like France, however, and he concluded by saying that Germany was lost. To his ethnologic antisemitism he even admixed the metaphysical antisemitism which, if I may say so, Schopenhauer had professed,[172] the antisemitism consisting in combating the optimism of the Jewish religion, an optimism which Schopenhauer found low and degrading, and with which he contrasted Greek and Hindu religious conceptions.

But Schopenhauer and Marr are not the only representatives of philosophical antisemitism. The whole of German metaphysics combated the *Jewish spirit,* which it considered essentially different from the *Germanic spirit,* and which for it stood for the past as contrasted with the present. While the Spirit is realized in the world's history, while it advances, the Jews remain at a lower stage. Such is the Hegelian thought, that of Hegel and also of his disciples of the extreme left—Feuerbach, Arnold Ruge and Bruno Bauer.[173] Max Stirner[174] developed these ideas with much precision. To his mind, universal history has until now passed through two ages : the first, represented by antiquity, during which we had to work out and eliminate "the negro stage of the soul;" the second, that of *Mongolism,* represented by the Christian period. During the first age man depended upon things, during the second he is swayed by ideas, waiting until he can dominate them and free himself. But the Jews, these precociously wise children of antiquity, have not passed out of this *negro stage of the soul.* In Dühring we find another more ethical than metaphysical form of philosophical antisemitism. In several treatises, pamphlets and books,[175] Dühring assails the Semitic spirit and the Semitic conception of the divine and of ethics, which he contrasts with the conception of the Northern peoples. Pushing the deductions from his premises to their logical end and still following up Bruno Bauer's doctrine, he assails Christianity which is the last manifestation of the Semitic spirit : "Christianity," says he, "has above all no practical morality such as is not capable of ambiguous interpretation and thus might be available and sane. The nations will, therefore, not be done with the Semitic spirit until they have expelled from their spirit this present second aspect of Hebraism."

After Dühring, Nietzsche,[176] in his turn, combated Jewish and Christian ethics, which, according to him, are the *ethics of slaves* as contrasted with *the ethics of masters.* Through the prophets and

Jesus, the Jews and the Christians have set up low and noxious conceptions which consist in the deification of the weak, the humble, the wretched, and sacrificing to it the strong, the proud, the mighty.

Several revolutionary atheists, Gustave Tridon[177] and Regnard[178] among them, have espoused, in France, this Christian antisemitism which, in its final analysis, is reduced to the ethnologic antisemitism, just like the strictly metaphysical antisemitism.

The different varieties of antisemitism may, then, be reduced to three : Christian antisemitism, economic antisemitism, and ethnological antisemitism. In our examination just made we have pointed out that the grievances of the antisemites were religious grievances, social grievances, ethnologic grievances, national grievances, intellectual and moral grievances. To the antisemite the Jew is an individual of a foreign race, incapable of adapting himself, hostile to Christian civilization and religion; immoral, antisocial, of an intellectuality different from the Aryan intellectuality, and, to cap it all, a depredator and wrongdoer.

We shall now examine these grievances in regular order. We shall see whether they are well-founded, *i.e.,* whether the real causes of contemporary antisemitism correspond to them, or whether they are but prejudices. Let us first turn to the study of the ethnologic grievance.

THE RACE

THE Jew is a Semite, he belongs to a strange, noxious, disturbing and inferior race—such is the ethnologic grievance of the antisemites. What does it rest upon? It rests upon an anthropological theory which had given rise or at least justification to an historical theory: the doctrine of the inequality of races, of which we must speak first of all.

Since the eighteenth century attempts have been made to classify men and distribute them under well-defined, distinct and separate categories. As a basis for it quite different indices were taken: the section of the hair—oval section for negroes with woolly hair, or round section;[179] the shape of the skull—broad or elongated;[180] the colour of the skin. This last classification has prevailed: nowadays three races of mankind—the negro, the yellow, and the white race —are distinguished. Different aptitudes are ascribed to these races, and they are arranged in the order of their superiority in a ladder of which the negro race occupies the lowest and the white race the highest round.

Race is, however, a fiction. No human group exists that can boast of having had two original ancestors and having descended from them without any adulteration of the primitive stock through mixture; human races are not pure, *i.e.,* strictly speaking, there is no such thing as a race. "There is no unity," says Topinard:[181] "the races have divided, scattered, blended, intercrossed in all degrees and directions since thousands of centuries; most of them gave up their language in favour of that of their conquerors, then gave the same up for a third, if not a fourth language; the principal masses have disappeared and now we find ourselves face to face with peoples and not races." The anthropologic classification of mankind has consequently no value whatever.

Nevertheless, and however untenable this doctrine of the inequality of races, whether from the linguistic or from the anthropologic point of view, it has been quite dominant in our times, and

nations have chased and still chase this chimera of ethnologic unity,
which is but the heritage of an ill-informed past and, truth to tell,
a form of regress.

Whatever they be, true or false, these ethnologic principles
which concern us, have, by the very fact of their existence—been
one of the causes of antisemitism; they have supplied a scientific
appearance to a phenomenon which we shall later recognize as
national and economic and, through them, the grievances of the
antisemites were fortified with pseudo-historical and pseudo-
anthropological arguments. Indeed, not only was the existence
admitted of three races—negro, yellow and white—ranged in hier-
archic order, but even in these races sub-divisions, categories, were
established. At first it was asserted that the white race alone and
some families of the yellow race were capable of founding superior
civilizations; presently this white race was divided into two
branches : the Aryan race and the Semitic race; finally it was
maintained that the Aryan must be considered the most perfect
race. Even in our days the Aryan race has been subdivided into
groups, and this enabled anthropologists and chauvinistic ethnolo-
gists to declare either that the Celtic or the Germanic group must
be considered as the pure wheat of this Aryan race, already superior as it was. Thus, consciously or unconsciously, history is modelled
after the ethnic tables of Genesis—tables also met with among the
Babylonians and the primitive Greeks—which accounted in a rudi-
mentary way for the diversity of human groups, by the existence
of sprouts issued from single parents, each sprout then producing a
nation. Thus it is the Bible again that lends assistance to the antisemites, for in ethnography and history we are still clinging to the
explanations of the Genesis—Shem, Ham and Japhet, only replaced
by the Semite, the Turanian and the Aryan, however impossible it
may be to justify these divisions linguistically, anthropologically or
historically.

Without stopping to discuss whether the negro races are capable
of civilization or not we must see what is understood under the
names Aryans and Semites.

Aryans is the name of all peoples whose language is derived
from Sanskrit, a language spoken by a human group called arya.
Now, this group "presents no scientifically demonstrable unity
except from the exclusively linguistic point of view." All anthropologic unity is undemonstrable : the cranial measurements, indices,

numbers, furnish no proof. In this Aryan chaos are found Semitic types, Mongolian types, all types and all varieties of types, from the one which is capable of developing morally, intellectually and socially, up to the one that remains in everlasting mediocrity. There may be observed dolichocephals and brachycephals, men with brown skin, others with yellowish and yet others with white skin. Still, despite the fact that some tribes of Aryan language had no development perceptibly superior to that of some agglomerations of negroes, it is not a whit less energetically asserted that the Aryan is the most beautiful and noblest of the races, that it is the productive and creative race *par excellence,* that to it we are indebted for the most wonderful metaphysics, the most magnificent lyric, religious and ethical productions and that no other race ever was or is susceptible of a like expansion. To arrive at such a result, an abstraction is naturally made from the indisputable fact that all historical organisms had been formed of the most dissimilar elements, whose respective share in the common work it is impossible to determine.

The Aryan race, then, is superior, and it has proven its superiority by resisting the rule of a fraternal and rival race—the Semitic. This latter is a ferocious, brutal race, incapable of creative power, devoid of any ideal, and Universal History is represented as the history of the conflict between the Aryan and the Semitic race, a conflict which we witness even at present. Each antisemite affords proof of this secular conflict. Even the Trojan War becomes, with some, the struggle between the Aryan and the Semite, and through the exigencies of the case, Paris becomes a Semitic brigand who ravishes Aryan beauties. Later on the Median Wars form a phase of this great contest, and the great king is pictured as the leader of the Semitic Orient falling upon the Aryan Occident; then it is Carthage disputing with Rome over the Empire of the World; then Islam advances against Christendom, and all through it is pointed with pleasure that the Greek has defeated the Trojan and Artaxerxes, that Rome triumphed over Carthage, and Charles Martel checked Abder-Rahman.

The Christian antisemites have thus reconciled their faith with their animosity, and not stopping short even before heresy, they have admitted that the prophets and Jesus were Aryans,[182] while the anti-Christian antisemites consider the Galilean and the *nabis* (prophets) as deserving condemnation and inferior Semites.

Does what we know of the history of ancient and modern nations give us the right to accept as genuine this rivalry, this struggle, this instinctive opposition between the Aryan and the Semitic race? By no means, since Semites and Aryans have intermingled in a continuous way, and since the Semitic share in all so-called Aryan civilizations is considerable. From this point of view, the history of Hellenic myths is curious and instructive, and this Semitic contribution may be grasped by comparing Hercules to Melkart, or Ashtoreth to Aphrodite. Likewise, the Phoenician cups and vases, exported in great numbers by the merchants of Tyre and Sidon, served as models for the Greek artists, and thus enabled the subtle mind of the Ionians and Dorians to interpret the myths represented on them, and the Phoenician image-trade helped out much the Greek iconologic mythology.

Still the modern antisemites would rigorously admit the importance of the Semites in the history of civilization, but would make a classification even there. There are, they say, superior and inferior Semites. The Jew is the latter type, of the Semites, essentially unproductive, from whom men have received nothing and who can give nothing. It is impossible to accept this assertion. It is true that the Jewish nation has never displayed any great aptitudes for the plastic arts, but, through the voice of its prophets, it has accomplished a moral work by which every nation has been benefited; it has worked out some of those ethical and social ideas which are the leaven of humanity; if it has not had any divine sculptors and painters, it has had wonderful poets, it has, above all, had moralists who had worked for universal brotherhood, prophetic pamphleteers who made living and immortal the idea of justice, and Isaiah, Jeremiah, Ezekiel, despite their violence, fierceness even, have made heard the voice of suffering which wants not only to be protected against execrable force, but to be freed from it.

However, if the Phoenician element had incorporated itself with the Pelasgian, Hellenic, Latin, Celtic and Iberian elements, the Jewish element, by intermingling with others, has also contributed to the formation of those agglomerations which later on united to form the modern nations. The Jew, too, came to sink and disappear in that enormous crucible which Asia Minor presented, and where the most diverse nations were cast. Slowly hellenized, the Jews in Alexandria turned the city into one of the most active centres of Christian propaganda. They were among the first to convert; they formed the nucleus of the primitive Church in Alexandria, Antioch, Rome, and after the disappearance of the Ebionites they were absorbed in the total mass of Greek and Roman converts.

Throughout the Middle Ages Jewish blood was intermingling with Christian blood. Cases of wholesale conversion were exceedingly numerous, and it would make interesting reading to recount those of the Jews of Braine,[183] of Tortosa,[184] those of Clermont converted by Avitus, the 25,000 converted, as tradition goes, by Vincent Ferrer—all of whom disappeared in the midst of the nations among whom they lived. If the Inquisition hindered, or at least tried to hinder, judaization, it favoured the absorption of the Jews, and were the Christian antisemites logical they would curse Torquemada and his successors, who helped to pollute Aryan purity by the adjunction of the Jew. The number of Marranos in Spain was enormous. In nearly all Spanish families, a Jew or a Moor is found at some point of their genealogy; "the noblest houses are full of Jews," they said,[185] and the cardinal Mendoza y Bovadilla wrote in the sixteenth century a pamphlet on the flaws in Spanish lineages.[186]

We have thus made answer to those who maintain the purity of the Aryan race; we have pointed out that this race, like all the others, was a product of countless mixtures. Not to speak of the prehistoric times we have made it clear that the Persian, Macedonian and Roman conquests made worse the ethnologic confusion which increased in Europe still further during the invasions. The so-called Indo-Germanic races, stock-full of alluvions even before, intermingled with Chudians, Ugrians, Uralo-Altaians. Those among the Europeans who believe themselves descended in line direct from Aryan ancestors do not keep in mind those so diverse lands which these ancestors had traversed in their long journeys, nor all the tribes which they had swept along with them, nor all those which they found settled wherever they tarried—tribes of unknown races and of uncertain origin, obscure and unknown tribes whose blood is still running in the veins of those who boast themselves heirs of the legendary and noble Aryans, as the blood of the yellow Dasyus and black Dravidians flows under the skin of the white Arya-Hindoos.

At present, the Jews—who consider themselves the highest incarnation of Semitism—help in perpetuating this belief in the inequality and hierarchy of races. The ethnologic prejudice is universal, and those even who suffer from it are its most tenacious upholders. Antisemites and philosemites join hands to defend the same doctrines, they part company only when it comes to award the supremacy. If the antisemite reproaches the Jew for being a part of a strange and base race, the Jew vaunts of belonging to an elect and superior race; to his nobility and antiquity he attaches the highest importance and even now he is the prey of patriotic pride. Though no longer a nation, though protesting against those who see in him the representative of a nation encamped among strange nations, he nevertheless harbours in the depth of his heart this absurdly vain conviction, and thus he is like the chauvinists of all lands. Like them he claims to be of pure origin, while his assertion is no more well-founded, and we have to examine closely the assertion of Israel's enemy and of Israel himself : to wit, that the Jews are the most united, stable, impenetrable, irreducible nation.

We possess no documents to determine the ethnology of the nomadic Bene-Israel, but probable it is that the twelve tribes constituting this people, according to the tradition, did not belong to a single stock. They were doubtless heterogeneous tribes, for, in spite of its legends, the Jewish nation cannot, any more than the other nations, boast of having originated from a single couple, and the current conception which represents the Hebrew tribe as subdividing into sub-tribes[187] is but a legendary and traditional conception—that of the Genesis—and one which a portion of historians of the Hebrews have wrongly accepted. Already composed of various unities among which doubtless were Turanian and Kushite groups, *i.e.*, yellows and blacks, the Jews added still other strange elements while living in Egypt and in the land of Canaan which they conquered. Later on Gog and Magog, the Scythians, coming in Josiah's reign to Jerusalem's gates, probably left their impress on Israel. But starting with the first captivity the mixtures grow in number. "During the Babylonian captivity," says Maimonides,[188] "the Israelites mingled with all sorts of foreign races and had children, who formed, owing to these unions, a kind of a new confusion of tongues," and yet this Babylonia, where there were cities like Mahuza, almost entirely peopled by Persians converted to Judaism, was deemed to contain Jews of a purer race than the Jews of Palestine. Said an old proverb : "For the purity of the race, the difference between the Jews of the Roman provinces is just as perceptible as the difference between dough of mediocre quality and dough made of the flour of meal; but, compared to Babylonia, Judea itself is like mediocre dough."

This means that Judea had undergone many vicissitudes. It had always been the transit ground for the Mizraim and Assur; afterwards, on returning from captivity, the Jews united with the Samaritans, Edomites and Moabites. After the conquest of Idumea by Hyrcan, there were Jewish and Idumean unions, and it was said that, during the war with Rome, the Latin conquerors had begotten sons. "Are we perfectly sure," said Rabbi Ulla, melancholically, to Judah-ben Ezekiel, "that we are not descended from pagans who dishonoured the young daughters of Zion after the capture of Jerusalem?"

But what was most conducive to the introduction of foreign blood into the Jewish nation was proselytism. The Jews were a propagandist nation *par excellence,* and from the construction of the Second Temple and particularly after the dispersion, their zeal was considerable. They were exactly those of whom the Gospel says, that they ran over "earth and sea to make a proselyte,"[189] and with perfect right could Rabbi Eliezer exclaim : "Wherefore has God scattered the Jews among the nations? To recruit for Him proselytes everywhere."[190] There are abundant proofs of the proselyting ardour of the Jews, [191] and during the first centuries before the Christian era Judaism spread with the same vigour as characterized Christianity and Mohammedanism later on. Rome, Alexandria, Antioch—where nearly all the Jews were converted gentiles—Damask, Cyprus were the centres of fusion, as I have already pointed out.[192] Nay, more, the Hasmonide conquerors compelled the vanquished Syrians to circumcise; kings, carrying their subjects along, converted, as, e.g., the family of Adiabenus, and the population was very mixed in certain cantons of Palestine itself, as was the case with Galilea, in that "circle of gentiles" where Jesus was to be born.

All over Europe the Jews attracted proselytes, thus rejuvenating their blood by the admixture of new blood. They made converts in Spain where successive councils at Toledo forbade mixed marriages; in Switzerland, where a decree of the fourteenth century sentenced young girls to wearing Jewish hats for having begotten children by Israelite fathers; in Poland, in the sixteenth century, in spite of Sigismund I's edicts, if we are to believe the historian

Bielski.[193] And they not only made these unions with the so-called Aryan nations in Europe, but also with the Uralo-Altaians and Turanians; there the infiltration was more considerable.

On the shores of the Black and the Caspian Sea, the Jews had established themselves in great antiquity. The story goes that during the war he waged against King Tachus (361 B.C.) in Egypt, Artaxerxes Ochus wrested the Jews from their land and transferred them to Hyrcania on the Caspian shore. Even if their establishment in this region is not so old as claimed by this tradition, they still were settled there long before the Christian era, witness the Greek inscriptions of Anape, Olbia and Panticapea. They emigrated in the seventh and eighth centuries from Babylonia and came to the Tartar cities, Kertsh, Tarku, Derbend, etc. About 620 they converted there a whole tribe, the Khazars,[194] whose territory was in the neighbourhood of Astrakhan. Legend seized upon this fact, which greatly stirred up the Jews of the West, but, despite of this, there can be no doubt about it. Isidore of Seville, a contemporary of the event, mentions it, and afterwards Chasdai Ibn-Shaprut, minister of the Khalif Abd-er-Rahman, corresponded with Joseph, the last Khagan of the Khazars, whose kingdom was destroyed by Svyatoslav, prince of Kieff. The Khazars exercised a great influence over the neighbouring Slav tribes, the Polyane, Syeveryane and Vyatichi, and made numerous proselytes among them.

The Tartar peoples of the Caucasus also embraced Judaism in the twelfth century, according to the report of the traveller Petachya of Ratisbon.[195] In the fourteenth century, there were numerous Jews in the hordes, which, with Mamay at their head, invaded the lands surrounding the Caucasus. It was in this nook of Eastern Europe that actively went on the fusion of Jews and Uralo-Altaians; here the *Semite* mixed with the *Turanian,* and even now, in studying the nations of the Caucasus, one meets with traces of this mixture among the 30,000 Jews of that country and the tribes surrounding them.[196]

Thus this Jewish race represented by Jews and antisemites as the most unassailable, most homogeneous of races, is strongly multifarious. Anthropologists would in the first place divide it into two well-defined parts : the dolichocephals and the brachycephals. To the first type belong the Sephardic Jews—the Spanish and Portuguese Jews as well as the greater part of the Jews of Italy and Southern France; to the second may be assigned the Ashkenazim, *i.e.,* the Polish, Russian and German Jews.[197] But the Sephardim and the Ashkenazim are not the only two known varieties of Jews; these varieties are numerous.

In Africa are found agricultural and nomadic Jews, allied with the Kabyls and Berberians, near Setif, Guelma and Biskra, at the frontier of Morocco; in caravan they go as far as Timbuctoo, and some of their tribes, on the borders of Sahara, like the Daggatouns, are black tribes,[198] as also are the Fellah Jews of Abyssinia.[199] In India, one finds white Jews in Bombay, and black Jews in Cochin China, but the white Jews have in them melanian blood. They settled in India in the fifth century, after the persecutions of the Persian King Pheroces, who banished them from Bagdad. Their settling is at all events assigned to a more remote date : the coming of the Jews into China, i.e., before Christ. As to the Jews of China, they are not only related to the Chinese surrounding them, but they have also adopted the practices of the Confucian religion.[200]

The Jew, consequently, has incessantly been transformed by the environments in which he stayed. He has changed because the different languages which he has spoken, have introduced into his mind different and opposite notions; he has not remained such as a united and homogeneous people ought to be, but, on the contrary, he is, at present, the most heterogeneous of all nations, one that presents the greatest varieties. And this pretended race whose stability and power of resistance friend and foe agree in extolling, affords us the most multifarious and most opposite types, since they range from the white to the black Jew, passing by way of the yellow Jew, not to speak of the secondary divisions—Jews with blond and red hair, and brown Jews with black hair.

Consequently, the ethnologic grievance of the antisemites does not rest upon any serious and real foundation. The opposition of the Aryans and the Semites is artificial; it is not correct to say that the Aryan race and the Semitic race are pure races, and that the Jew is a single and unvarying people. Semitic blood has mingled with Aryan blood and Aryan blood has mixed with Semitic blood. Aryans and Semites have both, furthermore, received an admixture of Turanian blood and Hamite, Negro or Negroid blood, and in the Babel of nationalities and races which the world is at present, the preoccupation of those who seek to discover who among his neighbours is an Aryan, a Turanian, a Semite, is a vain pursuit.

In spite of this there is a portion of truth in the grievance which we have examined, or, rather, the theories of the antisemites about the inequality of races and Aryan superiority, in one word, the anthropologic prejudices are but the veil which covers some real causes of antisemitism.

We have said that there are no races, but there are peoples and nations. What is improperly called a race is not an ethnologic unit, but is an historic, intellectual and moral unit. The Jews are not an *ethnos,* but they are a nationality, they are diversified types, it is true, but what nation is not diversified? What makes a people is not unity of origin, but unity of sentiments, ideas, ethics. Let us see whether the Jews do not present this unity, and whether we cannot find therein, in part, the secret of the animosity shown them.

ELEVEN

NATIONALISM AND ANTISEMITISM

THERE are about eight million Jews scattered over the face of the earth, nearly seven-eighths of which inhabit Europe. Among these Jews figure the Bedoween Jews living on the confines of Sahara, the Daggatouns of the desert, the Fellahs of Abyssinia, the black Jews of India, the Mongoloid Jews of China, the Kalmuk and Tartar Jews of the Caucasus, the blond Jews of Bohemia and Germany, the brown Jews of Portugal, Southern France, Italy and the Orient, the dolichocephalous Jews, the brachycephalous and sub-brachycephalous Jews, all Jews, who, according to the section of their hair, the shape of their skull, the colour of their skin, could be classified, on the strength of the best principles of ethnology, into four or five different races, as we have just shown.

Still, proceeding in this way, we shall really have proven that the race is not an ethnologic unity, *i.e.*, that no people is a descendant of common parents, and that no nation has been formed from the aggregation of cells of this kind. But we shall by no means have proven that there exists no French people, a German people, an English people, etc., and we should not be able to do it, since there exists an English literature, a German literature, a French literature, different literatures all of them, expressing in a different way common sentiments, it is true, but whose objective and subjective play upon the various individuals affected by them is not the same, sentiments common to human nature, but ones which each man and each collection of men feels and expresses in a different way. We have had to reject the anthropologic notion of race, a notion which is erroneous and which we shall see to have given origin to the worst opinions, the most detestable and least justifiable vanities, that anthropologic notion which tends to make of each people an association of proud and egoistic recluses, but we are forced to admit the existence of historical units *i.e.*, separate nations. For the idea of race we substitute the idea of nation, and again we have to make an explanation, for the nineteenth century based its belief in nationalities on its belief in race, and an innate race at that.

To sum up. Customarily a nation is called an agglomeration of individuals having in common their territory, language, religion, law, customs, manners, spirit, historic mission. Now, we have seen that a common race, innate race, a race implying the same origin and purity of blood is but a fiction; the idea of race is not necessarily linked with the conception of a nation—proof that the Basques, Bretons, Provencals, belong all to the French nation, though very different anthropologically. As for territorial community, it is not a whit more necessary; the Poles, *e.g.*, possess no common territory, and yet there is a Polish nation. Language, too, does not seem indispensable, and indeed one may refer to Switzerland, Austria, Belgium, in which countries two or several languages are spoken but these countries, organized—with the exception of Switzerland—federatively, permit us on the contrary, to assert that language is clearly the sign of nationality, since in all of them those speaking the same language strive to group together, in other words, that one language tends to become preponderant and destroy the others. Religion was formerly one of the most important forces that contributed to the formation of peoples. We cannot possibly realize what Rome, Athens or Sparta had been, if we disregard the Gods of Olympus and the Capitolium; the same is true of Memphis, Nineveh, Babylon and Jerusalem, and what becomes of the Middle Ages if we leave out Christianity?

Nations, consequently, do exist. These nations may sometimes not be organized under the same government; they may have lost their fatherland, their language, but the nation continues as long as this self-consciousness and the consciousness of that community of thought and interests which they represent by the fictitious background of race, filiation, origin and purity of blood have not disappeared.

Now let us turn to the Jew. We have seen that he does not exist, as far as race is concerned, and those are in error who say: "There is no longer a Jewish people, there is a Jewish fellowship closely united with a race."[201] It remains to inquire whether the Jew is not a part of a nation composed, like all nations, of various elements, and nevertheless possessing unity. Now, if we leave aside the Abyssinian Fellaheen, some little known nomadic Jewish tribes of Africa, the black Jews of India, and the Chinese Jews, we arrive at the conclusion that by the side of the pointed out differences which distinguish these Jews they possess also common peculiarities, a common individuality and a common type. Still, the Jews have lived in quite contrasting countries, they were subjected to very diverse climatic influences, they were surrounded by very dissimilar peoples. What is it that succeeded in keeping them such as they have remained until today? Why do they continue to exist otherwise than as a religious confession? This is due to three causes : one depending on the Jews—religion; another for which they are partly responsible—their social condition; the third, which is external—the conditions which have been forced upon them.

No religion has ever moulded soul and spirit as has the Jewish religion. Nearly all religions have had a philosophy, ethics, a literature alongside of their religious dogmas; with Israel religion was simultaneously ethics and metaphysics, nay, more, it was law. The Jews had no symbolic independence from their legislation; no, after the return from the second captivity, they had Yahweh and his Law, each inseparable from the other. To become part of the nation one had to accept not its God only, but also all legal prescriptions emanating from Him and bearing the stamp of sanctity. Had the Jew had only Yahweh, he would probably have vanished in the midst of the different peoples that had received him, just as had vanished the Phoenicians who carried only Melkart with them. But the Jew had something more than his God—he had his Torah, his law, and by it he has been preserved. He not only did not lose this law when losing his ancestral territory, but, on the contrary, he has strengthened its authority; he has developed it; he has increased its power as well as its property. After the destruction of Jerusalem the law became the bond of Israel; he lived for and by his law. But this law was minute and meddlesome, it was the most perfect manifestation of the ritual religion—into which the Jewish religion turned under the influence of its doctors, an influence which may be contrasted with the spiritualism of the prophets whose tradition Jesus carried on. These rites which foresaw every act in life, and which the Talmudists made infinitely complicated, have given shape to the Jewish brain, and everywhere, in all lands, they have shaped it in the same manner. Though scattered, the Jews thought the same way in Seville, York, Ancona, Ratisbon, Troyes and Prague; they had the same feelings and ideas about human beings and things; they viewed things through the same eye-glasses; they judged according to similar principles. The Jewish type has been formed in a way analogous to that in which were formed and are still forming the type of a physician, the type of a lawyer, etc., types produced by the identity of the social and psychic function. The Jew is a confessional type; such as he is he has been made by the law and the Talmud; more powerful than blood or climatic varieties, they have developed in him the characteristics which imitation and heredity have perpetuated.

Social characteristics were added to these confessional characteristics. We have spoken[202] of the role played by the Jew during the Middle Ages, how internal and external causes, proceeding from economic and psychological laws, led them to become almost exclusively traders, and above all dealers in gold at a time when capital was forced to be creditor in order to be productive. This role was general; the Jews filled it in all countries, not in any particular one only. To their common religious preoccupations were consequently added common social preoccupations. As a religious being the Jew was already thinking in a certain way wherever he was; as a social being he again thought identically; thus other peculiarities were created, which, too, spread peculiarities, the formation of which was general and simultaneous with all Jews. In Spain, France, Italy, Germany, Poland, the legislation against the Jews was identical, a fact quite easy of explanation as in all these lands the legislation was inspired by the church. The Jew was placed under the same restrictions, the same barriers were built around him, he was ruled by the same laws. The Jew obtained a territory on the day he was imprisoned in these Jewries, and the Israelites lived since then exactly like a people that had a fatherland of its own; in these special quarters they preserved their customs, manners and secular habits, scrupulously transmitted by an education which was everywhere guided by the same invariable principles.

This education did not preserve the traditions only, it was preserving the language. The Jew spoke the language of the country he inhabited, but he spoke it only because it was indispensable in his business transactions; once at home he made use of a corrupt Hebrew or of a jargon of which Hebrew formed the basis. For writing purposes he employed Hebrew, and the Bible and the Talmud do not constitute the whole of Hebrew literature. The Jewish literary productivity from the eighth to the fifteenth century was very great. There has been a neo-hebraic poetry of the synagogue, which was particularly copious and brilliant in Spain,[203] there has been a Jewish religious philosophy which was born with Saadiah in Egypt and which Ibn Gebirol and Maimonides developed afterwards; there has been a Jewish theology since the time of Joseph Albo and Jehuda Halevi, and Jewish metaphysics—that is the Kabbala. This literature, this philosophy, this theology, these metaphysics were the common property of the Israelites of all countries.

Thus, consequently, the Jews had the same religion, manners, habits and customs, they were subjected to the same civil, religious, moral and restrictive laws; they lived in similar conditions; in each city they had their own territory, they spoke the same language, they enjoyed a literature, they speculated over the same persisting and very old ideas. This alone was sufficient to constitute a nation. They had even more than that: they have had the consciousness of being a nation, that they had never ceased to be one. After they had left Palestine, in the first centuries before the Christian era, a bond always tied them to Jerusalem; after Jerusalem had been plunged in flames, they had their exilarchs, their *Nassis* and *Gaons,* their schools of doctors, schools of Babylon, Palestine, then Egypt, finally of Spain and France. The chain of tradition has never been broken. They have ever considered themselves exiles and have deluded themselves with the dream of the restoration of Israel's kingdom on earth. Every year, on the eve of the Passover they have chanted from the depth of their whole beings, three times the sentence: *"Leshana haba b'Yerushalaim"* (the next year in Jerusalem!). They have preserved their ancient patriotism, even their chauvinism; in spite of disasters, misfortunes, outrages, slavery, they have considered themselves the elect people, one superior to all other peoples, which is characteristic of all chauvinist nations, the Germans as well as the French and English of today. At one time in the beginning of the Middle Ages, the Jew was really superior, because, he, the inheritor of an already ancient civilization, the possessor of a literature, philosophy and above all experience, which should have given him the advantage, came into the midst of barbarian children. He lost that supremacy, and in the fourteenth century even, his was already a culture lower than the general culture of those in the same class with him. But he has religiously kept this idea of supremacy, has kept on looking with

disdain and scorn upon all those who were strangers to his law.
However, he was taught to be such by his book, the Talmud pervaded by a narrow and ferocious patriotism. The book has been
charged with being anti-social, and there is some truth in this
accusation; it has been claimed that it is the most abominable code
of law and ethics, and therein lay the error, since it is neither more
nor less execrable than all particularist and national codes. If it is
anti-social, it is so only in that it represented and still represents
a spirit differing from that of the laws in force in the country
where the Jews lived and that the Jews wanted to follow their
code before following the one to which every member of society
was amenable, and again it is unsocial only in a relative sense, as
the law was not always uniform and custom invariable in all parts
of the States. At one moment of history it appeared fatally anti-
human, because it remained immutable while everything was
changing. Its brutality has been exposed by the Christian antisemites, because this brutality shocked them directly, but in saying,
"Kill even the best of Goyim," Rabbi Simon ben Jochai was no
more cruel than was Saint Louis, who thought that the best way
of arguing with a Jew was to plunge a dirk in his belly, or than
the Pope Urban III when he wrote in his bull: "Everybody is
allowed to kill an excommunicate if it is done from zeal for the
church."

One thing, besides, has to be taken into account. Some modern
Jews and philosemites have rejected with horror those aphorisms
and axioms that had been national aphorisms and axioms. They
say that the invectives against the *goyim,* the Mineans, were
directed at the Romans, the Hellenes, the Jewish apostates, but
they were never aimed at the Christians. There is a great deal of
truth in these assertions, but there is also a great deal of error.
When Judaism was fought by the rising Christianity, all the hatred
and wrath of hired assassins, patriots, pious people turned upon
the Jews who were converting themselves—the Mineans. When
deserting the national faith they deserted the battle against Rome
and the enemy; they were traitors to their country, to the Jewish
religion; they lost interest in a struggle that was vital for Israel;
gathered around their new temples they looked with an eye of
indifference upon the fall of the national glory, the disappearance
of their autonomy, and not only did they not fight against the
she-wolf, but they even unnerved the courage of those listening

to them. Against them, against these anti-patriots, formulas of malediction were drawn up; the Jews placed them under the ban of their society, it was lawful to kill them, just as it was lawful to kill "the best of *goyim.*" Similar exhortations would be found at all periods of patriotic struggles, among all nations; the proclamations of the generals, the calls to arms of the tribunes of all ages contain just as odious formulas. When the French, for instance, invaded the Palatinate, it must have been a rule, nay, even a duty, for all Germans to say : "Death even to the best of Frenchmen !"

There came a day when the Jew had but one enemy in Europe —the Christian—who persecuted, hunted, massacred, burned, martyrized him. As a consequence he could not experience any very tender feeling toward the Christian, the more so that all the efforts of the Christian were bent on destroying Judaism, on annihilating the religion which from that time on constituted the Jewish fatherland. The *goy* of the Maccabees, the Minean of the doctors, turned into the Christian, and to the Christian all the words of furious hatred, wrath and despair found in the book, were applied. To the Christian, the Jew was a despicable being, but to the Jew the Christian became the *goy,* the execrable stranger, who fears no pollution, who maltreats the elect nation, one through whom Judah suffers. This word *goy* comprehended all the passions, scorns, hatreds of persecuted Israel—against the stranger, and this cruelty of the Jews toward the non-Jew is one of the things that best prove how long-lived the idea of nationality was among the children of Jacob. They have always believed themselves a people. Do they still believe it at present?

Among the Jews who receive a Talmudic education, and this means the majority of the Jews in Russia, Poland, Galicia, Hungary, Bohemia and the Orient, the idea of nationality is still as alive at present as it had been during the Middle Ages. They still form a people apart, fixed, rigid, congealed by the scrupulously observed rites, by the unvarying customs and the manners; hostile to every innovation, to every change, rebelling against all attempted efforts to detalmudize him. In 1854 the rabbis anathematized the Oriental schools founded by French Jews, where profane sciences were taught; at Jerusalem, an anathema was hurled, in 1856, against the school established by Doctor Franckel. In Russia and Galicia, sects like those of the New Chassidim are still opposing all attempts made to civilize the Jews. In all these countries only a minority escapes the Talmudic spirit, but the mass persists in its isolation, and however great its abjection and its humiliation, it ever holds itself the chosen people, the nation of God.

This intolerant aversion toward the stranger has disappeared among the Western Jews, the Jews of France, England, Italy and a great portion of the German Jews.[204] The Talmud is no longer read by these Jews, and the Talmudic ethics, at least the nationalist ethics of the Talmud, have no longer any hold on them. They no longer observe the 613 laws, have lost their fear of impurity, a horror which the Eastern Jews have preserved; the majority no longer know Hebrew; they have forgotten the meaning of the antique ceremonies; they have transformed the rabbinic Judaism into a religious rationalism; they have given up the familiar observances, and the religious exercise has been reduced by them to passing several hours in the year in a synagogue listening to hymns they no longer understand. They can't attach themselves to a dogma, a symbol; they have none of it; in giving up the Talmudic practices they have given up what made their unity, that which contributed to forming their spirit. The Talmud had formed the Jewish nation after its dispersion; thanks to it, individuals of diverse origin had constituted a people; it had been the mould of the Jewish soul, the creator of the race; it and the restrictive laws of the various societies have modelled it. It appears that with the legislators abolished, the Talmud left in disdain, the Jewish nation should inevitably have died, and yet the Western Jews are Jews still. They are Jews, because they have kept perennial and living their national consciousness; they still believe they are a nation, and, believing that, they preserve themselves. When the Jew ceases to have the national consciousness he disappears; so long as he has this consciousness, he continues to be. He practices his religious faith no longer, he is irreligious, often even an atheist, but he continues to be, because he has a belief in his race. He has kept his national pride, he always fancies himself a superior individuality, a different being from those surrounding him, and this conviction prevents him from assimilating himself, for, being always exclusive, he generally refuses to mix through marriage with the peoples surrounding him. Modern Judaism claims to be but a religious confession; but in reality it is an *ethnos* besides, for it believes it is that, for it has preserved its prejudices, egoism and vanity as a people—a belief, prejudices, egoism and vanity which make it appear a stranger to the peoples in whose midst it exists, and here we touch upon one of the most profound causes of antisemitism. Antisemitism is one of the ways in which the principle of nationalities is manifested.

What is this question of nationalities? By it is understood "the movement which carries certain populations, of the same origin and language, but constituting a part of different States—to unite in such a way as to make a single political body, a single nation."[205]

Simultaneously with proclaiming the rights of the land, formerly the property and domain of the peoples the Revolution overthrew the old conception of rule and dynasty on which the nations were founded; the land, formerly the property and domain of the kings, now became the domain of the people that occupied them. The royal government in itself constituted the national unity—the representative, constitutional government placed that unity somewhere else : in the community of origin and language. The artificial bond being broken, a natural bond was sought for; there have been efforts on the part of nations to acquire an individuality; they all strove for the unity they lacked. It was about 1840 that nationalist ideas especially manifested themselves, they began the work, and contemporary Europe was founded through them. The theory of a National State was wrought out by the savants, historians, philosophers, poets of a whole generation.

On these ideas of nationalities Russia and Germany have been and are resting to make up their empire, Pangermanic or Panslavic; and is not this Panslavism, and this Pangermanism what agitates the East of Europe, do not the destinies of that part of Europe depend on this remote or near clash of theirs?

It would be out of place to discuss here the legitimacy or illegitimacy of this movement. It will suffice for our purpose merely to state its existence. How do the peoples construe this tendency into unity? In two ways : either by uniting under the same government all individuals who speak the national language, or by reducing all heterogeneous elements coexisting in the nations, for the benefit of one of these elements which becomes preponderant and whose characteristics henceforth become the national characteristics. Thus the Germans have endeavoured to assimilate the Alsatians and Poles; the Russians compel the Poles to maintain the Russian universities which denationalize them; in Austria the Germans try to absorb the Czechs; in Hungary, "Slovak orphans are taken from the places where their native tongue is spoken and removed to Magyar comitats."[206] If these heterogeneous elements do not let themselves be absorbed, there comes a struggle, a violent struggle often, which is manifested in many various ways—from persecution down to expulsion in some cases.

Now, in the midst of the European nations the Jews live as a confessional community, believing in the latter's nationality, having preserved a peculiar type, special aptitudes and a spirit of their own. In their struggle against the heterogeneous elements which they contained, the nations were led to struggle against the Jews, and antisemitism was one of the manifestations of the effort made by the peoples in order to reduce these strange individualities.

To these nationalist egotists, to these exclusivists, the Jews appeared a danger, because they felt that the Jews were still a people, a people whose mentality did not agree with the national mentality, whose concepts were opposed to that ensemble of social, moral, psychological, and intellectual conceptions, which constitutes nationality. For this reason the exclusivists became antisemites, because they could reproach the Jews with an exclusivism exactly as uncompromising as theirs, and every antisemitic effort tends, as we have seen already,[207] to restore those ancient laws restricting the rights of the Jews who are considered strangers. Thus is realized this fundamental and everlasting contradiction of nationalist antisemitism : antisemitism was born in modern societies, because the Jew did not assimiliate himself, did not cease to be a people, but when antisemitism had ascertained that the Jew was not assimilated, it violently reproached him for it, and at the same whenever possible it took all necessary measures to prevent his assimilation in the future.

At all events, there exist contrary, opposing tendencies by the side of these nationalist tendencies. Above nationalities there is mankind; now, this mankind, so fragmental at the start, composed of thousands of inimical tribes that were devouring one another, is becoming a very homogeneous mankind. The different peoples possess a common ground, despite their differences; a general conscience is formed above all the national consciences; formerly there had been civilizations, now we advance towards *one civilization;* once upon a time Athens resisted its neighbour Sparta; from now on, even if dissimilarities between one nation and another persist, the similarities are accentuated. As by the side of his special qualities constituting his essence and personality, each individual in a nation possesses qualities in common with those who speak the same tongue and have the same interests as he, just so civilized mankind acquires similar characteristics, though each nation preserves its physiognomy. More frequent from day to day, the relations among the peoples bring on a more intimate communion. Science, art, literature, become more and more cosmopolitan. Humanitarianism takes its place by the side of patriotism, internationalism by the side of nationalism, and presently the idea of mankind will acquire more force than the idea of fatherland, which is being modified and is losing some of that exclusivism which the national egoists wish to perpetuate. Hence the antagonism between the two tendencies. To internationalism, which is already so powerful, patriotism is opposed with unheard of violence. The old conservative spirit is elated; it is in training against cosmopolitanism which will some day defeat it; it fiercely fights those who are in favour of cosmopolitanism, and this is again a cause of antisemitism.

Though often exceedingly chauvinist, the Jews are essentially cosmopolitan in character; they are the cosmopolitan element of mankind, says Schaeffle. This is quite true, since they have always possessed in a high degree that mark of cosmopolitanism—the extreme facility of adaptation. On their arrival into the Promised Land they adopted the language of Canaan; after a seventy year sojourn in Babylonia, they forgot Hebrew and re-entered Jerusalem, speaking an Aramaic or Chaldee jargon; during the first century before and after the Christian era, the Hellenic tongue pervaded the Jewries. Once dispersed the Jews fatally became cosmopolites. Indeed they did not again attach themselves to any territorial unit, and have had only a religious unity. True, they have had a fatherland, but this fatherland, the most beautiful of all, as, however, every fatherland is, was placed in the future, it was Zion renewed, with which no land is compared or comparable; a spiritual fatherland which they loved so ardently that they became indifferent to every land, and that every land seemed to them equally good or equally bad. Finally they lived under such and so terrible circumstances that they could not be expected to have a fatherland of their choice, and, with the aid of their instinct of solidarity, they have remained internationalists.

The nationalists have been led to consider them as the most active propagators of the ideas of internationalism; they even found that the example alone of these countryless laymen was bad, and that by their presence they undermined the idea of fatherland, that is any special idea of fatherland. For this reason they became antisemites or rather for this reason their antisemitism took on added force. They not only accused the Jews of being strangers, but even destructive strangers. The conservatism of the exclusivists connected cosmopolitanism with revolution; it upbraided the Jews first for their cosmopolitanism, and then for their revolutionary spirit and activity. Has the Jew, indeed, any leaning toward revolution? We shall examine that.

TWELVE

THE REVOLUTIONARY SPIRIT
IN JUDAISM

To inquire into the revolutionary tendencies of Judaism does not mean to examine Jewish Communism. Moreover, from the fact that the so-called Mosaic institutions had been inspired by socialistic principles it should not necessarily be inferred that the revolutionary spirit has always guided Israel.

Communism and revolution are not inseparable terms, and if nowadays we cannot utter the first word without fatally evoking the other—this is due to the economic conditions governing us and to the fact that the transformation of the present-day societies, based as they are on individual property, is considered impossible without a violent tearing up. In a capitalistic State the communist is looked upon as a revolutionist, but it is not taken into account that a partisan of private capital would be treated in similar fashion in a communistic State.

If it can be said, with Renan, of the Jews that they have been an element of progress or at least of transformation, if they could be regarded as the ferments of revolution, and that, too, at all times, we shall see, it is not because of these laws on gleaning, on the workmen's wages, on the sabbatic and jubilee years, which are found in the Exodus, Numbers, Leviticus, etc.,[208] but because they have always been malcontents.

I do not mean to claim thereby that they were mere mudslingers and systematic opponents of all government, for they were not wrought up against an Ahab or Ahaziah only—but the state of things did not satisfy them; they were forever restless, in the expectation of a better state which they never found realized. Their ideal not being one of those which are satisfied with hope— they had not placed it high enough for that—they never could lull their ambitions with dreams and phantoms. They thought they had a right to demand immediate satisfactions and not remote promises. Hence this constant agitation of the Jews, which had manifested itself not only in prophetism, Messianism and Christianity that was its supreme consummation, but as well since the time of the dispersion, and then in an individual manner.

The causes that gave birth to this agitation, which kept it up and perpetuated it in the souls of some modern Jews, are not external causes such as the tyranny of a ruler, of a people or ferocious code; they are internal causes, *i.e.*, such as pertain to the very essence of the Hebrew spirit. The reasons of the sentiments of revolt with which the Jews were animated must be sought in the idea they had of God, in their conception of life and death.

To Israel, life is a boon, the existence granted to man by God is good; to live is in itself good luck.

By contrast, death is the only evil that can afflict man, it is the greatest of calamities; it is so horrible, so frightful that to be struck by it is the most terrible of punishments. "May death serve me as expiation," the dying would say, for he could not conceive of a more serious punishment than that consisting in death. The only recompense that the pious earnestly desired was that Yahweh might make them die sated with days, after years passed in abundance and jubilation.

Besides, what recompense other than this could they have expected? They did not believe in the future life, and it was late, perhaps only under the influence of Parsism, that they began to admire the immortality of the soul. For a Jew, his existence ended with life, he was sleeping till the day of resurrection, he had nothing to hope for except from existence, and the punishments that threatened vice, just as the satisfactions that accompanied virtue, were all of this world.

Having no hope of future reward the Jew could not resign to the misfortunes of life; it was only at a very late date that he could console himself in his misfortunes by dreaming of celestial happiness. To the scourges befalling him he replied neither with the Mohammedan's fatalism, nor with the Christian's resignation, but with revolt. As he possessed a concrete ideal, he wanted to realize it, and whatever retarded its advent aroused his wrath.

The peoples that believed in a world beyond, those who deluded themselves with sweet and consoling chimaeras and let themselves be lulled to sleep with the dream of eternity; those that possessed the dogma of rewards and punishments, of paradise and hell, all these peoples accepted poverty and sickness with bowed heads. The dream of future rejoicing kept them up, and without anger they put up with their sores and their privation. They consoled themselves of the injustices of this world by thinking of the mirth that would be their *idyllic* pleasures, they consented to bend, without complaint, before the strong who tyrannized them.

But this idea of the continuity and persistence of the personality contributed nothing to the formation of the moral being with the Jews. In earliest times they did not share the hopes of the later Pharisees; after Yahweh had closed their eyelids, they expected only the horror of Sheol. Acordingly, life was for them the important thing; they sought to beautify it with all blessings, and these mad idealists, who had conceived the pure idea of one God, were, by a startling yet explicable contrast, the most untractable of sensualists. Yahweh had assigned to them a certain number of years on earth; in this existence, always too short to suit the Hebrew, He demanded of them a faithful and scrupulous worship; in return, the Hebrew claimed positive advantages from his Lord.

The idea of contract dominated the whole of Jewish theology. When the Israelite fulfilled his duties toward Yahweh, he demanded reciprocity. If he thought himself wronged, if he considered his rights had not been respected, he had no good reason to temporize, for the minute of happiness he lost was a minute stolen from him, one which could never be returned to him. Accordingly, he looked to a punctual fulfilment of mutual obligations; he wanted a correct balance to exist between his God and himself; he kept a strict account of his duties and his rights, this account was part of the religion, and Spinoza could justly say :[209] "With the Jews the religious dogmas did not consist in instructions, but in rights and prescriptions; piety meant justice, impiety meant injustice and crime."

The man whom the Jew lauds is not a saint, not a resignee : it is the just man. The charitable man does not exist for those of Judah's people; in Israel there can be no question of charity, but only of justice : alms is but a restitution. Besides, what did Yahweh say? He has said : "Just balances, just weights, a just *ephah,* and a just *hin* shall ye have;"[210] he has also said : "Thou shalt not respect the person of the poor, nor honour the person of the mighty; but in righteousness shalt thou judge thy neighbours."[211]

From this conception of the primitive times of Israel came the law of retaliation. Simple spirits, imbued with the idea of justice, were obviously bound to come to: "An eye for an eye, a tooth for a tooth." The rigour of the code softened only then when a more exact idea of equity was obtained.

The Yahwehism of the prophets reflects these sentiments. What the God they praise wants is: "Let judgment run down as waters and righteousness as a mighty stream;"[212] he says: "I am the Lord which exercise lovingkindness, judgment and righteousness in the earth; for in these things I delight."[213] To know justice is to know God,[214] and justice becomes an emanation from divinity; it takes on the character of a revelation. With Isaiah, Jeremiah, Ezekiel it formed part of the dogma, it had been proclaimed during the Sinaitic theophanies, and little by little is born this idea: Israel must realise justice.

On returning from Babylon, the Jewish population formed a considerable nucleus of *poor, just, pious, humble, and saints.* A great portion of the Psalms came from this midst. These Psalms are for the most part violent diatribes against the rich; they symolize the struggle of the *ebionim* against the mighty. When addressing the possessors, the *sated,* the Psalmists readily say with Amos: "Hear this, O ye that swallow up the needy, even to make the poor of the land to fail,"[215] and in all these poems written between the Babylonian exile and the Maccabees (589-167) the poor is glorified. He is God's friend, His prophet, His anointed; he is good, his hands are pure; he is upright and just; he is part of the flock of which God is the shepherd.

The rich is the wicked, he is the man of violence and blood; he is knavish, perfidious, haughty; he does evil without motive; he is contemptible, for he exploits, oppresses, persecutes and devours the poor. But his great crime is that he does not do justice; that he has bribed judges who condemn the poor beforehand.[216]

Incited by the words of their poets, the *ebionim* did not slumber in their misery, they did not delight in their misfortunes, they did not resign to poverty. On the contrary, they dreamed of the day that would avenge the iniquities and opprobriums heaped upon them, the day when the wicked would be hurled down and the just exalted: the day of the Messiah.

When Jesus comes he will repeat what the *ebionim* Psalmists had said, he will say: "Blessed are they which do hunger and thirst after righteousness, for they shall be filled;"[217] he will anathematize the rich, and will exclaim: "It is easier for a camel to go through the eye of a needle than for a rich man to enter the Kingdom of God."[218] On this point the Christian doctrine will turn out to be purely Jewish, not at all Hellenic, and Jesus will find his first adherents among the *ebionim*.

Thus the conception the Jews formed of life and death furnished the first element of their revolutionary spirit. Starting with the idea that good, that is justice, was to be realized not beyond the grave—for beyond the grave there is sleep, until the day of the resurrection of the dead—but during life, they sought justice, and never finding it, ever dissatisfied, they were restless to get it.

The second element was given them by their conception of divinity. It led them to conceive the equality of men, it led them even to anarchy; a theoretic and sentimental anarchy, since they always had a government, but a real anarchy, for they never accepted with cheerful heart this government, whatever it were.

Whether worshipping Yahweh as their national God, or when they rose with their prophets to the belief in one and universal God, the Jews never speculated over the essence of Divinity. Judaism never set for itself any essential metaphysical questions, whether about the "beyond" or the nature of God. "Sublime speculations have no connection with the Scripture," says Spinoza, "and, as far as I am concerned, I have not and could not learn, from the Holy Writ, any of the eternal attributes of God",[219] and Mendelssohn adds : "Judaism has not revealed unto us any of the eternal truths."[220]

The Jews looked upon Yahweh as a celestial monarch, who would give a charter to his people and enter into engagements with it, demanding, in return, obedience to his laws and prescriptions. In the eyes of the ancient Hebrews and, later on, the Talmudists, the Bene-Israel alone could enjoy the prerogatives granted by Yahweh; in the eyes of the prophets, all nations could lawfully claim these privileges, because Yahweh was the God Universal, and not the equal of Dagon or Beelzebub.

But Yahweh was "the supreme head of the Hebrew people",[221] He was the all-powerful and formidable lord, the only king, jealous of His authority, cruelly punishing those who showed themselves rebellious against His omnipotence. In good luck, as in ill-luck, a pious Jew had ever to have recourse to Him. To turn to men and not to God Yahweh was a crime, and having made an alliance with Rome and Mithridates I, Judas Maccadaeus in-

curred this anathema of Rabbi José, son of Johanan : "Accursed
be he who places his reliance in creatures of flesh and who removes
his heart from Yahweh !" Yahweh is thy fort, thy shield, thy
citadel, thy hope, say the Psalms.

All Jews are Yahweh's subjects; He has said it Himself : "For
unto me the children of Israel are servants."[222] What authority can,
then, prevail by the side of the divine authority? All government,
whatever it be, is evil since it tends to take the place of the government of God; it must be fought against, because Yahweh is the
only head of the Jewish commonwealth, the only one to whom the
Israelite owes obedience.

When insulting the Kings, the prophets represented the sentiment of Israel. They were giving expression to the thoughts of the
poor, the humble, all those who, being directly ill-used by the
power of the Kings or of the rich, were more inclined, for that very
reason, to criticize or deny the good coming from this tyranny.

Holding Yahweh alone as their lord, these *anavim* and *ebionim,*
were ever driven to revolt against human magistracy; they could
not accept it, and during the periods of uprising Zadok and Judah
the Galilean were seen carrying with them the zealots by their cry :
"Call none your master !" Zadok and Judah were logical : if we
place our tyrant in heavens we cannot endure one down here.

God himself commands this equality, and again the mighty are
the obstacle to its realization. The humble, who live in common,
practice it; they follow the communistic precepts of Leviticus,
Exodus, Numbers, precepts inspired by preoccupations with
equality. As for the rich, they forget that God had made all men
from the same clay, they disown the equality proclaimed by God.
Thus they oppress the people, they fill their houses with the spoils
of the poor, they browse his vineyard, they make of widows their
prey, of orphans their booty,[223] and owing to them inequality
exists.

At them, at these possessors and these grandees the prophets
hurl the anathema; the psalmists thunder : "O Lord God, to whom
vengeance belongeth; O God, to whom vengeance belongeth, show
thyself !"[224] they cry. They rebuke the rich for the abundance of
his treasures, his luxury, his love of pleasures; whatever contributes
to raise him materially above his brethren; whatever can give him
the impious arrogance of deeming himself made of other dust than
that of which is made the mountain-shepherd who pastures his

sheep and fears God; whatever makes him forget this divine truth; men are equal to one another, since they are the children of Yahweh who pretended giving each of his subjects an equal share of the earth they tread on, an equal share of joys and blessings.

After Yahweh they believed in self only. To the unity of God there corresponded the unity of being; to God absolute—absolute being. Accordingly, subjectivity has ever been the fundamental trait of the Semitic character; it has often led the Jews to egoism, and having once exaggerated this egoism, certain Talmudists ended with recognizing, in the matter of duties, nothing but duties to one's self. This subjectivity, as much as monotheism, accounts for the incapacity shown by the Jews in all plastic arts. As for their literature it was purely subjective; the Jewish prophets, like the psalmists, like the poets of Job and the Song of Songs, like the moralists of the Ecclesiastes and the Book of Wisdom, knew only themselves and generalized their feelings or their personal sensations. This subjectivity also makes us understand why the Jews have at all times, even in our days, shown so much aptness for music—that most subjective of all arts.

Thus they were undeniably individualists, and these men, so eager to pursue earthly interests, appear to us—thanks to their uncompromising conception of existence—as untractable idealists. Now, an individualist imbued with idealism is and will always be in revolt. He will never want to allow anybody to violate his sacred self, and no will can prevail over his.

Notwithstanding their long bondage, despite the years of martyrdom which have been their lot, in spite of the centuries of humiliation, which have debased their character, depressed their brains, cramped their intelligence, changed their tastes, their customs, their aptitudes, the debris of Judah have not abjured their so vivid dream, which had been their support and inspiration during the wars for independence.

The funeral-piles, massacres, spoliations, insults, everything contributed to make dearer to them the justice, the equality and the liberty which during many long years were for them the emptiest words. The great voice of the prophets proclaiming that the wicked will be punished one day has always found an echo in these tenacious souls that did not like to bend, and despised this so miserable reality in order to delude themselves with the idea of the future time; that future time, of which Amos and Isaiah, Jeremiah and

Ezekiel, and all those have spoken who sang *Mizmorim* (*psalms*), to their own accompaniment on stringed instruments. However gloomy the present, Israel never ceased to believe in the future.

The Jews were told: "Why do you await Messiah; obdurate, know ye not that he has come?" They answered with sarcasm, they shrugged their shoulders and replied: "The Messiah has not come, for we are suffering, for famine desolates the land, for the black pest and the nobleman burden the sorrowful wretches!" But when they would be told that their Meshiach would never come, they would lift up their bowed down heads and, stubborn that they were, would say: "Meshiach will come one day and on that day will be understood the word of the Psalmist: 'I have seen the wicked in great power and spreading himself like a green bay tree. Yet he passed away and lo! he was not; yea, I sought him, but he could not be found'[225] and the poor, the just are those who will possess the earth."

The narrow practices into which their doctors had pressed the Jews, have put to slumber their instincts of revolt. Under the bonds of the Talmudic laws, they felt tottering in them the ideas that had ever sustained them, and it could be said that Israel could be vanquished only by himself. Still the Talmud did not debase all Jews; among those who rejected it there were some who persisted in the belief that justice, liberty and equality were to come to this world; there were many of them who believed that the people of Yahweh was charged with working for this coming. This makes it plain why the Jews were implicated in all revolutionary movements, for they took an active part in all revolutions, as we shall see when we study their role during all periods of trouble and change.

It remains now to know how the Jew has manifested these revolutionary tendencies, whether he was actually (as he is accused) an element of disturbance in modern societies; and thus we are led to examine the religious, political and economic causes of anti-semitism.

THIRTEEN

THE JEW AS A FACTOR IN THE TRANSFORMATION OF SOCIETY

THUS it would seem as if the grievance of the antisemite were well founded; the Jewish spirit is essentially a revolutionary spirit, and consciously or otherwise, the Jew is a revolutionist. Not content, however, with this, antisemitism would have it that the Jews are the very cause of revolution. Let us see what truth there is in the charge.

Taking him as he was, the tendencies of his nature and the direction of his sympathies made it inevitable that the Jew should play an important part in the revolutions of history; and such a part he has not failed to play. Nevertheless it would be too much to say, with the great mass of Israel's enemies, that every public commotion, every uprising, every political overturning has originated with the Jews, or has been provoked or occasioned by the Jews, and that governments change and take on new forms because the Jew in his secret counsels has plotted such changes and transformations. In maintaining such a proposition we violate the simplest of historical laws, by assigning to a minute cause a totally disproportionate effect, and concentrating our attention upon one phase of historical development to the exclusion of a thousand others of its manifold aspects. Had the Jews perished to a man behind the walls of Zion, the destiny of nations would not have been changed, and though the Jewish element were wanting to this wondrous totality which we call progress, society would have developed notwithstanding. Other forces would have taken the place of the Jews and accomplished what the Jews have accomplished in the general scheme. Given the Bible and Christianity, the intellectual and moral mission of the Jew would have been carried out without him.

Theologians who resort to reason for the defence of dogma, will inevitably end by asserting the superiority of reason to dogma, with fatal results to the latter. Exegesis and freedom of investigation are powerful destroyers, and it is the Jews who originated biblical

exegesis, just as they were the first to criticize the forms and
doctrines of Christianity. The importance of the controversial
literature of the Middle Ages has already been shown. If we study
closely we find in it all the arguments advanced by the scholars of
our own day. It might, indeed, be maintained in denial of the
revolutionary role said to have been played by the Jews, that the
greater part of their exegesis was addressed to Jews only, and that
it consequently could not have been a means of inciting to change,
inasmuch as the Jew knew well how to reconcile the results of
textual criticism with the minutiae of his practices and the integrity
of his faith. This, however, is not altogether true, for Jewish doctrines did find their way out of the synagogue, and this in two
different ways. In the first place the Jews could always find an
opportunity for proclaiming their ideals, thanks to the prevalence
of public disputation. In the second place, they were the means of
disseminating the Arabian philosophy, and were its expounders at
a time, twelfth century, to be precise, when Al Farabi and Ibn Sina
were being anathematized in the mosques, and orthodox Mussul-
mans were feeding the fires with the writings of the Arabian
Aristotelians. The Jews of this period translated the writings of
Aristotle and of the Arabian philosophers into Hebrew, and these,
retranslated into Latin, afforded the scholastics an opportunity for
becoming acquainted with Greek thought. The most famous of the
scholastics, "men like Albertus Magnus and St. Thomas Aquinas,
studied the works of Aristotle in Latin versions made from the
Hebrew."[226]

The Jews did not stop there. They preached the materialism of
the Arabian philosophers which was to prove so destructive to the
Christian faith, and carried abroad the spirit of scepticism. Their
activity was such as to give rise to a general belief in the existence
of a secret society sworn to the destruction of Christianity.[227] During
the thirteenth century, a century which witnessed the rapid development of that complex of humanism, scepticism and paganism
which we call the Renaissance, at a time when the Hohenstaufen
defended the cause of science against dogma, and showed themselves the protectors of Epicureanism, the Jews occupied the first
place among scholars and rationalist philosophers. At the Court of
the Emperor Frederick II, "that hotbed of irreligion," they were
received with favour and respect. It was they, as Renan has
shown,[228] that created Averroism; it was they who established the

fame of that Ibn-Roshd, that Averroes whose influence was destined to become so great. Without doubt they had their share, too, in the dissemination of the "blasphemies" of the impious Arabians; blasphemies which an Emperor, fond of science and of philosophy, encouraged. These find their type in the so-called "Blasphemy of the Three Impostors," Moses, Jesus and Mahomet, invented by the theologians, and their spirit is tersely summed up in the saying of the Arabian soufis, "What care I for the Kaaba of the Mohammedan, the synagogue of the Jew, or the convent of the Christian!" Truly has Darmesteter written : "The Jew was the apostle of unbelief, and every revolt of the mind originated with him, whether secretly or in the open. In that immense foundry of blasphemy maintained by the Emperor Frederick and the princes of Suabia and Aragon, he acted a busy part."[229]

Another thing also is worthy of notice. If the Jews as followers of Averroes, or as unbelievers, sceptics and blasphemers, sapped the foundations of Christianity in spreading the doctrines of materialism and rationalism, they were also the creators of that other enemy of Catholic dogma, pantheism. In fact the *Fons Vitae* of Avicebron was the well at which numerous heretics drank. It is even quite possible that David de Dinant and Amaury de Chartres, were influenced by the *Fons Vitae* which they knew in a Latin translation made in the twelfth century by the archdeacon Dominique Gundissalinus. It is certain that Giordano Bruno borrowed from the *Fons Vitae,* whence his pantheism came in part.[230]

If, therefore, the Jews were not solely responsible for the destruction of religious doctrine and the decay of faith, they may at least be counted among those who helped to bring about such a state of desuetude and the changes which followed. If they had never existed, the Arabians and the heterodox theologians would have filled their place; but they did exist, and existing they were not idle. Moreover the Hebrew genius worked not only through them, for their Bible became a powerful aid to all advocates of freedom of thought. The Bible was the soul of the Reformation, just as it was the soul of the religious and political revolution in England. Bible in hand, Luther and the English recusants blazed the path to liberty, and it was through the Bible that Luther, Melanchthon and others broke the yoke of Roman theocracy and overthrew the tyranny of dogma. But they made use, too, of that Jewish scholarship which Nicholas de Lyra had transmitted to the Christian world. *Si Lyra non lyrasset, Lutherus non saltasset,* it used to be said, and Lyra had studied with the Jews; in fact, he was so steeped in the science of Hebrew exegesis that he was taken for a Jew himself.

In like manner we would have to inquire what was the importance, I will not say of the Jew, but of the Jewish spirit throughout the period of fierce revolt against Christianity which characterized the eighteenth century. We must not forget that in the seventeenth century, scholars like Wagenseil, Bartolocci, Buxtorf and Wolf, had brought forth from oblivion old volumes of Hebrew polemic, written in refutation of the Trinity and the Incarnation and attacking all dogmas and forms of Christianity with a bitterness entirely Judaic, and with all the subtlety of those peerless casuists who created the Talmud. They gave to the world not only treatises on questions of doctrine and exegesis, like the *Nizzachon* or the *Chizuk Emunah,*[231] but published blasphemous tractates and pseudo-lives of Jesus, of the character of the *Toldoth Jesho*. The eighteenth century repeated, concerning Jesus and the Virgin, the outrageous fables invented by the Pharisees of the second century; we find them in Voltaire and in Parney, and their rationalist satire, pellucid and mordant, lives again in Heine, in Boerne and in Disraeli; just as the powerful logic of the ancient rabbis lives again in Karl Marx, and the passionate thirst for liberty of the ancient Hebrew rebels breathes forth again in the glowing soul of Ferdinand Lassalle.

I have sketched here, and that in the broadest strokes, the function performed by the Jews in the development of certain ideas which helped to bring on the general revolution; but I have not yet shown how the activity of the Jew revealed itself in the very work of revolution. I believe I have established the fact, on more than one occasion, that the Jews acted as a leaven upon the economic development of the age,[232] even though their influence may have proved to be, as the partisans of the old régime assert, a source of disorder; order and stability being represented by the Christian monarchical state. If we are to believe Barruel, Crétineau-Joly, Gougenot des Mousseaux, Dom Deschamps, Claudio Jannet, all those who see in history the mere work of secret societies, the role played by the Jews in the political and social upheavals of history has been one of capital importance.

True it is that, during the last years of the eighteenth century, secret associations exercised a great influence on the course of events, and though they may not have been formulators of the humanitarian, rationalistic and revolutionary theories of the time, such societies certainly were the cause of the enormously widespread dissemination of revolutionary ideas. They were, in fact, great centres of agitation. It cannot be denied that Free Masonry and Martinism were powerful agents in bringing about the revolution, but it must be remembered that their importance increased only as the theories for which they stood became predominant in society, and that, far from being the creators of that spirit of the times which was the fundamental cause of the Revolution, they were in themselves but one of its effects, though an effect to be sure which reacted in its turn upon the course of events.

What then was the connection between these secret societies and the Jews? The problem is a difficult one to solve, for respectable documentary evidence on the subject there is none. It is clear, however, that the Jews were not the dominant factors in these associations, as the writer whom I have just now quoted would have it; they were not "necessarily the soul, the heads, the grandmasters of Free Masonry," as Gougenot des Mousseaux maintains.[233] It is true, of course, that there were Jews connected with Free Masonry from its birth, students of the Kabbala, as is shown by certain rites which survive. It is very probable, too, that in the years preceding the outbreak of the French Revolution, they entered in greater numbers than ever, into the councils of the secret societies, becoming, indeed, themselves the founders of secret associations. There were Jews in the circle around Weishaupt, and a Jew of Portuguese origin, Martinez de Pasquales, established numerous groups of illuminati in France and gathered a large number of disciples, whom he instructed in the doctrines of reintegration.[234] The lodges which Martinez founded were mystic in character, whereas the other orders of Free Masonry were, on the whole, rationalistic in their teachings. This might almost lead one to say that the secret societies gave expression in a way to the two fold nature of the Jew, on the one hand a rigid rationalism, on the other that pantheism which, beginning as the metaphysical reflection of the belief in one God, often ended in a sort of Kabbalistic theurgy. There would be little difficulty in showing how these two tendencies worked in harmony; how Cazotte,

Cagliostro,[235] Martinez, Saint-Martin, the Comte de Saint Gervais, and Eckartshausen were practically in alliance with the Encyclopaedists and Jacobins, and both, in spite of their seeming hostility, succeeded in arriving at the same end, the under-mining, namely, of Christianity.

This, too, then, would tend to show that though the Jews might very well have been active participants in the agitation carried on by the secret societies, it was not because they were the founders of such associations, but merely because the doctrines of the secret societies agreed so well with their own. The case of Martinez de Pasquales is an exceptionable one, and even with regard to him, it should be remembered that before he became the founder of lodges, Martinez had already been initiated into the mysteries of the illuminati and the Rosicrucians.

During the Revolution the Jews did not remain inactive, considering how few their numbers were in Paris; the position they occupied as district electors, officers of legion, and associate judges, was important. There were eighteen of them in the capital, and one must wade through provincial archives to determine what part they played in affairs. Of these eighteen some even deserve official mention. There was the surgeon Joseph Ravel, member of the General Council of the Commune, who was executed on the ninth Thermidor; Isaac Calmer, President of the Committee of Safety at Clichy, executed on the 29th Messidor, Year II; and Jacob Pereira, who had held the post of commissioner of the Belgian government with the army of Dumouriez, and who as a follower of Hébert, was brought to trial and condemned at the same time as his chief, and was executed on the 4th Germinal, Year II.[236] We have seen how, as followers of Saint Simon, they bought about the economic revolution in which the year 1789 was but a step,[237] the important position occupied by d'Eichthal and Isaac Pereira in the school of Olinde Rodriguez. During the second revolutionary period, which begins in 1830, they displayed even greater ardour than during the first. They were actuated by motives of personal interest, for in the great number of European countries they were not as yet completely emancipated. Those, therefore, who were not revolutionists by temperament or principle, became such through self-interest. In labouring for the triumph of liberalism, they were looking for their own good. It is beyond a doubt that the Jews, through their wealth, their energy and their talents, supported and furthered the progress of the European revolution. During this period Jewish bankers, Jewish manufacturers, Jewish poets, journalists, and orators, stirred perhaps by quite different motives, were, nevertheless, all striving towards the same goal. "With stooping form, unkempt beard, and flashing eye," writes Crétineau-Joly,[238] "they might have been seen breathlessly rushing up and down everywhere in those countries which were unhappy enough to be afflicted with them. Contrary to their usual motives, it was not the desire for wealth that spurred them on to such activity, but rather the thought that Christianity could no longer withstand the repeated shocks which were convulsing society, and they were preparing to wreak on the cross of Calvary revenge for eighteen hundred and forty years of well-deserved suffering."

Nevertheless, it was not such feeling that animated Moses Hess, Gabriel Riesser, Heine, and Boerne in Germany, Manin in Italy, Jellinek in Austria, Lubliner in Poland, and many others besides who fought for liberty in those days. To discover in that all-embracing crusade which agitated Europe until the aftermath of 1848 the work of a few Jews intent on revenging themselves on the Nazarene, argues a remarkable mental attitude. Still, whatever may have been the end pursued, self-interest or idealism, the Jews were the most active, the most zealous of missionaries. We find them taking part in the agitation of Young Germany; large numbers of them were members of the secret societies which constituted the fighting force of the Revolution; they made their way into the Masonic lodges, into the societies of the Carbonari, they were found everywhere in France, in Germany, in England, in Austria, in Italy.

Their contribution to present-day socialism was, as is well known, and still is very great. The Jews, it may be said, are situated at the poles of contemporary society. They are found among the representatives of industrial and financial capitalism, and among those who have vehemently protested against capital. Rothschild is the antithesis of Marx and Lassalle; the struggle for money finds its counterpart in the struggle against money, and the worldwide outlook of the stock-speculator finds its answer in the international proletarian and revolutionary movement. It was Marx who gave the first impulse to the founding of the International through the manifesto of 1847, drawn up by himself and Engels. Not that it can be said that he "founded" the International, as is maintained by those who persist in regarding the International as a secret society controlled by the Jews. Many causes led to the organization of the International, but from Marx proceeded the idea of a Labour Congress, which was held at London in 1864, and resulted in the founding of that society. The Jews constituted a very large proportion of its members, and in the General Council of the society, we find Karl Marx, Secretary for Germany and Russia, and James Cohen, secretary for Denmark.[239] Many of the Jewish members of the International took part subsequently in the Commune,[240] where they found others of their faith. In the organization of the socialistic party, the Jews participated to the greatest extent. Marx and Lassalle in Germany,[241] Aaron Libermann and Adler in Austria, Dobrojan Gherea in Roumania, are or were at one time its creators and its leaders. The Jews of Russia deserve special notice in this brief résumé. Young Jewish students, scarcely escaped from the Ghetto, have played an important part in the Nihilistic propaganda; some, among them women, have given up their lives for the cause of liberation, and to these young Jewish physicians and lawyers, we must add the large number of exiled workingmen who have founded in London and in New York important labour societies, which serve as centres of socialistic and even of anarchistic propaganda.[242]

Thus have I briefly depicted the Jew in his character as a revolutionist, or at least have attempted to show how we might approach the subject. I have described his achievements both as an agent in the dissemination of revolutionary ideas, and as an actual participant in the struggle, and have shown how he belongs to both those who prepare the way for revolution through the activity of the mind, and those who translate thought into action. The objection may be raised that, in joining the ranks of revolution, the Jew as a rule, turns atheist, and ceases practically to be a Jew. This, however, is true only in the sense that the children of the Jewish radical lose themselves more easily in the surrounding population, and that as a result the Jewish revolutionist is more easily assimilated. But as a general thing, the Jew, even the extreme Jewish radical, can not help retaining his Jewish characteristics, and though he may have abandoned all religion and all faith, he has none the less received the impress of the national genius acting through heredity and early training. This is especially true of those Jews who lived during the earlier half of the nineteenth century, and of whom Heinrich Heine and Karl Marx may serve as fitting examples.

Heine, who in France was regarded as a German, and was reproached in Germany with being French, was before all things a Jew. As a Jew he sang the praises of Napoleon, for whom he entertained a fervent admiration common to all the German Jews, who had been freed from their disabilities by the Emperor's will. Heine's disenchantment, his irony, are the disenchantment and the irony of the Ecclesiastes; like Koheleth he bore within him the love for life and for the pleasures of the earth; and before sorrow and disease ground him down death to him was the worst of evils. Heines' mysticism came to him from the ancient Job. The only philosophy that ever really attracted him was pantheism, a doctrine which seems to come naturally to the Jewish philosopher who in speculating upon the unity of God by instinct transforms it into a unity of substance. His sensuousness, that sad and voluptuous sensuousness of the *Intermezzo,* is purely oriental, and has its source in the Song of Songs. The same is true of Marx. The descendant of a long line of rabbis and teachers he inherited the splendid powers of his ancestors. He had that clear Talmudic mind which does not falter at the petty difficulties of fact. He was a Talmudist devoted to sociology and applying his native power of exegesis to the criticism of economic theory. He was inspired by that ancient Hebraic materialism, which, rejecting as too distant and doubtful the hope of an Eden after death, never ceased to dream of Paradise realized on earth. But Marx was not merely a logician, he was also a rebel, an agitator, an acrid controversalist, and he derived his gift for sarcasm and invective, as Heine did, from his Jewish ancestry.

The Jew, therefore, does take an active part in revolutions; and he participates in them in so far as he is a Jew, or more correctly in so far as he remains Jewish. Is it for this reason, then, that the conservative elements among Christians are antisemites, and is this predisposition of the Jews for revolutionary ideas a cause of antisemitism? We may say at once that the great majority of conservatives overlook entirely the historic and educative role of the Jews. It is appreciated only, and that very imperfectly, by the theorists and the literary men among the antisemites. The hatred against Israel does not come from the fact that the Jews were instrumental in bringing about the Terror, or that Manin liberated

Venice, or that Marx organized the International. Antisemitism, the antisemitism of the Christian conservatives, says: "If modern society is so different from the old régime; if religious faith has diminished; if the political system has been entirely changed; if stock-gambling, if speculation, if capital in its industrial and financial forms, knowing no spirit of nationality dominates now and is to dominate in the future, the fault rests with the Jew." Let us clearly examine this point. The Jew has been living for centuries in the midst of those nations which, so it is said, are now perishing on account of his presence. Why, it may be asked, has the poison taken such a long time to work? The usual answer is, because formerly the Jew was outside of society; because he was carefully kept apart. Now that the Jew has entered into society, he has become a source of disorder, and, like the mole, he is busily engaged in undermining the ancient foundations upon which rests the Christian state. And this accounts for the decline of nations, and their intellectual and moral decadence: they are like a human body which suffers from the intrusion of some foreign element which it cannot assimilate and the presence of which brings on convulsions and lasting disease. By his very presence the Jew acts as a solvent; he produces disorders, he destroys, he brings on the most fearful catastrophes. The admission of the Jew into the body of the nations has proved fatal to them; they are doomed for having received him. Such is the very simple explanation which the anti-semites advance to account for the changes which society is undergoing.

The accusation has not been limited to this alone. The Jew, it is said, is not only a destroyer, but also an up-builder; arrogant, ambitious and domineering, he seeks to subject everything to himself. He is not content merely to destroy Christianity, but he preaches the gospel of Judaism; he not only assails the Catholic or the Protestant faith, but he incites to unbelief, and then imposes on those whose faith he has undermined his own conception of the world, of morality and of life. He is engaged in his historic mission, the annihiliation of the religion of Christ. Are the Christian antisemites right or wrong in this respect? Has the Jew retained his ancient notions; is he still in his actions anti-Christian? I say in his actions, because he is necessarily anti-Christian, by definition, in being a Jew, just as he is anti-Mohammedan, just as he is opposed to every principle which is not his own. The answer is that the Jew has retained his ancient animosities precisely where he has been kept outside of society; wherever he herds apart; in the Ghettoes, where he lives under the guidance of his rabbis, who unite with the powers in authority to prevent him from attaining light; everywhere, in fact, where the Talmud still dominates, and especially in eastern Europe where official antisemitism still prevails. In western Europe where the Talmud nowadays has lost its influence and the Jewish *cheder* has given place to the public school, the hereditary hatred of the Jew for the Christian has disappeared in the same proportion as the hatred of the Christian for the Jew. For we must not forget that though we speak frequently of the animosity of the Jew against the Christian, we speak very rarely of the animosity of the Christian against the Jew, a feeling which always thrives. Prejudice against the Jew, or, better still, the numerous prejudices against the Jew are not dead. We find in the publications of the antisemites all the ancient charges, which were brought forward in the Middle Ages, and which the seventeenth century revived, accusations which find support in popular belief. The most persistent of all accusations, however, and the one which typifies best the historic struggle of Judaism against Christianity, is the charge of ritual-murder. The Jew, it is maintained to the present day, has need of Christian blood in order to celebrate his Passover. What is the origin of this accusation which goes back to the twelfth century?

The first instance of such an accusation being brought against the Jews occurred at Blois, in 1171, when they were accused of having crucified a child during their celebration of Passover. Count Theobald of Chartres, after having caused the accuser of the Jews to undergo the ordeal by water, which proved favourable to him, condemned thirty-four Jewish men and seventeen Jewish women to be burnt.

We can see clearly enough why the Romans should have brought the identical charge against the early Christians. It arose from a materialistic conception of the Lord's Supper, from a literal interpretation of the words employed in consecrating the flesh and blood of Jesus. But how could the Jews, whose sacred books breathe forth a horror of blood, have given occasion, and still give occasion, for such a belief? This question must be discussed to the very bottom. We must examine the theories advanced by those who would have it that human sacrifice is a Semitic institution, whereas, as a matter of fact, it is found among all peoples at a certain stage of civilization. In this manner we would prove, as has in fact been proven, that the Jewish religion does not demand blood. Can we, however, prove, in addition, that no Jew ever shed blood? Of course not, and throughout the Middle Ages there must have been Jewish murderers, Jews whom oppression and persecution drove to avenge themselves by assassinating their persecutors or even perhaps their children. To this general belief there were added the accusations, often justified, which were brought against the Jews as being addicted to the practice of magic. Throughout the Middle Ages the Jew was considered by the common people as the magician *par excellence*. As a matter of fact, a number of Jews did devote themselves to magic. We find many formulas of exorcism in the Talmud, and the demonology both of the Talmud and the Kabbala is very complicated. Now it is well known the blood played always a very important part in the arts of sorcery. In Chaldean magic, it was of the utmost consequence; in Persia it was considered as a means of redemption, and it delivered all those who submitted themselevs to the practices of Taurobolus and Kriobolus. The Middle Ages were haunted by the idea of blood as they were haunted by the idea of gold; for the alchemist, for the enchanter blood was the medium through which the astral light could work. The elemental spirits, according to the magicians, utilized outpoured blood in fashioning a body for themselves, and it is in this sense that Paracelsus speaks when he says that "the blood lost by them brought into being phantoms and larvae." To blood, and especially to the blood of a virgin, unheard of powers were assigned. Blood was the curer, the redeemer, the preserver; it was useful in the search for the Philosopher's Stone, in the composition of potions, and in the practice of enchantments. Now it is quite probable, certain, in fact, that Jewish magicians may have sacrificed children, and thence the genesis of ritual murder. The isolated acts of certain magicians were attributed to them in their character as Jews. It was maintained that the Jewish religion which approved of the Crucifixion of Christ, prescribed in addition the shedding of Christian blood; and the Talmud and the Kabbala were zealously searched for text that might be made to justify such a thesis. Such investigations have succeeded only through deliberate misinterpretation, as in the Middle Ages, or through actual falsifications like those recently committed by Dr. Rohling, and proven spurious by Delitzch. The result, therefore, is this, that whatever the facts brought forward, they cannot prove that the murder of children constituted, or still constitutes, a part of the Jewish ritual any more than the acts of the maréchal de Retz and of the sacrilegious priests who practised the "black mass" would prove that the Church recommends in its books assassination and human sacrifice.

Are there still in existence in the East sects maintaining such practices? It is possible. Do Jews constitute a part of such societies? There is nothing to support such a contention. The general accusation of ritual murder, therefore, is shown to be utterly baseless. The murder of children, I speak of cases where murder was actually proved, and these are very rare, can be attributed only to vengeance or to the practices of magicians, practices which were no more peculiar to Jews than to Christians.

Among the nations of the West, the orthodox Jew likewise affords evidences of his conservatism. He holds to the law and to the regulations of society. He knows how to reconcile his Judaism with a spirit of patriotism, which in its excess amounts at times almost to Jingoism. As we have seen, it was only a minority of emancipated Jews who took part in the French Revolution. These emancipated Jews, even though they might abandon their faith, could not for all that cease to be Jews. And, indeed, how could they have done otherwise? By embracing Christianity, it is said, a course of action followed by some, but from which the majority have recoiled, as merely hypocrisy on their part, inasmuch as the emancipated Jew speedily arrives at a state of irreligion. They have therefore remained Jews by apathy. All those revolutionaries of the first half of the nineteenth century, of whom I have spoken, were brought up in Judaism, and if they abandoned Judaism in the sense that they no longer practised it, they remained its adherents in retaining the spirit of their nation.

The emancipated Jew, being no longer bound by the faith of his ancestors, and owning no ties with the old forms of a society in the midst of which he had lived an outcast, has become in modern nations a veritable breeder of revolutions. Now it has happened that the emancipated Jew has drawn perceptibly nearer to the Christian unbeliever; but instead of observing that the Christian has allied himself with the Jew, because he, too, like the Jew, has lost his religion, the antisemites would have us believe that the

Jew, by his very contact, has undermined the faith of the
Christians who have joined him. The Jews, therefore, are made
responsible for the disappearance of religious belief, and the
general decay of faith; and in doing so, moreover, the antisemite
does not distinguish between the Jew who is still faithful to his
religion and the emancipated Jew. To the impartial observer, however, it is not the Jew that is destroying Christianity. The
Christian religion is disappearing like the Jewish religion, like all
religions, which we may now observe in their slow agony. It is
passing away under the blows of reason and of science. It is dying
a natural death, because it essentially was in harmony with only
one period of civilization, and because the further we advance,
the less in harmony it is with changing conditions. From day to day
our yearning for the irrational and our need of the supernatural
is disappearing, and with them our need for religion, especially for
the rites of religion: for those even who believe in God, do not
believe in the necessity nor in the efficacy of worship.

These, then, in brief, are the political and religious mainsprings
of antisemitism. First and fundamental are hereditary dislike and
prejudice; then, as a result of these prejudices, an exaggerated
conception of the role which the Jews have played in the development and organization of modern society; a conception in which
the Jews appear as the representatives of the revolutionary spirit,
against the spirit of established order; of change against tradition;
a conception which makes them responsible in this age of transition for the fall of antiquated institutions and the disappearance of
ancient beliefs.

The nineteenth century witnessed the last effort on the part of
the Christian state to retain its dominance. Antisemitism represents
one phase of the struggle between the feudal state, based upon unity
of belief, and the opposite notion of a neutral and secular state,
upon which the greater number of political entities are at present
based. The Jew is the living testimony of the disappearance of that
state which had its foundations in theological principles and the
restoration of which is the dream of the Christian antisemite. The
day when the Jew was first admitted to civil rights the Christian
state was in danger. This is true, and the antisemites who say that
the Jews have destroyed the idea of State could more justly say that
the entrance of the Jew into society marked the destruction of the
State, meaning by State, the Christian State.

FOURTEEN

THE ECONOMIC CAUSES OF ANTISEMITISM

AFTER being assailed as a Semite, as a stranger, as a revolutionist, as an enemy to Christianity, the Jew is attacked as a factor in economic affairs. This has been the case ever since the dispersion. Already before our era the Romans and the Greeks were jealous of the privileges which permitted the Jews to carry on trade under more favourable conditions than the rest of the people,[243] and during the Middle Ages the usurer was hated as much as, if not more than, the murderer of Christ.[244] The condition of the Jews was changed at the end of the eighteenth century; and so favourable was the change to them that it tended to confirm, if not to increase, the feeling of antipathy with which they were regarded. Economic antisemitism to-day is stronger than it ever was, for the reason that to-day, more than ever, the Jew appears powerful and rich. Formerly he was not seen: he remained hidden in his Ghetto, far from Christian eyes. He had but one care, to conceal his wealth, that wealth of which tradition regarded him as the gatherer, and not the proprietor. The day he was freed from his disabilities, the day the restrictions put to his activities fell away, the Jew showed himself in public. Indeed, he showed himself with ostentation. He wished, after centuries of imprisonment, after years of oppression, to appear a man; and he had the naive vanity of the savage. That was his way of re-acting upon centuries of humiliation. On the eve of the French Revolution, they saw him humble, timid, an object of general contempt, exposed to insult and injury. They found him after the tempest, free, liberated from every constraint, and from a slave, become a master. Such a rapid exaltation was offensive. People were affronted by the wealth which the Jews had now attained the right to pile up, and recourse was had at once to the old accusation of the fathers, the charge that the Jew was an enemy to society. The wealth of the Jew, it was said, is gained at the expense of the Christian. It is acquired through deception, through fraud, through oppression, by all means and principally by detestable means. This is what I shall call the moral charge of the antisemites, and it may be summed up thus: the Jew is more dishonest than the Christian; he is entirely unscrupulous, a stranger to loyalty and candour.

Is this charge well founded? It was true and still is true in all those countries where the Jew is kept outside of society; where he receives only the traditional Talmudic education; where he is exposed to persecution, to insult, and to oppression; where people refuse to recognize in him the dignity and the independence of the human being. The moral condition of the Jew is due partly to himself, and partly to exterior circumstances. His soul has been moulded by the law which he imposed on himself, and the law which has been forced upon him. Throughout the centuries he lived twice a slave: he was the bondman of the law, and the bondman of everyone. He was a pariah, but a pariah whom teachers and guides united to keep in a state of servitude more complete than the ancient bondage of Egypt. From without a thousand restrictions impeded his way, arrested his development, restrained his activity; within he was confronted by an elaborate system of prohibitions. Outside the Ghetto he experienced the constraint of the law; within the Ghetto he suffered the oppression of the Talmud. If he attempted to escape from the one, a thousand punishments awaited him; if he ventured to depart from the other, he exposed himself to the *Cherem,* that awful excommunication which left him alone to the world. It would have been vain to attack these two hostile powers boldly; and therefore the Jew attempted to triumph over them by guile. Both forms of oppression developed in him the instinct of cunning. He attained to an unequalled talent for diplomacy, to a subtelty rarely found. His natural finesse increased, but it was employed for base purposes—to deceive a tyrannical God and despotic rulers. The Talmud and anti-Judaic legislation united to corrupt the Jew to his very depths. Impelled by his teachers, on the one hand, by hostile legislation on the other, by many social causes besides,[245] to the exclusive occupation of commerce and of usury, the Jew became degraded. The pursuit of wealth ceaselessly prosecuted, debauched him, weakened the voice of conscience within him, taught him habits of fraud. In this war of self-preservation which he was forced to carry on against the world and against the secular and religious law, he could conquer only by intrigue, and the unhappy wretch, given over to humiliations, to insults, forced to bow his head under blows and curses and persecution, could avenge himself on his enemies, his tormentors, his executioners only by guile. Robbery and bad faith became his weapons; they were the only weapons of which he could possibly make use, and therefore he exerted himself to elaborate them, to sharpen them, and to conceal them.

When the walls of the Ghetto were overthrown, the Jew, such as he had been made by the Talmud and the legislative and social restrictions imposed upon him, did not change all at once. Upon the morrow of the Revolution he lived just as he had lived upon its eve, nor did he alter his customs, his manners, and, above all, his spirit, as quickly as his condition in life had been altered. Liberated, he retained the soul of a slave, that soul which he is losing day by day as one by one the memories of his degradation are disappearing.

I have already shown how in the course of time the bourgeoisie found in the Jew a powerful and marvellously endowed ally. During long centuries, while society was still plunged in the barbarism of the Middle Ages, the Jew, the trader of old, well armed, well provided with a fine mental equipment, and rich in the possession of ages of experience, was either the representative of capital as employed in commerce and in usury, or else aided in its creation. Nevertheless, these forms of capital did not attain their greatest influence until the labour of centuries had prepared the way for their domination and had transformed them into industrial and bonded capital. To accomplish this Capital needed those two great movements, the Crusades and the discovery of America, followed by the manifold colonial enterprises of Spain, of Portugal, of the Netherlands, of England, and of France, all the activity, in fact, of the age of commercial development. It needed the establishment of public credit and the rise of great banking institutions. It needed the rise of manufactures and the scientific discoveries which brought about the invention and the perfection of machinery. It needed all the elaborate legislation looking towards the restriction of the labourer's rights and wages, until the moment came when the proletariat was deprived even of the right of association; it needed all that and many other causes besides, causes historic, religious and moral, in order to make present-day society what it is.

Those who maintain that the Jews are the sole cause of the present state of things succeed only in establishing their own absurdly marvellous ignorance.

Of course, as I have just said, the part played by the Jews in the development of modern society, was important, but its true character is very little known, or, at least, very imperfectly known, and that especially to the antisemites. It is not to this very elementary knowledge of the economic history of the Jews that antisemitism must be attributed. Our knowledge of the Jews since their emancipation is more complete; in France, under the Restoration and the July Monarchy, they stood at the head of the financial and industrial enterprise, and were among the founders of the great canal, railway and insurance companies. In Germany their activity was exceedingly great. They were at the bottom of all the legislation favourable to the carrying on of banking and exchange, the practice of usury and speculation. It was they who profited by the abolition, in 1867, of the ancient laws limiting the rate of interest. They were active in bringing about the enactment of the law of June 1870, which exempted stock companies from government supervision. After the Franco-German War, they were among the boldest speculators, and at a time when German capitalists were carried away by a passion for the creation of industrial combinations, they acted a no less important part than had the Jews of France, from 1830 to 1848.[246] Their activity persisted until the financial panic of 1873, when the country squires and the small traders who had been ruined by the excesses of this *Gründer Periode* (the era of promoters) in which the Jew had played the most important part, gave themselves up to the most violent antisemitism, such, indeed, as proceeds only from injured interests.

Once the important part played by the Jews of this period had been proven, and, indeed, their importance was undeniable, people proceeded to the conclusion that the Jew was the possessor of capital *par excellence*. This became an added cause of hatred against him. The Jews, it was asserted, held everything, and the word Jew, after having been a synonym for knave, malefactor and usurer, came to be used as equivalent to rich. Every Jew is a capitalist; such is the common belief. The error of course is deep.

There remain, about two million Jews in Western Europe and in the United States, who may be said to belong to the middle class. Of these two millions, however, it must be admitted that if they were of very little importance a hundred years ago, they are of very great importance to-day. Through their wealth, through their education, through their relations to one another, they occupy a place far out of proportion to their numbers. Compared with the general body of the population they are but a handful, and yet their position in life is such that they are to be seen everywhere, and in number seem to be legion. It is true that we must avoid the common error of comparing them with the total population of any country, inasmuch as they do not generally live outside of towns, but confine themselves to the cities where they play a correspondingly important part. If we would arrive at some exact statistical basis we must compare them to the Christian population of their own class, that is, to the bourgeoisie of commerce, industry and finance. And yet even when we reduce the comparison to these two factors, the Jew versus the bourgeoisie, it is still in favour of the Jew. Wherefore, then, this preponderance? Some Jews are in the habit of ascribing their economic supremacy to their intellectual superiority. This boast of Jewish superiority is not altogether true, or, at least, requires explanation. In the present bourgeois society, which is founded upon the exploitation of capital and upon exploitation by capital, where the power of wealth is supreme, where stock-jobbing and speculation are all-powerful, the Jew is certainly better equipped for success than any other body. Though he may have been degraded by his exclusive devotion to commerce through the ages, his experience has nevertheless endowed him with certain qualities which have become of surpassing value in the new organization of society. He is cold and calculating, supple and energetic, persevering and patient, clear and exact, qualities which he has inherited all from his ancestors, the money changers and traders of mediaeval times. When he devotes himself to commerce or to finance, he naturally profits by the education which his ancestors have undergone through centuries, an education which has rendered him, perhaps, not more suited for certain pursuits as his vanity suggests, but certainly more adaptable to them. In the present industrial struggle, he is better endowed, man for man—I am speaking in general terms—than his competitors, and all things being equal, he must suceed because of his superior equipment. He has no need to make use of fraud, or, at least, to make more use of it than his neighbours, since his personal and inherited qualities are sufficient to assure him the victory.

Still the possession of such personal gifts is not sufficient to explain the preponderance of the Jews. Among the Christians, too, there are ancient merchant families; a section of the bourgeoisie has inherited qualities very similar to those of the Jews, and therefore it would seem, should be able to challenge the Jews successfully. The answer is that there are other, farther reaching causes, arising both from the nature of the Jew and from the character of modern society. Bourgeois society is based entirely upon competition between man and man in the field of the daily necessities of life. It affords us the spectacle of individuals fighting bitterly one against the other, of isolated units stubbornly disputing the victory and making use of their own individual resources. In this state of society Darwin's principle of the struggle of life dominates. This spirit governs the actions of every man, and tacitly it is recognized that victory ought to belong to the strongest, to him, that is, who is best equipped, whose body and whose spirit are most perfectly adjusted to the social conditions of existence. If we conceive, then, in the midst of such a community, based upon egoistic action, associations of citizens strongly organized and gifted, animated for many centuries by the spirit of common action, and knowing by instinct and experience, the advantages which they may derive from union, it is certain that such organizations by directing their activity towards the same end as that pursued by the scattered individuals around them will possess such an advantage in the struggle as to assure them an easy victory. This is just the role which is being played by the Jews of the middle class in modern society. They are desirous of winning the same prizes of life as the Christian; they enter the same field of battle; they have the same ambitions; they are just as keen, just as greedy, just as hungry for wealth, just as foreign to any form of justice that is not the justice of their caste, or that does not defend them against the classes they hold in subjection; they are, to sum up, just as immoral at bottom as the Christian in the sense that they consider only the advantages which they may obtain for themselves, and that the sole ambition of their lives is the acquisition of material goods, of which each hopes and strives to obtain the maximum. But in this daily struggle, the Jew, who, personally, as we have already seen, is better endowed than his competitors, increases his advantage by uniting with his co-religionists possessed of similar virtues, and thus augments his powers by acting in common with his brethren; the inevitable result being that they out-distance their rivals in the pursuit of any common end. In the midst of a disunited middle class, whose members are engaged in a perpetual struggle against one another, the Jews stand united as one. This is the secret of their success. Their solidarity is all the stronger in that it goes so far back. Its very existence is denied, and yet it is un-deniable. The links in the chain have been forged in the course of ages until the flight of centuries has made man unconscious of their existence. It is worth our while to see how this bond of union was formed and how it was perpetuated.

Jewish solidarity dates from the Dispersion. Jewish emigrants and colonists took up their residence in foreign countries, and wherever they made their home they constituted a distinct society. Their communities centred around their houses of prayer, which they built in every town where they formed a nucleus. Everywhere they possessed numerous important privileges (see Chapters II and III.). The Diasporoi were invaluable allies of the Greeks in carrying on the work of eastern colonization, and strangely enough the Jews who adopted Hellenism, assisted in turn in Hellenizing the East. As a recompense they were allowed to retain their national homogeneity, together with full powers of self-government. This was the case in Alexandria, in Antioch, in Asia Minor, and in the Greek cities of Ionia. In almost every city they constituted corpora-tions at the head of which was an ethnarch or patriarch, who, with the assistance of a council of leaders and a special tribunal, exercised all the powers of civil authority and of justice. The synagogues were "veritable small republics." They were, in addi-tion, the centres of religious and public life. The Jews came together in their synagogues, not only to listen to the reading of the Law, but also for the discussion of their private affairs and for the purpose of exchanging views upon the general course of events. All the synagogues were closely connected in a vast federa-tion which included within its scope the entire ancient world, progressing parallel with the expansion of the Macedonian power and Hellenistic civilization. They communicated with one another by messengers and kept one another in constant touch with events, the knowledge of which was likely to prove useful. In every city the Jewish traveller could count upon the aid of the community;

when he arrived as an immigrant or as a settler, he was received as a brother, succoured in his need and assisted in his designs, he was permitted to take up his home wherever he desired and he enjoyed the protection of the community which put all its resources at his disposal. He did not come as a stranger bound upon a difficult conquest, but as one well equipped and with protectors, friends, and brothers by his side. Throughout Asia Minor, the Archipelago, Cyrenaica and Egypt, a Jew might travel in perfect security; everywhere he was treated as a guest, everywhere he proceeded straight to the house of prayer, where he was sure to find a welcome. The Essenes carried on their propaganda in the same manner. They, too, created their little social centres, little associations in the very heart of the Jewish communities, and in this fashion they travelled from city to city, at their own free will taking no thought of the morrow.

At Rome, where they lived in considerable numbers,[247] the Jews were as firmly united as in the cities of the Orient. "They are bound together by indissoluble bonds by the ties of loving sympathy," says Tacitus.[248] Thanks to their solidarity, they had acquired at Rome, as in Alexandria, such power that political parties feared them and sought their support. "You know," says Cicero,[249] "how great is the multitude of the Jews, how firm their union and their sympathy, how striking their political skill and their sway over the crowd in the assemblies."

When the Roman Empire fell, when the barbarian hosts invaded the ancient world, and triumphant Catholicism entered upon its career of expansion, the Jewish communities did not change. They were still powerful organisms and the activity of their common life was such as to lend them great powers of resistance. In the midst of the universal upheaval they preserved their religious and social unity, two inseparable bonds to which they owe their prosperity. The members of the Jewish synagogues drew still more closely together. It was owing to this mutual support that they suffered nothing from the great changes that were going on about them. For some time, even after the Gothic and German kingdoms had been established Jewish communities preserved a certain degree of self-government. They were placed under a special jurisdiction and in the midst of those new societies they constituted veritable trading corporations in which none of the ancient solidarity was wanting. In proportion as the nations became more hostile to the

Jews, in proportion as persecution and oppressive legislation increased, their solidarity increased. The external and internal forces which tended to imprison the Jews within the narrow circumference of their Ghettoes, only served to foster the spirit of union among them. Isolated from the world, they only tightened the bonds which held them together. Their common life nourished the desire for, and the need of, fraternal action. In other words, the Ghettoes developed the spirit of Jewish solidarity. In addition, the synagogues had succeeded in preserving their authority, so that while the Jews were subject to the harsh laws of king and of emperor, they had also a government of their own, councils of elders, and tribunals, to whose decisions they submitted. Their general synods forbade, in fact, any Jew under the pain of anathema, from citing a fellow Jew before a Christian tribunal.[250] Everything drove them to unity in those long years of horror and cruelty known as the Middle Ages. Had they been disunited they would have suffered still more. By common action they could defend themselves the more easily and escape some of the calamities that threatened them without end. In the eleventh century a Rabbinical synod at Worms, forbade a Jewish landlord to rent out his house, occupied by a Jew, to a Gentile without the consent of the tenant[251] and a council of the twelfth century forbade a Jew, under the pain of anathema, to bring a fellow Jew before a Christian tribunal. The Jewish community, or Kahal, made use of a powerful weapon against those who proved themselves lacking in the spirit of solidarity; it struck them with anathema and pronounced against them the *Cherem Hakahal* (the ban of the community).

In this manner, the action of time, the influence of hostile legislation and of religious persecution, and the need for mutual defence, have intensified the feeling of fellowship among the Jews. In our own day the powerful institution of the Kahal exerts its influence wherever the Jew is subjected to a rigorous regime, and even the reformed Jew, who has broken away from the narrow restrictions of the synagogue, and yields no obedience to the will of the community, has not forgotten the spirit of solidarity.[252] Once having acquired the sentiment of union and fostered it by the habit of ages, they could not get rid of it in getting rid of their faith. It had become a social instinct, and social instincts, slowly formed, are slow to disappear. A Jew will always obtain assistance from his co-religionists, provided he be found faithful to the ties of Jewish brotherhood; but, if on the contrary, he prove hostile to the sentiment of Jewish unity, he will meet with nothing but hostility. The Jew, even though he may have departed from the synagogue, is still a member of the Jewish free-masonry,[253] of the Jewish clique, if you will.

United, then, by the strongest feelings of solidarity, the Jews can easily hold their own in this disjointed and anarchic society of ours. If the millions of Christians by whom they are surrounded were to substitute this same principle of co-operation for that of individual competition, the importance of the Jew would immediately be destroyed. The Christian, however, will not adopt such a course, and the Jew must inevitably, I will not say dominate, the favourite expression of the antisemites, but certainly possess the advantage over others, and exercise that supremacy against which the antisemites inveigh, without being able to destroy it, seeing that its reason lies not only in the middle class among the Jews, but in the Christian bourgeoisie as well.

If we keep in mind, then, this conception of Jewish fellowship and the fact that the Jews at present, constitute an organized minority, we are not unjust in concluding that antisemitism is, in part, a mere struggle among the rich, a contest among the possessors of capital. In truth, it is the capitalist, the merchant, the manufacturer, the financier, among the Christians, who feels himself injured by the Jews, and not the Christian proletariat, who suffer no more from the class of Jewish employers than from their Christian masters; less, indeed, if we consider that in a case like this, where numbers count, the entrepreneur class among the Jews by comparison with the Christians amounts to little. This will explain why antisemitism is essentially the sentiment of the middle classes, and why it is so rarely met with, except in the form of a vague prejudice among the mass of the peasants and the working classes.

This war within the ranks of capital does not reveal itself after the same fashion; it presents rather two aspects, according as it arises from the hostility between the landowning class and the capitalist class in the narrower sense, or from competition within the industrial class itself.

The agrarian capitalist, in his contest against the captain of industry, has embraced antisemitism, because to the territorial lord, the Jew is the representative of commercial and industrial capitalism. For this reason, in Germany, the Agrarian Protectionists, are bitter enemies of the Jews, who are among the most conspicuous champions of free trade. By instinct and self-interest the Jews are opposed to the physiocratic theory which would vest political power only in the owners of land; they maintain rather the theory of modern industrialism, which makes political power go hand in hand with industrial development. Jews and Agrarians both are probably unconscious, as individuals, of the part they are playing in the economic struggle, but their mutual hatred comes from this source, nevertheless. The man of the lower middle class, the small tradesman whom speculation has probably ruined has much clearer ideas of why he is an antisemite. He knows that reckless speculation, with its attendant panics, has been his bane, and for him, the most formidable jugglers of capital, the most dangerous speculators are the Jews; which, indeed, is very true. Those even whose downfall has not been caused by speculation, ascribe their misfortunes indirectly to this cause which has destroyed a great part of the industrial and commercial capital of the world. But here, as everywhere, they make the Jew responsible for a state of things, of which he is far from being the sole cause.

The other form of economic antisemitism is more simple. It arises from the direct competition between Jewish and Christian brokers, manufacturers, and merchants. The Christian capitalist, acting for the most part, independently of his fellows, when confronted by the harmonious, if not united, opposition of the Jewish capitalists, finds himself necessarily at a disadvantage, and in the daily struggle for life frequently succumbs to his adversaries. He, therefore, suffers directly, from the rise of Jewish manufacturers and merchants. Hence his extreme animosity against the Jews, and the desire to break the power of his fortunate rivals. This is the most violent, the most bitter of all the manifestations of antisemitism, because it is the expression of the sentiments of those who feel themselves injured in their personal interests.

This prejudice against the Jews has prevailed to the present day, secret, instinctive rather than deliberate, and acquired by heredity. People still feel an intense bitterness against the deicides, and glance with no favourable eye at their riches, for they still find it difficult to understand how this tribe of miscreants and murderers, doomed to perdition, can legitimately be the owners of wealth.

The belief is still held that the Jew cannot acquire wealth without plundering the sons of the soil—every owner of land looking upon himself as its child. If economic antisemitism therefore must be regarded as the manifestation of a struggle within the ranks of capital, we must not forget, too, that it is an outcome of the opposition between national and foreign wealth.

FIFTEEN

THE FATE OF ANTISEMITISM

WE have seen then that the causes of antisemitism are, in their nature, ethnic, religious, political and economic. They are all causes of far reaching importance, and they exist not because of the Jew alone, nor because of his neighbours alone, but principally because of prevailing social conditions. Ignorant of the real cause of their sentiments, those who profess antisemitism, justify their opinion by accusations against the Jew which, as we have seen, do not at all agree with facts. Charges racial, charges religious, charges political and economic, none of these grievances of antisemitism are well founded. Some, like the ethnic grievance arise from a false conception of race; others like the religious and political charges, are due to a narrow and incomplete interpretation of historical evolution; and last of all, the economic count, has its justification in the necessity of concealing the strife going on within the capitalist class. None of these accusations is justified. It is no more correct to say that the Jew is a pure Semite than it would be to say that the European peoples are pure Aryans.

Still though the Jews are not a race, they were, until our own days, a nation. They did not fail to perpetuate their national characteristics, their religion and their theological code, which was at the same time a social code. Though they were never guilty of working for the destruction of Christianity, and were never organized in a secret conspiracy against Jesus, they did lend aid to those who assailed the Christian religion, and in all attacks on the Church, they were ever in the front rank. In the same way, even if they did not constitute a vast secret society, implacably pursuing through the centuries as its object, the undermining of monarchy, they did render important aid to the cause of Revolution. In the nineteenth century they were among the most ardent adherents of the liberal, social, and revolutionary parties, to which they contributed men like Lasker and Disraeli, Crémieux, Marx and Lasalle, not counting the obscure herd of agitators. To the revolutionary cause, too, they contributed their wealth. Finally, as I have just said, if they did not, by themselves, erect the throne of triumphant capitalism on the ruins of the old regime they were instrumental in its erection. Thus are the Jews found at the opposite poles of modern society. On the one hand they labour assiduously at that enormous concentration of wealth, which, no doubt, is bound to result in its expropriation by the State; on the other hand, they are among the most bitter foes of capital. Opposed to the Jewish money baron, the product of exile, of Talmudism, of hostile legislation and persecution, stands the Jewish revolutionist, the child of biblical and prophetic tradition, that same tradition which animated the fanatic Anabaptists of Germany in the sixteenth century, and the Puritan warriors of Cromwell. In the midst of the many transformations which our age has witnessed, they have not remained inactive; indeed, it is their activity which has, I will not say caused, but rather perpetuated, antisemitism, for antisemitism is but the successor of the anti-Judaism of the Middle Ages. Long ago, in Spain, the persecution of the Moriscoes and the Marranos was an attempt to eliminate a foreign element in the Spanish nation; and in the same way the Jews were regarded as a strange tribe, a horde of deicides, whose aim was by propaganda to infuse their spirit into the Christian peoples, and in addition, to obtain possession of great wealth, the importance of which was becoming apparent even during the early years of the Mediæval period. Antisemitism, at present, finds different expression from that of former times; the charges brought against the Jew have also varied, in that they are formulated after a different fashion and are given a basis of ethnologic and anthropologic theory; but the causes have not altered appreciably, and modern antisemitism differs from the anti-Judaism of former times only in that it is more self-conscious, more pragmatic, and more deliberate. At the bottom of the antisemitism of our own days, as at the bottom of the anti-Judaism of the thirteenth century are the fear of, and the hatred for, the stranger. This is the primal cause of all anti-semitism, the never failing cause. It appears in Alexandria under the Ptolemies, in Rome during the lifetime of Cicero, in the Greek cities of Ionia, in Antioch, in Cyrenaica, in feudal Europe, and in the modern state whose soul is the spirit of nationality.

Let us leave now this old anti-Judaism and concern ourselves only with the antisemitism of modern times. A product of the spirit of national exclusiveness and of a reaction on the part of the conservative spirit against the tendencies set into motion by the Revolution, all the causes which have brought it about, or have served to maintain it, may be reduced to this one only: the Jews are not as yet assimilated; that is to say, they have not yet given up their belief in their own nationality. By the practice of circumcision, by the observation of their special rules of prayer and their dietary regulations, they still continue to differentiate themselves from those around them; they persist in being Jews. Not that they are incapable of the sentiment of patriotism—the Jews in certain countries, as in Germany, have contributed more than anybody else to the realization of national unity—but they seem to solve the apparently unsolvable problem of constituting an integral part of two nationalities; if they are Frenchmen, or if they are Germans, they are also Jews.

Why is this so? Because everything has contributed to maintain their peculiar characteristics as a people; because they have been the possessors of a religion which is national in character, and which had its perfect reason for existence while the Jews constituted a people, but which ceased to be of service after the Dispersion and now tends only to keep them apart from the rest of the world; because all over Europe they have established colonies jealous of their prerogatives, and clinging firmly to their customs, to their religious practices, to their manners of life; because they have been living for ages under the domination of a theological code, which has rendered them immobile; because the laws of the numerous countries in which they have made their abode, together with prejudice and persecution, have prevented them from mingling with the body of the people; because since the second exodus, since their departure, that is, from Palestine, they have raised around themselves, and others have raised around them rigid and insurmountable barriers. Such as they are they are the result of a slow process of creation, on their own part, and on the part of others: their intellectual and moral life is what it is, because others made it their object to differentiate the Jews from the world, and the Jews themselves devoted themselves to the same object. They feared defilement through contact, and they were feared in turn as a source of defilement. Their doctors forbade them to unite with the Christians, and the Christian lawmakers forbade all union with the Jews. Of their own impulse they devoted themselves to the occupation of money-changing, and they were forbidden to exercise any other profession than that; of their own accord, they separated themselves from the world, and they were forced by others to remain in the Ghettoes.

Here we find ourselves confronted with a most serious objection. The antisemites are not content with saying that the Jew belongs to a different race, and is therefore a stranger, but they declare that he is by nature an element which can never be assimilated; and even if some of them admit that the Jew may become a constituent part in the composition of nations, they would have it that such an amalgamation is only detrimental to that nation. The Semite, it is maintained, saps the strength of and destroys the Aryan, and this in spite of the antisemitic theory that the superior race is bound to overcome the inferior race without being in the least affected by it. Are the Jews then incapable of assimilation? Not the least in the world, and their entire history proves the contrary. It shows us[254] how large is the number of Jews who have become mixed with the other nations through baptism, how numerous were their conversions in the Middle Ages; how many Jews have been absorbed by the surrounding population, going over of their own free will to Christ, or driven to the baptismal font by the violence of monks and fanatical kings. Jews, in short, of whom we can no longer find any trace, just as we can no longer find any traces of the Goths, the Alamani and the Suevi, who with many other peoples united to form the French nation. At all times the Jew, like all Semites, has been in touch with the Aryan; at all times there has been inter-communication between the two races, and nothing can serve better to prove that their assimilation is possible. If we find certain resemblances between the Spanish Jew and the Jew of Russia[255] we find also marked differences, and these differences are due not only to the absorption of other races, attracted and converted by the Jew, but are the result also of the Jew's natural environment, social, moral, and intellectual. The Jewish type has varied not only geographically, but has changed through time; it is a truism that the Jew of the Roman Ghetto was not the same as the Jew who fought under Bar-Cochba, just as the Jew of our great European cities does not resemble the Jew of the Middle Ages. The Jew has been no exception to this law of human evolution, and it is not the snows of Poland, or the burning suns of Spain that have been the principal factors in his development. He has been reduced to a state of petrifaction by the hostile laws of the nations in which he lived, and by his religion, a puissant and fearful religion, like all non-metaphysical religions which are characterized predominantly by a ritual and a Law. For the Jew this religion and this Law have always been the same, in all times and all places. They have been constant forces in his development, both externally and internally.

But during the last hundred years, these seemingly constant factors have undoubtedly undergone a change.[256] There are no longer external legislative restrictions on the Jew; the special laws to which he was formerly subjective have been abolished, and henceforth, he is amenable only to the laws of the country of which he is a citizen (and these laws, let me remark, differing with every country constitute in themselves a factor of differentiation for the Jew). With the disappearance of discriminating laws, his own peculiar laws have also disappeared. The Jew no longer lives apart, but shares in the common life; is no longer a stranger to the civilization of the countries which have received him; has no longer a literature of his own; nor manners that mark him as different from others. In short, he has adapted himself to the mode of life of whatever nation he adheres to. And as these modes of life differ from nation to nation, they serve to create marked differences among the Jews themselves, with the progress of time creating more and more striking variety among them. Day by day they are departing from the class of occupations and the type of religion peculiar to the Jew.

Still more important, however, is the fact that the Talmudic spirit is slowly vanishing. Such schools of the Talmud as still exist in Western Europe are disappearing day by day: the modern Jew is not even able to read Hebrew; freed from the bonds of the rabbinical code, the synagogue of the present day professes at most a sort of ceremonial deism, and deism itself is losing its strength with the modern Jew, making every reformed Jew ready for rationalism. Nor is it only Talmudism that is dying, but the Jewish religion itself is in its death agony. It is the oldest of all existing religions, and it would seem right that it should be the first to disappear. Direct contact with the Christian world has started it upon its course of dissolution. For a long time it has endured as all bodies endure which are deprived of light and air: but once a breach is made in the cavern in which it has been sleeping, the sun and the fresh breath of the outside air have entered and it has

fallen apart. Together with the Jewish religion, the Jewish spirit
is vanishing. True it is that that was the spirit which animated
Heine and Boerne, Marx and Lassalle, but they were still the
products of the Jewry; they were cradled in traditions which the
young Jews of to-day overlook or despise. At the present time, if
there is still such a thing as Jewish personality, it tends to
disappear. What religious persecution could not bring about, the
decline of religious faith, based upon national ideal has accomplished. The emancipated Jew, freed alike from hostile legislation
and obscurant Talmudism, far from being an element to absorb
others, has become an element that can be readily absorbed. In
certain countries, as in the United States, the distinction between
Jews and Christians is rapidly disappearing.[257] It is vanishing from
day to day, because from day to day the Jews are abandoning their
ancient prejudices, their peculiar modes of worship, the observance of their special laws of prayer and their dietary regulations.
They no longer persist in the belief that they are destined always
to remain a people; they no longer dream—a touching dream,
perhaps, but ridiculous—that they have an eternal mission to
fulfill. The time will come when they shall be completely eliminated; when they shall be merged into the body of the nations, after
the same manner as the Phoenicians, who, having planted their
trading stations all over Europe disappeared without leaving a
trace behind them. By that time, too, antisemitism will have run
its course. The moment, to be sure, is not near; the number of
orthodox Jews is still great, and as long as they exist it would seem
that antisemitism must exist.

If Judaism, then, is in the process of dissolution, neither is
Catholicism or Protestantism gaining in strength, and we may
venture to say that every external form of religion is losing its
influence. On the one hand, we are advancing towards a narrow
and stupid materialism, opposed to all religious feeling; on the
other, our way is towards a state of philosophic and moral un-
religion which shall be "a degree higher than religion or civilization
itself."[258] At the same time while these tendencies are increasing,
religious prejudice is tending to disappear, and the prejudice of
Christian against Jew, and of Jew against Christian, persistent, in
its way, as the prejudice of the Catholic against the Protestant,
cannot possibly be the only one to remain. Even now it is decreasing in intensity, and the time is near, no doubt, when every Jew

will no longer be held responsible for the sufferings of Jesus on Calvary. With the steady extinction of religious animosities, one of the causes of antisemitism must disappear, and antisemitism itself must lose much of its violence, though exist it will, so long as the economic and ethnic causes which have made it, endure.

The spirit of national egotism and self-sufficiency, however strong it may be at present is also showing signs of decay. Other ideas have arisen, which from day to day are gaining in influence; they enter into the spirits of men, they impress themselves upon their understanding, they engender new conceptions and new forms of thought. The brotherhood of nations which formerly was a mere chimera, may be dreamt of now, without transcending the limits of common sense. The sentiment of human solidarity is growing stronger; and the number of thinkers and writers who labour at furthering its growth is increasing from day to day. The nations are coming into closer touch, and are learning to know one another better, admire one another, love one another. Increased facilities of communication tend to favour the development of the cosmo-politan spirit, and this spirt of cosmopolitanism will unite one day the most diverse of races in a peaceful Federation of definite entities, substituting universal altruism for selfish patriotism. The Jews are bound to profit by this decline of national exclusiveness, in that it must coincide with the partial elimination of their own peculiar characteristics. The progress of internationalism must bring about the decay of antisemitism. Parallel with the decline of national prejudices the Jews will witness the economic causes of antisemitism losing their force. At present the Jews are assailed as the representatives of foreign wealth. It is therefore just to suppose that when the animosity against things foreign shall have dis-appeared, Jewish capital will no longer be an object of attack for Christian capital. Competition will, of course, persist in spite of all this, and those Jews who persist in maintaining their national identity, will always remain the objects of an hostility based upon this competitive struggle.

Other events, however, and other changes may bring about the disappearance of these economic causes. In the struggle which is now on between the proletariat and the industrial and financial classes, we shall possibly see Jewish and Christian capitalists forgetting their differences to unite against a common enemy. If present social conditions persist, however, such a union of the

Christian and Jewish bourgeoisie can only bring about a temporary truce. From the battle which must inevitably be fought out, the indications are that Capital cannot come out the victor. Founded upon egoism, upon selfishness, upon injustice, upon lies, and upon theft, our present society is doomed to disappear. However brilliant it may appear, however resplendent, refined, luxurious, magnificent, it is striken with death. It has been weighed morally and found wanting. The bourgeoisie which exercises all political power because it holds control of all economic agencies, will draw upon its resources in vain; in vain will it appeal to all the armies that defend it, to all the tribunals of justice that watch over it, to all the legal codes that protect it; it will not be able to withstand the inflexible laws which day by day are working towards the substitution of communal property for the capitalistic régime.

Everything is tending to bring about such a consummation. Such is the irony of things that antisemitism which everywhere is the creed of the conservative class, of those who accuse the Jews of having worked hand in hand with the Jacobins of 1789 and the Liberals and Revolutionists of the nineteenth century, this very antisemitism is acting, in fact, as an ally of the Revolution. Drumont in France, Pattai in Hungary, Stoecker and von Boeckel in Germany are co-operating with the very demagogues and revolutionists whom they believe they are attacking. This antisemitic movement, in its origin reactionary, has become transformed and is acting now for the advantage of the revolutionary cause. Antisemitism stirs up the middle class, the small tradesmen, and sometimes the peasant, against the Jewish capitalist, but in doing so it gently leads them toward Socialism, prepares them for anarchy, infuses in them a hatred for all capitalists, and, more than that, for capital in the abstract. And thus, unconsciously, antisemitism is working its own ruin, for it carries in itself the germ of destruction.

Such, then, is the probable fate of modern antisemitism. I have tried to show how it may be traced back to the ancient hatred against the Jews; how it persisted after the emancipation of the Jews, how it has grown and what are its manifestations. In every way I am led to believe that it must ultimately perish, and that it will perish for the various reasons which I have indicated, because the Jew is undergoing a process of change; because religious, political, social, and economic conditions are likewise changing;

but above all, because antisemitism is one of the last, though most long lived, manifestations of that old spirit of reaction and narrow conservatism, which is vainly attempting to arrest the onward movement of the Revolution.

REFERENCES

1 *Tractatus theologico-politicus.*
2 When I say "Moses assigned," it is not to maintain that Moses himself elaborated all the laws which pass under his name, but merely because he is credited with having revised them.
3 *Cod. Theod.*, book II, title VIII, §2. *Cod. Just.*, book I, title IX, §2.
4 Philo, *Legat. ad Cai.*
5 *Dig.*, book I, title III, §3. (Decisions by Septimius Severus and Caracalla.)
6 Spinoza, *Tractatus theologico-politicus.*
7 The *Dibre Sopherim.*
8 Mark, vii, 27.
9 Derembourg, *Geographie de la Palestine.*
10 Graetz, *Histoire des Juifs,* b. II, p. 469.
11 *Ant. Jud.*, xx, 9.
12 The Jewish thought still had a few lights in the fifteenth and sixteenth century. But those among the Jews who produced anything mostly took part in the struggle between philosophy and religion, and were without influence upon their co-religionists; their existence is therefore no denial of the spirit inculcated on the masses by the rabbis. Besides, one meets, throughout that period, none but unimportant commentators, physicians and translators; there appears no great mind among them. One must go as far as Spinoza to find a Jew truly capable of high ideas; it is well-known how the Synagogue treated Spinoza.
13 *"Insolentia Judaeorum,"* spoken of by Agobard, Amolon and the polemists of the Middle Ages means nothing but the pride of the Jews, who consider themselves the chosen people. This expression has not the sense forced into it by modern antisemites, who, it may be noted, are poor historians.
14 The Roman laws, the Visigothic ordinances and those of the Councils will probably be cited; yet nearly all these measures proceeded principally from Jewish proselytism. It was not until the thirteenth century that the Jews were radically and officially separated from the Christians, by ghettos, by symbols of infamy (the hat, the cape, etc.). See Ulysse Robert, *Les Signes d'infamie au moyenage.* (Paris, 1891.)
15 Inscription of Aahmes, chief of the mariners, cited in Ledrain's *Histoire du peuple d'Israel,* I, p. 53.
16 *In Flaccum.*
17 *Preparatio Evangelica.*
18 Josephus, *Contra Apionem*, book II, ch. 6.
19 Philo, *In Flaccum.*
20 Valerius Maximus, I, 3, 2.

21 I *Maccab.* viii., 11, 17-32; xii, 1-3; xiv, 16-19, 24.—Josephus, *Antiqu. Jud.*, xii, 110; xiii, 5, 7, 9 Mai; *Script. vet.*, 111, part 3, p. 998.

22 *Pro Flacco.*

23 *Sat.*, V.

24 *Ars amatoria*, I, 75, 76.

25 *Fragm. poet.*

26 Tac., *Hist.*, v. 4, 5.

27 Juvenal, *Sat.*, xiv, 96, 104.

28 *Hist. nat.*, xiii, 4.

29 *Epistle* xv.

30 *De superstitione,* fragm. xxxvi.

31 Suetonius, Claud., 25.

32 *Demonstratio Evangelica.*

33 *Testimonium adversus Judaeos ex Tetere Testamento,* Migne, P. G., XLVI.

34 *Oratio adversus Judaeos,* Migne, P. L. XLII.

35 *De Tobia.* Migne, P. L. XIV.

36 *Ep. CLI, Quaest.* 10, Migne, P. L. XXII.

37 *Ep. CLI, Quaest,* 10, Migne, *P. G.,* XXXIII.

38 *Adversus Judaeos,* 10, Migne, *P. G.,* XLVIII.

39 Eusebius, *Vita Constantini,* III, 18, 20.

40 *Codex Justinianeus,* l. I, tit. IX, 16.

41 *Codex Theodosianus,* l. XVI, tit. IX, 3, 4, 5.

42 *Codex Justinianeus,* l. I, tit. IX, 6.

43 *Cod. Theod.,* b. XVI, tit. viii, 5.

44 *Code Theodosien,* l. XVI, tit. VIII, 28.

45 *Codex Justinianeus,* l. I, tit. IX, 17 and *Cod. Theodos.,* l. XVI, tit. VIII, 14.

46 *Codex Justinianeus,* l. I, tit. IX, 18.

47 Justinianus, *Novellae,* 45.

48 *Codex Justinianeus,* l. I, tit. IX, 15.

49 *Codex Justinianeus* l. I, tit. IX, 13, and *Cod. Theod.,* l. VIII, tit. IX, 8.

50 His course was probably influenced by his Minister Cassiodorus, who seems to have had scant sympathy for the Jews—he characterized them as scorpions, wild asses, dogs and unicorns.

51 *Leges Visigoth,* l. XII, tit. II, 5.

52 *Lex Burgundionum,* tit. XV, 1, 2, 3.

53 *Vie de Saint Cesaire,* Migne. *Patrologie latine,* t. LXVII.

54 *Sidonius Apollinaris,* l. III, ep. IV, and l. IV, ep. V.

55 Fredegaire (*Chronique,* XV), and Aumoin (*Chroniqua Moissiacensis,* XLV) relate that, at the instigation of Emperor Heraclius, Dagobert gave to the Jews the choice between death, exile and baptism. (*Gesta Dagoberti,* XXIV). The same is reported of the Visigothic King Sisebut (see appendix to the Chronicle of Bishop Marius, A.D. 588; Dom Bouquet, t. II, p. 19). Chilperich forced many Jews to be baptized. (Gregoire de Tours, H. F., l. VI, ch. XVII). Bishop Avitus compelled the Jews of Clermont to renounce their faith, or leave the city. Gregoire de Tours, H. F., l. V, ch. XI). Other bishops resorted to force, and it required the interference of Pope St. Gregory to stop or at least moderate their zeal. "The Jews must not be baptized by force, but brought over by sweetness," says he in his letters addressed to Virgil bishop of Arles, to Theodore, bishop of Marseilles, and to Paschasius, bishop of Naples. (*Regesta Pontificum Romanorum,* ed. Jafle, nos. 1115 and 1879.) But the authority of the Pope was not always effective.

56 *De Insolentia Iudaeorum* (Patrologie Latine, t. CIV).

57 *Gesta Philippi Augusti.*

58 For the position of Southern Jews at the time of Philip the Fair, cf. Simeon Luce (*Catalogue des documents du Tresor des Chartes* (Revue des Etudes Juives, t. I, 3).

59 "Thou shalt not lend upon usury to thy brother; usury of money, usury of victuals, usury of anything that is lent upon usury : unto a stranger (*nokhri*) thou mayest lend upon usury." Deuter. XXIII, 19-20.
Nokhri means a transient stranger; a resident stranger is *ger*.
"And if thy brother be waxen poor, and fallen in decay with thee; then thou shalt relieve him : *yea, though he be* a stranger, or a sojourner; that he may live with thee. Take thou no usury of him or increase." Levit. XXV, 35-36.
"Lord, who shall abide in Thy tabernacle? . . . *He that* putteth not out his money to usury." (Psalm, XV, 1-5). "Even to a non-Jew," adds the Talmudic commentary (*Makkoth* XXIV). Consult also : Exod. XXII 25; Philo, *De Charitate;* Josephus, *Antiquitates Judaeorum,* l. IV, ch. VIII; Selden, l. VI, ch. IX.

60 The Hebrew Sibyl speaks of "the execrable thirst for gold, of the passion for sordid gain which goads the Latins on to the conquest of the world."

61 Cf. S. Munk, *Melanges de philosophie juive et arabe.*

62 *Guide des Egarés* (Translated by S. Munk).

63 Peter the Venerable, abbot of Cluny : *Tractatus adversus Judaeorum inveteratam duritiam* (Bibl. des Peres Latins, Lyons).

64 Title XXIV.

65 *General Statute of Ladislas Jagellon.* Art. XIX.

66 Loc. cit.

67 *The Jews and their Lies.* Wittenberg, 1558.

68 The confederate shoe.

69 Abraham de Balmes translated into Latin the greatest part of Averroes's writings, and his translations were in use in the Italian universities until the end of the seventeeth century.

70 On this point consult Duguet, *Regles pour l'intelligence des Saintes Ecri ures,* 1723. Bossuet, *Discours sur l'Histoire universelle,* part II. Rondet, *Dissertation sur le rappel des Juifs,* Paris, 1778. Anonymous, *Lettre sur le proche retour des Juifs,* Paris, 1789, etc.

71 Gregoire, *Histoire des sectes religieuses,* t. II (Paris, 1825).

72 In Russia, Poland and Galicia they are extant even to-day.

73 Consult Wolf, *Bibliotheca Hebraea,* v. II, p. 798. Hamburg.

74 *Exemplar vitae humanae.* (Published by Limbroch, 1687).

75 *Tractatus Theologico.-Politicus.*

76 Consult the *Spicilegium* by Achery, vols. X and XV.

77 Isidore of Seville, *De Fide Catholica ex vetere et novo Testamento contra Judaeos* (Opera, vol. VII). Migne, P. L., lxxxiii.

78 *Disputatio contra Judaeos*. Opera, Editio Basileensis, p. 180.

79 *Contra Judaeos.* Lib. VI.

80 Migne, P. L., Ch. CLIX.

81 *Liber contra perfidia Judaeorum.* Opera, Paris, 1519.

82 Augustin Giustiniani, *Linguae Hebreae* (1566).

83 *Pugio Fidei* (Paris, 1651). (Cf. Quetif, *Bibl. Scriptorum dominicanorum,* v. I, p. 396, and the edition of Carpzon, Leipzig, 1687).

84 *Victoria adversus impios Hebreos et sacris litteris* (Paris, 1629). Wolf, *Bibl. Hebr.* v. I, p. 1124.

85 Consult Fabricius, *Bibliotheca Latina,* on Peter of Barcelona (Petrus Barcinonensis).

86 *De Arcanis catholicae veritatis libris* (Soncino, 1518).

87 Throughout the Middle Ages they believed in this fourfold meaning of the Scriptures, and the following distich expressed its import:

> *Littera gesta docet, quid credas, allegoria;*
> *Moralis, quid agas quo tendas anagogia.*

88 For the antisemitic literature of the Jewish apostates consult Wolf, *Bibl. Hebr.,* v. I.

89 Cf. Wolf, *Bibl. Hebr.,* I, p. 1004; and Joseph Rodriguez de Castro, *Bibliotheca espanola* (Madrid, 1781), vol. I, p. 235.

90 *Tractatus Zelus christi contra Judaeos, Saracenos et infideles* (Venice, 1542).

91 *Hostis Judaeorum* (Cologne, 1509).

92 *Hebreomastyx* (Frankfort, 1601).

93 Juda Hallevy, *Liber Cosri.* Translated by John Buxtorf, Jr., 1660—a German translation with an introduction was published by H. Jolowicz and D. Cassel, *Das Buch Kuzari,* 1841, 1853.

94 *De Insolentia Judaeorum* (Patrologie latine v. CIV).

95 *Epistola seu liber contra Judaeos* (Patrologie latine, v. CXVI).

96 *Gesta Philippi Augusti,* 12-16.

97 *Tractatus adversus Judaeorum inveteratam duritiam* (Bibliotheque des Peres latins. Lyons).

98 *Les Jours caniculaires* (*Dierum canicularium*) translated by F. de Rosset (Paris, 1612).

99 Agobard, *loc. cit.*

100 Amolon, *loc. cit.*

101 Pierre de Cluny, *loc. cit.*

102 Agobard, *loc. cit.*—Rigord, *loc. cit.*

103 S. Maiol, *loc. cit.*

104 *The Jews and their lies* (Wittenberg, 1558).

105 *Fortalitium Fidei* (Nuremberg, 1494). Wolf, *Bibl. Hebr.,* v. I, p. 1116.

106 *L'Incredulite et mecreance du sortilege pleinement convaincue* (1622).

107 *Centinela contra Judios* (Cf. Loeb, *Revue des Etudes Juives,* v. V).

108 Bibliotheque Nationale, Spanish section, Ms. No. 356 (Loeb, *Revue des Etudes Juives* v. XVIII).

109 *Centinela contra Judios.*

110 Pierre de Lancre, *loc. cit.*

111 Lavocat, *Proces des Freres de l'ordre du Temple*, Paris, 1888.

112 Lavocat, *loc. cit.*

113 Loeb, *Revue des Etudes Juives*, v. XVIII.

114 Shem-Tob ben Isaac Shaprut, *The Touchstone* (Loeb, *loc. cit.*).

115 Wagenseil in his *Tela ignea Satanae* (Altdorf, 1681), reproduces all these treatises in print.

116 Zadoc Kahn, *The Book of Joseph the Zealot* (Revue des Etudes Juives, vols. I and III).

117 For the *Toldot Jesho*, cf. *Tela ignea Satanae*, Wagenseil, v. II, p. 189, and B. de Rossi, *Biblotheca Judaica antichristiana* (Parma, 1800), p. 117.

118 Wagenseil, *loc. cit.*

119 *Magna Biblothica Rabbinica* (Rome, 1693-95).

120 Solomon ben Adret, of Barcelona, refuted the *Pugio Fidei*.

121 Chayimibn Musa refuted Nicholas de Lyra in his *Shield and Sword* (Graetz, *loc. cit.*)

122 *Letter of Combat* (Graetz, *loc. cit.*, and Rossi, *Bibloth. antichrist*, p. 100).

123 *Dialogue against the Apostates* (Loeb, *loc. cit.*)

124 *Alteca Boteca* (Loeb, *loc. cit.*)—De Rossi, *Dizionario Storico degli autori Ebrei* (Parma, 1802), p. 89.

125 *Disputationes Selectae* (Utrecht, 1663).

126 *Theologia Judaeorum* (1647).

127 *Benachrichtung wegen einiger die Judenschaft engehenden Sachen* (Altdorf, 1709).

128 *Dictionn, chaldeo-talmudico-rabbinique* (Basiliae, 1639) and *Synagogua Judaica* (Hanau, 1604).

129 Pean de la Croullardiere, *Methode facile pour convaincre les heretiques* (Paris, 1667), which contains a "method of assailing and converting the Jews"; Thomas Bell, Hader, *Dottrina facile e breve per reduire l'Hebreo al conoscimento del vero Messia e Salvator del Mondo* (Venetia 1608).

130 Conrad Otton, *Gali Razia* (Secrets unveiled), (Nurenberg, 1605).

131 *Judaism Unveiled* (Frankfort, 1700).

132 *Compendium Historiae Judaicae* (Frankfort, 1700) and *Judaeus Christicida gravissime peccans et vapulans* (1700).

133 *Revue des Etudes juives*, v. V, p. 57.

134 *Loc. cit.*

135 *A Case of Conscience* (London 1655).

136 Mention must be made that, as in the Middle ages, the Alsatian Jews were the "dummies" and intermediaries of the Christian usurers (Cf. Halphen, *Recueil des lois et decrets concernant les Israelites* (Paris, 1851), and the *Petition des Juifs etablis en France addressee a l'Assemblee nationale le 28 janvier* 1790).

137 On the Alsatian Jews before and after the Revolution, consult: Gregoire, *Essai sur la Regeneration des Juifs;* Dohm, *De la Reforme politique des Juifs;* Paul Fauchille, *La Question Juive en France Sous le premier Empire* (Paris, 1884).

138 Halphen, *Recueil des lois et decrets.*

139 Halphen, *loc. cit.*

[140] At this moment the Jews entered suit against the city of Frankfort to contest the legality of the city's decisions. This suit was the occasion of violent anti-Jewish polemics.

[141] The constitution of March 4, 1849, proclaimed the equality before the law. But as this constitution was abolished in 1851, an ordinance of July 29, 1853, restored the old legislation against the Jews. Successive Amendments were added to it, and the Constitution of 1867 finally restored equality before the law and liberated the Jews.

In Hungary the law emancipating the Jews was also voted in 1867 by the Chamber of Deputies, on motion by the Government. (Cf. Wolf, *Geschichte der Juden in Wien*, Vienna, 1876; Kaim, *Ein Jahrhundert der Judenemancipation*. Leipzig, 1869.)

[142] The German Constituent Assembly voted the equality of all citizens before the law, on May 20, 1848. The Parliament of Frankfort did likewise, and the principle of this equality was incorporated in the German constitution of 1849. At any rate many States retained the restrictions against the Jews till the time of the Law of the Northern Federation of July 3, 1869, which abolished all the "restrictions of civil and political rights that still existed and were based on difference in religion." (Cf. Kaim, *loc. cit.* and *Allegemeine Zeitung des Judenthums* for the years 1837, 1849, 1856, 1867, 1869). After the Franco-German war, this way was forced upon those States like Bavaria, *e.g.*, which had not adopted it before the organization of the Empire.

[143] Desjardins, *Les Juifs de Moldavies* (Paris, 1867).—Isidore Loeb, *La Situation des Israelites en Turquie, en Serbie et en Roumanie* (Paris 1877).

[144] N. de Gradovski, *La Situation legale des Israelites en Russie* (Paris, 1891).—Tikhomirov, *La Russie politique et sociale* (Paris, 1888).—*Les Juifs de Russie* (Paris, 1891).—Prince Demidoff-San-Donato, *La question juive en Russie* (Bruxelles, 1884).—Anatole Leroy-Beaulieu, *L'Empire des Tzars et les Russes* (Paris, 1881-82-89). [English translation, London and New York, 1894].—Weber et Kempster, *La Situation des Juifs en Russie* (Resumé of a report to the United States Government by its delegates).—Leo Errera, *Les juifs Russes* (Bruxelles, 1893).—Harold Frederic, *The New Exodus* (1892).

[145] The condition of the Jews in Russia, compared with that of the native people, is absolutely the same as in the Middle Ages. The Russian peasant and the workingman are pretty nearly as wretched as the Jew. They, too, are subjected to annoyances and arbitrary rule, but they are not persecuted, and have, to a certain degree the right of migrating.

[146] Tikhomirov, *loc. cit.*

[147] Saint-Simon, *Du Systeme industriel* (Paris, 1821).

[148] Saint-Simon, *Catechisme des Industriels,* 1er *Cahier* (Paris, 1823).

[149] The anxiety for the future role of the Jews is expressed in a striking book by Leon Bloy, *Le Salut par les Juifs* (Paris, 1892). In the volume of documents and notes written as a sequel to Dom Deschamps' work on *Secret Societies,* Claudio Jannet expresses the opinion that the Jews are

undoubtedly destined to lead the world back to God. This is exactly the ancient theological belief.

150 Eng. translation. A. Rohling, *Le Juif selon le Talmud* (Paris, 1888). Translated from the German.

151 Louis Blanc, *Histoire de la Revolution Francaise,* vol. II, p. 74.

152 *Recherches historiques et politiques qui prouvent l'existence d'une secte revolutionnaire, son antique origine, son organisation, ses moyens ainsi que son but; et devoilent entierement l'unique cause de la Revolution Francaise,* par le Chevalier de Malet. Paris, Gide fils, libraire, 1817.

153 Barruel, *Memoires sur le Jacobinisme* (1797-1813). Father Barruel was the first to expound these ideas, and those who followed him have, properly speaking, only imitated or continued his work.

154 Eckert, *La Franc-Maconnerie dans sa veritable signification* (Liege, 1854).—*La Franc-Maconnerie en ellememe* (Liege, 1859).

155 Dom Deschamps, *Les Societes Secretes et la Societe,* with an introduction, notes and documents by Claudio Jannet. Paris, 1883.

156 Cretineau Joly, *L'Englise romaine avant la Revolution.* Paris 1863.

157 On the Hebrew traditions in Free-Masonry, and on the points of similarity between the Free-Masons and the ancient Essenians, cf. Clavel, *Histoire pittoresque de la Franc-Maconnerie* (Paris, 1843); Kauffmann et Cherpin, *Histoire philosophique de la Franc-Maconnerie* (Lyons, 1856) and an article by Moise Schwab on the Jews and the Free-Masons, published in the *Annuaire des Archives israelites pour l'an 5650* (1889-1890). Consult also the various works of J. M. Ragon on Free-Masonry (Paris, Dentu).

158 Gougenot des Mousseaux, *loc. cit.*

159 Rupert, *L'Eglise et la Synagogue* (Paris, 1859).

160 De Saint-Andre, *Francs Macons et Juifs* (Paris, 1880).

161 A Chabeauty, *Les Juifs nos Maitres* (Paris, 1883).

162 It must be noted that in his *France Juive* (I mean in its first chapters) Drumont does not quote Gougenot des Mousseau or Barruel even once; he quotes, in passing, Dom Deschamps three times and Cretineau de Joly's *Vendee Militaire* once, and yet he laid these writers under heavy contribution. Unless his "historical documents" had been furnished to him by the disciples of those I have just mentioned—that is quite possible. Let it be understood here, that this refers to Drumont as historian and not as polemist.

163 Fourier, *Le Nouveau Monde industrial et societaire* (Paris, libraire societaire, 1848).

164 In Karl Marx (*Annales franco-allemandes,* 1844, p. 211) and in Lassalle, the same estimates of the parasite Jew may be found as in Fourier and Proudhon.

165 Toussenel, *Les Juifs rois de l'Epoque* (Paris, 1847). Toussenel followed up this book with a violent campaign in the newspaper, *La Democratie pacifique.* However, the antisemitic movement was quite violent, under the July monarchy, and numerous pamphlets were published against the Jewish financiers.

166 Capefigue, *Histoire des grandes operations financieres* (Paris, 1855).

167 Otto Glagau, *Der Boersen und Grundergeschwindel in Berlin* (Leipzig,

1876). *Les besoins de l'Empire et le nouveau Kulturkampf* (Osnabruck, 1879).

168 During the last years of his life Renan had given up his theory of races, their inequality and their mutual superiority or inferiority. These theories will be found set forth quite clearly and lucidly in Gobineau's in many ways remarkable book, *L'inegalite des races* (Paris, Firmin Didot, 1884).

169 H. von Treitschke, *Ein Wort uber unser Judenthum* (*A Word about Our Jews*). Berlin, 1888.

170 Drumont is the type of the assimilator antisemite who has flourished in France these last years, and who has overrun Germany. A talented polemist, vigorous journalist and sprightly satirist, Drumont is a historian of poor documentary evidence, a mediocre sociologist and especially philosopher, and can under no circumstances be compared with men of H. von Treitschke's, Adolph Wagner's and Eugen Duhring's standing. Yet, in the development of antisemitism in France and Germany even he has played a considerable role, and he has exercised a great influence as a propagandist.

171 W. Marr, *Der Sieg des Judenthums uber das Germanthum* (Berne, 1879). In the *Journal des Debats* of Nov. 5, 1879, Bourdeau devoted an essay to this pamphlet.

172 "A God like that Jehovah," says Schopenhauer, "who, as *animi causa,* for its own pleasure and from the *joy of heart* produces this world of misery and lamentations, and who even glories in it—this is too much. Let us then, at this point, consider the religion of the Jews as the last among the religious doctrines of the civilized nations, and this will be in perfect accord with the fact that it is the only one that has absolutely not a trace of immortality." (*Parerga und Paralipomena*, v. II, ch. XII, p. 312, Leipzig 1874).

173 We shall return to this question in our *Economic History of the Jews,* when speaking of the role of the Jews in Germany in the nineteenth century.—Cf. Hegel, *Philosophie des Rechts;* Arnold Ruge, *Zwei Jahre in Paris;* Bruno Bauer, *Die Judenfrage;* L. Feuerbach, *Das Wesen des Christenthums.*

174 Max Stirner, *Der Einzige und sein Eigenthum.* Leipzig, 1882, pp. 22, 25, 31, 69.

175 Particularly in *The Parties and the Jewish Question. Die Judenfrage als Frage der Racenschaedlichkeit.*

176 Frierich Nietzche, *Human, all too Human* (1879), *Beyond Good and Evil; The Geneaology of Morality* (1887).

177 Gustave Tridon, *Du Molochisme juif.* (Bruxelles, 1884).

178 A. Regnard, *Aryens et Semites.* (Paris, 1890).

179 Ulotrichi and Leiotrichi.

180 Brachycephals and Dolichocephals.

181 L. Gumplowicz, *La Lutte des races* (Paris, 1893).

182 This theory, which has the immense advantage of not resting on any foundation, sprang up in Germany and passed from there into France and Belgium. De Biez and Edmond Picard have in turn upheld it, but

they did not bring any even illusory proof in support of their assertions. (Cf. *Antisemiten—Spiegel*, pp. 132, *et seq*, Danzig, 1892).

183 Saint-Prioux, *Histoire de Braine.*

184 The Jews of Tortosa converted in thousands after the conference opened at the instigation of Jerome de Santa Fe.

185 *Centinela contra Judios.*

186 Francisco Mendoza y Bovadilla, *El Tizon de la Nobleza Espanola, o maculas y sambenitos de sus Linajes* (Barcelona, 1880; Bibliotheca de obras raras).—Cf. also Llorente, *Histoire de l'Inquisition* (Paris, 1817).

187 Ernest Renan, *Histoire du peuple d'Israel*, v. I.

188 Maimonides, *Yad Hazaka* (the powerful hand), Part I, chap. 1, §4.

189 Matth. xxiii.

190 Talmud Babli, *Pesachim*, f. 87.

191 Horace, Sat. IV, 143.—Josephus *Bell. Jud.*, vii, III., 3.—Dio Cassius, xxxvii, xvii, etc., etc.

192 Cf. ch. II; ch. III and ch. IV.

193 Bielski, *Chronicon rerum Polonicarum.*

194 Vivien de Saint-Martin, *Les Kharzars* (Paris, 1851).—C. C. d'Ohsson, *Les Peuples du Caucase*, Paris, 1828.—*Revue des Etudes juives*, v. XX, p. 144.

195 Basnage, *Histoire des Juifs*, v. IX, p. 246; and Wagenseil, *Exercitationes.*

196 Among the Chechens inhabiting the East and Northwest of the Caucasus, as well as among the Andis of Daghestan, the Jewish type is very widespread. The Tats of the Caspian Sea are considered to be Jews, and there are many Jews among the Tatar tribes, as the Kumiks, for instance. (Cf. Eckert, *Der Kaukasus und seine Volker*, Leipzig, 1887).

197 For the dolichocephalous Jews of Africa and Italy, cf. the works of Pruner-Bey (*Memoire de la Societe d'anthropologie*, II, p. 432 and III, p. 82) and Lombroso.—For the brachycephalous Jews cf. Copernicki and Mayer, *Physical Characteristics of the Population of Galicia*, Cracow, 1876 (in Polish).

198 Mardochee Aby Serour, *Les Daggatouns*, Paris, 1880.

199 On the Fellahs cf. Abbadie, *Nouvelles annales des Voyages*, 1845, III, p. 84, and Ph. Luzzato, *Archives israelites*, 1851-1854.

200 Elie Schwartz, *God's Nation in China*. Strassburg, 1880.—Abbe Sionnet, *Essai sur les Juifs de la Chine*, Paris, 1837.

201 A. Franck, lecture on "Religion and Science in Judaism," in *Annuaire de la Societe des Etudes Juives*, 2nd year.

202 Chapt. VII.

203 Cf. Munk, *De la Poesie hebraique apres la Bible*, in *Temps* of Jan. 19, 1835, and the works of Zunz, Rappoport and Abraham Geiger. Cf. also Amador de los Rios, *Histoire des Juifs d'Espagne* (1875).

204 I leave apart the Polish Jews of Germany.

205 Laveleye, *Le Gouvernment dans la Democratie*, v. I, p. 53 (Paris, 1891).

206 J. Novicow, *Les luttes entre societies humaines*, Paris, 1893.

207 Ch. ix.

208 Leviticus, xix, xxv; Exodus, xxii; Numbers, xxv.

209 *Tract. Theolog. Polit.*, chap. xvii.

210 Levit., xix, 36.

211 Levit., xix, 15.

212 Amos, v, 24.

213 Jeremiah, ix, 24.

214 Jeremiah, xxii, 15-16.

215 Amos, viii, 4.

216 Psalms, xxvi, 10; lxxxii, 2-3; lviii, 2; xxii; xlviii; lxix; cii, 1, 2; cvii, etc.

217 Matth., v, 6.

218 Mark, x, 25.

219 Spinoza, *Letters,* xxxiv.

220 Mendelssohn, *Jerusalem.*

221 Munk, *Palestine.*

222 Levit., xxv, 55.

223 Isaiah, iii; x.

224 Psalms, xciv.

225 Psalms, xxxvii, 35-36.

226 S. Munk, *loc. cit.*

227 Cf. the poetic account of the *Descent of St. Paul into Hell,* cited by Ernest Renan in his *Averroes et l'Averroisme,* p. 284.

228 E. Renan, *loc. cit.*

229 James Darmesteter; *Coup d'oeil sur l'histoire du peuple juif,* Paris, 1881.

230 p. 582.

231 See Chap. vii.—Wolf, *Bibl. Hebr.,* vol. iv, p. 639.

232 I hope to establish the point still more completely in my *Economic History of the Jews,* of which *The Role of Jew in the French Revolution* forms but a part.

233 Gougenot des Mousseaux, *loc. cit.*

234 M. Matter, *Saint Martin et le philosophe inconnu.*

235 The statement is often made that Cagliostro was a Jew, but the assertion is based on no real evidence.

236 See Emile Campardon, *Le Tribunal revolutionnaire de Paris,* Paris, 1866.—*Proces instruit et juge au tribunal revolutionnaire contre Hebert et ses consorts* (1-4 Germinal), Paris, An. II.— Leon Kahn, *Les Juifs a Paris* (Paris, 1889).

237 Capefigue, *Histoire des grandes operations financieres.*—Toussenel, *Les juifs rois de l'epoque.*

238 Cretineau-Joly, *Histoire du Sonderbund,* p. 195 (Paris, 1850).

239 Besides Marx and Cohen, mention might be made of Neumayer, secretary of the bureau of correspondence in Austria; Fribourg, who was one of the directors of the Parisian Federation of the International to which belonged Loeb, Haltmayer, Lazare and Armand Levi; Leon Frankel, director of the German section at Paris; Cohen who acted as delegate from the Cigar Makers' Union of London to the Congress of the International held at Brussels in 1868; Ph. Coenen who, at the same Congress, represented the Antwerp section of the International, etc. See O. Testut: *L'Internationale,* Paris, 1871; and *L'Internationale au ban de l'Europe* (Paris, 1871-72); Fribourg, *L'Association internationale des travailleurs* (Paris, 1891).

240 Among the others Fribourg and Leon Frankel.

241 There are at present four Jewish social-democrats in the German Reichstag, and among the younger element in the ranks of the socialists, collectivists and communistic anarchists, the number of the Jews is very large. Of the reform part in Germany we may mention Doctor Hertzka, the founder of the Freiland colony, an attempt at realizing the ideal social organization. (See *Eine Reise nach Freiland*, von Theodor Hertzka.)

242 In April the members of the Jewish revolutionary party in London, celebrated the anniversary of the founding of heir club in Berners Street. In reviewing the history of the social movement among the Jews, the orator of the occasion declared that "during the last seven years, the Jew has made his entrance as a revolutionary; and now wherever there are Jews— in London, in America, in Austria, in Poland, and in Russia—there are Jewish revolutionists and anarchists." By seven years, the speaker was referring to the date when the proletarian class among the Jews first declared their adhesion to the revolutionary propaganda.

243 Chap. ii.

244 Chap. v.

245 Chap. v.

246 Otto Glagau, *loc. cit.*

247 E. Renan estimates the number of Jews in Rome at the time of Nero at from twenty to thirty thousand (*L'Antechrist*, p. 7, note 2).

248 *Hist.* v. 5.

249 *Pro Flacco*, xxviii.

250 These synods frequently met after the twelfth century, and constituted the first general assemblies of the Rabbis since the closing of the Talmud. Jacob Tam (Rabbenu Tam), the founder of the school of Tossafists, was the first to bring about the reunion of such assemblies, for the purpose, undoubtedly, of considering means of common resistance to persecution.

251 Jost, *Geschichte der Juden*, Berlin, 1820, Vol. 2.

252 The *Alliance Israelite Universelle*, founded in 1860 by Adolphe Cremieux, and numbering at present more than thirty thousand members, has served only to foster the fraternal spirit among the Jews. The aims of the *Alliance* are to ameliorate the intellectual and moral conditions of the Jews in the Orient by the establishment of schools, to take measures for their relief from oppression, and to bring about their complete emancipation.

253 I am not speaking, of course, of Masonic lodges, but use the word Free Masonry in the broad meaning of the term.

254 Chap. x.

255 I am speaking of the Jews who have remained true to their faith.

256 I must repeat once more that I am speaking now only of the Jews of Western Europe, who have been admitted to the rights of citizenship in the countries where they live, and not of the Jews of the East, who are still subject to discriminating laws, as in Roumania, in Russia, in Morocco, and in Persia.

257 Henry George, *Progress and Poverty*.

258 M. Guyau, *L'Irreligion de l'avenir*; Paris, 1893.

BIBLIOGRAPHY

1 Antisemitism in Antiquity

ANTI-JEWISH LITERATURE
Apion: *Tractatus contra Judaeos*
Cicero: *Pro Flacco*
Juvenal: *Saturnalia*
Ovid: *Ars amatoria*
Petronius: *Fragm. poet.*
Pliny: *Hist. nat.*
Seneca: *De superstitione*
Suetonius: *Claudius*
Tacitus: *Historia*

JEWISH APOLOGIA
Josephus, Flavius:
  Contra Apionem — Apologia —
  Antiquitates Judaeorum
Philo:
  Legatio ad Caium — In Flaccum
  — de Charitate
"The Sybylline Books"; mid 2nd
  to mid 1st century B.C.
"The Wisdom of Solomon";
  1st century B.C.

N. Bentwich: *Philo-Judaeus of Alexandria*, 1910.
Reinach, Theodore: *Textes d'Auteurs Grecs et Romains Relatifs au Judaisme*, 1895

2 Christian Anti-Judaism to the Reformation

CHRISTIAN APOLOGISTS, ANTI-JEWISH POLEMICS
Alfonso of Valladolid: *Batallos de Dios*
Alonzo de Spina: *Fortalitium Fidei*, 1494
Amolon: *Epistola seu liber contra Judaeos*
Ariston of Pella: *Altercation of Jason and Papiscus*
Cedrenus: *Disputatio contra Judaeos*
Commodian: *Instructiones adversus Gentium Deos*
Crepin, Gilbert: *Disputatio Judei cum Christiano de Fide Christiana*
Cyprian: *De Catholicae Ecclesiae Unitate*
Dagobard: *De Insolentia Judaeorum*
Eusebius: *Preparatio Evangelica*
Evagrius: *Altercation of Simon and Theophilus*
Francisco de Torrejoncillo: *Centinela contra Judios*
Isidore of Seville: *De Fide Catholica ex vetere et novo Testamento contra Judaeos*
Jerome de Santa Fe: *Hebreomastyx*
Justinianus: *Novellae*
Lactantius: *Divinae Institutiones*
Luther, M: *The Jews and their Lies*, 1558
Maiol, Simon: *Dierum canicularium*
Martin, Raymund: *Capistro Judaeorum — Pugio Fidei*
Nicholas de Lyra: *Postilla — De Messia*
Origen: *Contra Celsum*
Paul de Santa Maria: *Examination of the Holy Writ*
Paul de la Caballeria: *Tractatus Zelus Christi contra Judaeos, Saracenos et infideles*, 1542
Pierre de Blois: *Liber contra Perfidia Judaeorum*, 1519
Pierre de Cluny: *Tractatus adversus Judaeorum inveteratam duritiam*
Pfefferkorn: *Hostis Judaeorum*, 1509
Rigord: *Gesta Philippi Augusti*
St. Justin: *Dialogue with Tryphon — Letter to Diognetus*
Theophanus: *Contra Judeos*

JEWISH APOLOGISTS, ANTI-CHRISTIAN POLEMICS:

I SPAIN

Crescas Hasdai : *Tratado*
Duran Profiat : *Kelimmat ha-Goyim*
Duran Simon ben Zemah : *Keshet-u-Magen*
Kimhi, Joseph : *Nizzachon — Sefer ha-Berit*
Levi, Judah ha- : *Cuzari*
Maimonides, Moses : *Moreh Nebukhim*
Moses Cohen of Tordesillas : *Ezer-ha-Emunah*
Nahmanides : *Wikkuah*
Ibn Gabirol, Solomon ben Judah : *Fons Vitae*
Ibn Pulgar : *Ezer ha-Dat*
Jacob ben Reuben : *Sefer Mihhamot Adonai*
Shem-Tob ben Isaac ibn Shaprut : *Eben Bohan*
Troki, Isaac : *Hizzuk Emunah*, 2 vols. (tr. into Latin, German, Spanish, English)

II FRANCE

Isaac ben Nathan : *Tokahut Mat'eh*
  Mibzar Yizhuk
Meir ben Simon of Narbonne : *Milhemet Mizwah*
Mordecai ben Josiphiah : *Mahuzik ha-Emunah*

III ITALY

Brieli : *Hassugot 'al Sifre ha-Shilluhim*
Farissol, Abraham : *Magen Abraham*
Moses of Salerno : *Ma 'amar ha Emunah*
  Ta 'anot
Solomon ben Jekuthiel : *Mikhamot Adonai*

IV GERMANY

Lipman Mülhausen : *Nizzachon*
Reuchlin : *Mirror of the Eyes*

V HOLLAND

Isaac Cardoso : *Fuenta Clara las Excellencias y Calumnias de los hebreos*
Nahamios de Castro : *Tratado de Calumnia*
Saul Levi Morteira : *Tractado de la Verdad de la Ley*
Spinoza : *Tractatus Theologico-Politicus*

VI GENERAL

H. GRAETZ : *The Influence of Judaism on the Protestant Reformation,* 1867
I. Loeb : *La Controverse Religieuse entre les Chretiens et les Juifs du Moyen-age,* 1888
S. Munke : *Melanges de Philisophie juive et arabe*
L. I. Newman, Rabbi : *Jewish Influence on Christian Reform Movements,* 1925
Robert, Ulysse : *Les Signes s'infamie au Moyenage,* 1891
Roth, C. : *A History of the Marranos,* 1932
D. de Sola : "The Influence of some Jewish apostates on the Reformation," *Jewish Review,* 1911-1912

3 Reformation to the French Revolution

Acosta, Uriel : *Exemplar Vitae Humanae,* 1687
Bossuet : *Discours sur l'Histoire Universelle*
Croullardiere, Pean de la : *Methode facile pour convaincre les heretiques,* 1667

Duguet : *Regles pour l'Intelligence des Saintes Ecritures*
Dury, John : *A Case of Conscience*, 1655
Eisenmenger : *Judaism Unveiled*, 1700
Giustiniani, Augustin : *Linguae Hebreae*, 1656
Hallevy, Judah : *Liber Cosri*, 1660
Otton, Conrad : *Gali Razzia*, 1605
Piere de Lancre : *L'incredulite et mecreance du sortilege pleinement convaincue*, 1622
Rondet : *Dissertation sur le rappel des Juifs*, 1778
Roth, C. : *Menasseh Ben Israel*, 1945
Voetius : *Disputationes Selectae*, 1663
Voisin, Joseph de : *Theologia Judaeorum*, 1647
Wagenseil : *Tela ignea Satanae*, 1681
Wolf, L. : "Cromwell's Jewish Intelligencers", *Jewish Literary Annual*, 1904

4 The French Revolution

Barruel : *Memoires sur le Jacobinisme*, 1789
Blanc, Louis : *Histoire de la Revolution francaise*
Campardon, E. : *Le Tribunal Revolutionnaire de Paris*, 1866
Dohm : *De la Reforme Politique des Juifs*
Gregoire : *Essai sur la Regeneration des Juifs*
Kahn, Leon : *Les Juifs a Paris*, 1889
Malet, Chevalier de : *Essai sur la Secte des Illumines*, 1789
    Recherches Historiques, 1817
Petition des Juifs etablis en France addressee a l'Assemblee nationale, le 28 janvier, 1790
Webster, N. H. : *The French Revolution*, 1919

5 Antisemitism in Russia

Adler, C. : *Jacob Schiff—His Life and Letters*, 1929
Aubert, maitre : *Bolshevism's Terrible Record*, 1924
Errera, Leo : *Les Juifs Russes*, 1893
Fahey, Rev. Denis : *The Rulers of Russia*
Fejto, Ferenc (Francois) : *Les Juifs et l'Antisemitisme dans les Pays Communistes*, 1960
Frederic, Harold : *The New Exodus*, 1892
Gradovski, N. de : *La Situation legale des Israelites en Russie*, 1891
Lenin : *The Jewish Question*
Leroy-Beaulieu : *L'Empire des Tzars et les Russes*
Sarolea, Charles : *Impressions of Soviet Russia*, 1924
Tikhomirov : *Les Juifs de Russie*, 1891
"The Persecution of the Jews in Russia"—*Russo-Jewish Committee*, 1890
Weber et Kempster : *La Situation des Juifs en Russie*
Wilton, Robert : *Russia's Agony*, 1918
Yarmolinsky, Avrahm : *The Jews and other minorities under the Soviets*

6 Antisemitism and the Talmud

Drach (ex-Rabbi), Chevalier P. L. B. : *De l'Harmonie entre l'Eglise et la Synagogue*, 1844
Freedman, Benjamin : *Facts are Facts*, 1955
Gougenot des Mousseaux : *Le Juif, le Judaisme et la Judaisation des peuples chretiens*, 1869
Lemann, the Fathers : *La Question du Messie et le Concile du Vatican*, 1869
Mielziner, M. : *Introduction to the Talmud*
Nossig, Alfred : *Integrales Judentum*, 1922

Rodkinson, M.: *The History of the Talmud*
Rohling, A.: *Le Juif selon le Talmud*, 1888
Rupert: *L.Eglise et la Synagogue*, 1859

7   Antisemitism and Kabbalism and Magic

Christian, Dr.: *The Kabbalah*, 1920
Davies: *Magic, Divination and Demonology among the Hebrews and their Neighbours*, 1898
Ginsburg, C. D.: *Kabbalah*, 1865
Levi, Eliphas: *Histoire de la Magie*
Mathers, S. L. MacGregor: *The Kabbalah Unveiled*, 1887
Monod, Bernard: *Juifs, sorciers et heretiques au moyenage*, 1903
Rhodes, H. T. F.: *The Satanic Mass*, 1965
Vulliaud, Paul: *La Kabbale Juive*, 1923
A. E. Waite: *The Doctrine and Literature of the Kabbalah*, 1902
The Holy Kabbalah, 1929

8   Antisemitism and the Blood Accusation

AGAINST THE ACCUSATION

Menasse-ben-Israel: *Vindiciae Judaeorum*, 1656
Roth, C.: *The Ritual Murder Libel and the Jews*, 1935
Strack, H. L.: *The Jews and Human Sacrifice*, 1900

SUPPORTING THE ACCUSATION

Leese, A. S.: *Jewish Ritual Murder*, 1938
Monniot, A.: *Le Crime Rituel chez les Juifs*, 1914
Prynne, William: *A Short Demurrer to the Jewes long discontinued Remitter into England*, 1656

9   Antisemitism and Freemasonry

MASONIC WRITINGS

Clavel: *Historie Pittoresque de la Franc-Maconnerie*, 1843
Goodman, Paul: *B'nai B'rith*, 1936
Haute Vente Romaine (Alta Vendita) Correspondence of, 1846
Mackey, A. G.: *Encyclopedia of Freemasonry*, 1905, etc.
MARTIN, G.: *La Franc-Maconnerie francaise et la preparation de la revolution* 1925
Mellor, A.: *Nos Freres Separes*, Les Francs-Maçons, 1961
La Franc-Maconnerie a l'Heure du choix, 1963
Originalschriften des Illuminaten Ordens, 1787
Pike, Albert: *Morals and Dogma of the Ancient and Accepted Scottish Rite of Freemasonry*, 1880
Ragon: *Cours Philosophique*
Vindex: *Light Invisible*, 1964
A. E. Waite: *The Secret Tradition in Freemasonry*, 1911; etc.

NON-MASONIC WRITINGS

Cahill, Rev. E.: *Freemasonry and the Anti-Christian Movement*, 1959
Cretineau-Joly: *L'Eglise Romaine en face de la Revolution*, 1859.
Deschamps, Rev. N., S.J.: *Les Societes Secretes et la Societe*, 1881
Dillon, Mgr. G.: *Grand Orient Freemasonry Unmasked as the Secret Power Behind Communism*, 1965
Eckert: *La Franc-Maconnerie dans sa veritable signification*, 1854
Hannah, Rev. W.: *Darkness Visible*, 1963
Christian by Degrees, 1964
Lecouteux de Canteleu, Comte: *Les Sectes et societies secretes*, 1863
Leo XIII, Pope: *Humanum Genus*, 1884

Poncins, Vicomte Leon de : *The Secret Powers behind Revolution,* 1929
Webster, N. H. : *World Revolution,* 1921
    Secret Societies and Subversive Movements, 1964

10 Reference Books

Aumoin : *Chronique Moissiacensis*
Bartolocci : *Magna Bibliotheca Rabbinica,* 1693-95
Bielski : *Chronicon Rerum Ponolicarum*
Buxtorf : *Dictionnaire chaldeo-talmudico-rabbinique,* 1639
Catholic Encyclopedia, The
Codex Justinianus
Codex Theodosianus
Encyclopaedia Britannica, The (Art. "Antisemitism" by L. Wolf)
Fabricius : *Bibliotheca Latina*
Fredegaire : *Chronique*
Halphen: *Receuil des Lois et Decrets concernant les Israelites,* 1851
Jewish Encyclopedia, The, Funk & Wagnall Edition, New York, 1901-1906
    see Articles : Antisemitism, Apologists, Apostasy, Blood Accusation, Conversion, Disputations, Freemasonry, Polemics, Talmud
Kayserling : *Bibliotheca Espanola-Portugueza-Judaica,* 1890
Migne : *Patrologie latine* (P.L.)
    Patrologie grecque (P.G.)
Quetif : *Bibliotheca Scriptorum Dominicanorum*
Regesta Pontificum Romanorum, Jafle edition
Revue des Etudes Juives
Rodriguez, de Castro, Joseph : *Bibliotheca espanola,* 1781
Rossi, B. de : *Bibliotheca Judaica Antichristiana,* 1800
Transactions of the Jewish Historical Society
Wolf, J. C. : *Bibliotheca Hebreae,* 1721

11 General Bibliography

Abbott, G. F. : *Israel in Europe*
Amadore de los Rios : *Histoire des Juifs d'Espagne,* 1875
Basnage : *Histoire des Juifs*
Benamozegh, Elie: *Israel et l'Humanite,* 1961
Capefigue : *Histoire des grandes operations financiees,* 1855
Corti, Count : *The Rise of the House of Rothschild,* 1928
    The Reign of the House of Rothschild, 1928
Crosland : T. W. H. : *The Fine Old Hebrew Gentleman,* 1930
Darmesteter, J. : *Coup d'oeil sur l'histoire du peuple juif,* 1881
Dimont, Max I. : *Jews, God and History,* 1964
Drumont : *La France Juive,* 1886
    Testament d'un Antisemite, 1891
Fauchille, Paul : *La Question juive en France sous le premier Empire,* 1884
Fejto, Ferenc (Francois) : *Dieu et son Juif,* 1960
Fleg, E. : *Pourquoi je suis juif,* 1928
    Israel et moi, 1936
Fourier: *Le Nouveau Monde industriel et societaire,* 1848
Fribourg : *L' Association internationale des travailleurs,* 1891
Gobineau, Comte de: *L'Inegalite des races*
Golding, Louis : *The Jewish Problem,* 1938
Graetz, H. : *History of the Jews,* 2 vols., 1891-92
Gumplowicz, L. : *La Lutte des races,* 1893
Guyau, M. : *L'Irreligion de l'avenir,* 1893
Herford, R. Travers : *The Pharisees,* 1924
Herzl, T. : *The Jewish State,* 1936
Hyamson, A. M. : *History of the Jews in England,* 1929

Isaac, Jules: *Genese de l'Antisemitisme,* 1948, 1956
   Jesus et Israel, 1946, 1959
   The Christian Roots of Antisemitism, 1965 (Tr. by J. Parkes
Jacobs, J.: *Jewish Contributions to Civilisation,* 1919
Jehouda, Joshua: *L'Antisemitisme, Miroir du Monde,* 1958
Jost: *Geschichte der Juden,* 1820
Kadmi-Kohen, *Nomades,* 1929
Lavocat: *Proces des Freres de l'ordre du Temple,* 1888
Ledrain: *Histoire du peuple d'Israel*
Leroy-Beaulieu, A: *Israel parmi les nations,* 1893
Levison, Leon: *The Jew in History,* 1916
Lewisohn, Ludwig: *Israel,* 1925
Madaule, Jacques: *Les Juifs et le monde actuel,* 1963
Memmi, A.: *Portrait of a Jew,* 1963.
Mendoza y Bovadilla, Francisco: *El Tizon de la Nobleza Espanol,* 1880
Neumann: *Permanent Revolution,* 1942
Parkes, James: *The Conflict of the Church and the Synagogue,* 1934
   An Enemy of the People, Antisemitism, 1945
   The Emergence of the Jewish Problem, 1946
Poliakov, Leon: *Histoire de l'Antisemitisme*
Poncins, Vicomte Leon de: *Les forces secretes de la Revolution,* 1929
   La Franc-Maconnerie, d'apres ses documents secrets, 1934
   Le Probleme Juif face au Concile, 1965
Regnard, A.: *Aryens et Semites,* 1890
Reitlinger, G.: *The Final Solution,* 1953
Renan: *Le Judaisme comme Race et Religion,* 1883; etc.
Rennap, I.: *Antisemitism and the Jewish Question;* 1942
Roth, C.: *A Short History of the Jewish People,* 1936
   The Jewish Contribution to Civilisation, 1938
Sacks, George: *The Jewish Question,* 1937
Saint-Martin, Vivien de: *Les Khazars,* 1851
Saint-Simon: *Du Systeme Industriel,* 1821
Samuel, Maurice: *The Great Hatred,* 1943
Sartre, Jean-Paul: *Portrait of the Antisemite,* 1948
Schwartz, Elie: *God's Nation in China,* 1880
Sionnet, Abbe: *Essai sur les Juifs de la Chine,* 1837
Sombart, W.: *The Jews and Modern Capitalism*
Testat, O.: *L'Internationale,* 1871
Toulat, Abbe Jean: *Juifs mes Freres,* 1963 (Pref. by Cardinal Gerlier).
Unity in Dispersion—A History of the World Jewish Congress, 1948
Valentin, Hugo: *Antisemitism,* 1936
Wolf, Lucien: *The Myth of the Jewish Menace in World Affairs,* 1921
Zangwill, Israel: *The Voice of Jerusalem,* 1921
Zenker, E. V.: *Anarchism,* 1898
Zûkerman, W.: *The Jew in Revolt,* 1937

INDEX